First Nations and First Settlers in the Fraser Valley (1890-1960)

First Nations and First Settlers in the Fraser Valley (1890-1960)

Editors: Harvey Neufeldt,
Ruth Derksen Siemens and Robert Martens

Published by Pandora Press

Library and Archives Canada Cataloguing in Publication

First nations and first settlers in the Fraser Valley (1890-1960) / editors, Harvey Neufeldt, Ruth Derksen Siemens and Robert Martens.

Papers presented at a conference held June 5-7, 2003.
Includes bibliographical references and index.
ISBN 1-894710-54-1

1. Minorities--British Columbia--Fraser Valley--History--Congresses. 2. Mennonites--British Columbia--Fraser Valley--History--Congresses. 3. Ethnology--British Columbia--Fraser Valley--History--Congresses. 4. Fraser Valley (B.C.)--History--Congresses. I. Neufeldt, Harvey II. Siemens, Ruth Derksen III. Martens, Robert, 1949-

FC3845.F73F57 2005   971.1'37004   C2005-901070-3

The article "Transnational Communities: Japanese Communities of the Fraser Valley" by Anne Doré was previously published in *BC Studies* 135 (Summer 2002): 35-70. It is reprinted by permission.

Cover painting, "Fraser Valley Spectrum" by Hilda M. Goertzen is accompanied by the artist's statement:
Through the window entwined with a hop vine, we see images representing the various cultures:
the Natives fishing on the Fraser;
the Japanese watercraft;
the Sikhs sawmills;
the Mennonites farms and educational institutions

The red background epitomizes energy.
The sun that shone for our ancestors continues to radiate.
The mountains are still there to climb and conquer.
The orchards teems with fruitfulness.
The Fraser River is the life that flows through it all.

FIRST NATIONS, FIRST SETTLERS
IN THE CENTRAL FRASER VALLEY, 1890–1960

ISBN 1-894710-54-1

Printed and bound at: Pandora Press 33 Kent Avenue Kitchener, Ontario N2G 3R2 www.pandorapress.com

All Pandora Press books are printed on Eco-Logo certified paper.

Table of Contents

Part III: Community and Family in Yarrow

Part IV: Educational Institutions and the Arts

Part V: Economic Development and Urbanization of Ethnic Mennonites

Preface

First Nations and First Settlers in the Fraser Valley (1890-1960)

Dr. Harold (Skip) Bassford, President,
University College of the Fraser Valley

The Fraser Valley is one of the most ethnically and culturally diverse parts of Canada. Most people attribute this fact to the very large numbers of recent immigrants who have contributed to the explosive growth the region is undergoing. But, as the conference from which the present volume is derived demonstrated, the diversity has existed since earlier times. As the included essays show, the First Nations settlements were joined at the end of the nineteenth and in the early twentieth century by Japanese, Sikh and Mennonite settlers, all of whom contributed significantly to the Valley's development.

The current volume examines the interactions, positive and negative, of the early settlers. The articles trace the experiences of the diverse groups from the perspectives of community, religion, education and economics. Together they trace the historical development of the Fraser Valley communities, filling many *lacunae* in the previously existing narrative, and helping significantly to improve the understanding of the Valley's present.

It is worth noting that the First Nations and First Settlers Conference participants came from a broad section of the Fraser Valley's residents. Some were academics, but many were citizens with access to family and community history. As such, the conference can be seen as a community activity, whereby many community members came together to understand their past, and how it contributed to their present.

UCFV is a university which emphasizes interaction with its community. Because of that I was very pleased to have UCFV host the First Nations and First Settlers Conference in June, 2003. I am even more pleased to see the excellent collection of articles which has developed from the presentations. I believe they make a significant and accessible contribution not only to local history, but also to the history of Canada.

Introduction

Ruth Derksen Siemens
and Harvey Neufeldt

The central Fraser Valley, including the south shore of the Fraser River between Chilliwack and Abbotsford, as well as the Mission District along the Fraser's north shore, has attracted various groups of settlers and immigrants: First Nations, British, Sikhs, Japanese, and Russian-born Mennonites, among others. Water, in the form of rivers, streams and especially Sumas Lake, served not only as an essential transportation route, but also formed an obstacle to the various groups of settlers as they attempted to survive on the rich valley soils. The various writers of this volume attempt to reflect the diverse developmental phases of the area's settlement.

Most of the papers included in this volume were presented at *First Nations and First Settlers in the Fraser Valley (1890-1960)*, a conference jointly sponsored by the Yarrow Research Committee and University College of the Fraser Valley on June 5-7, 2003. However, in our attempt to reflect more diversity in this anthology, three papers have been added: Bob Smith's research examines the impact that the reclamation of the Sumas project had upon the surrounding region generally, and upon the small growing community of Yarrow specifically; Baljeet Dhaliwal's and Anne Doré's studies recognize the significant contribution of the Sikh and the Japanese settlers to the socio-cultural milieu of the Fraser Valley. While most papers are written in the genre of academic research,[1] several are more aptly presented in the genre of personal reflections. In his poignant opening address, Sonnie McHalsie introduces himself in light of the habitat of the *Stó:lō* Nation's territory, Catherine Marcellus, John Harder, and John Redekop's papers are also personal reflections that provide socio-political perspectives on settlement patterns in the Fraser Valley.

The first section, "Pre-Settlement and Early Settlement," includes five papers. Sonnie McHalsie, cultural advisor and acting executive director of the Aboriginal Rights and Title Department of the *Stó:lō* Nation, is not Scottish as his name suggests, but his naming reflects the influence of colonization on the aboriginal communities. McHalsie provides an overview of the areas of aboriginal settlements. He describes the *Stó:lō* people in terms of the language and micro-dialects of the region, he explains the territorial boundaries and family lineages, and he recites oral narratives of *Stó:lō* beginnings and ancestry.

Bob Smith traces the deliberations and implementation of the massive Sumas Lake reclamation project. The area known today as Sumas Prairie became inhabitable as a result of a massive dyking and drainage project managed by the provincial government in the early 1920s. Previously, Sumas Lake had extended to the western boundary of present-day community of Yarrow. Although the project had significant cost overruns, Smith argues that the workers were spared much of the exploitation characteristic of earlier public-private construction projects, most notably in the construction of railways. While the reclamation project resulted in thousands of acres of fertile land becoming available for agricultural pursuits, the project also dramatically altered the landscape and threatened wildlife habitats.

In her paper on the Japanese transnational communities, Anne Doré examines the settlement and socio-historical events that shaped her people in the Fraser Valley from 1904–1942. Doré asserts that "racialization was a dynamic force in sustaining these distinct communities." While the Euro-Canadian's social construction of race as applied to the Japanese immigrants was negative, the Japanese immigrants' concept of racialization, on the other hand, "was based on a positive interpretation of the same traits deemed negative by Euro-Canadians." Unlike the coastal urban centers, the central Fraser Valley witnessed a great deal of cooperation between the Japanese immigrants and their Euro-Canadian neighbours. The clamorous anti-Japanese voices, common to the coastal urban areas, were not commonly heard in the rural villages and small towns of the Fraser Valley. Japanese and Euro-Canadians joined together to establish the Pacific Cooperative Union in which Japanese farmers constituted seventy-five percent of the membership.

Baljeet Dhaliwal's paper describes the political and cultural structures of the Sikh people in Canada and specifically in the Fraser Valley prior to 1960. She begins with a description of the Sikhs' minority status in India, their struggle for religious survival in the era of the Moghul rulers, and their privileged yet inferior status in the British Empire. Interviews with local Sikhs provide the ethnographic perspective of the challenges many faced in arriving and settling on both the north and south sides of the Fraser River.

Catherine Marcellus, a local historian of the Mission area, specifically explores the history of the communities along the north shore of the Fraser River. Marcellus recounts the beginnings of communities such as Hatzic, Nicomen Island, Deroche and particularly Mission. She argues that the inhabitants of Mission, whose population, while characterized by diversity, had learned how to collaborate effectively and work for the benefit of the whole community.

The second section, "Early Religious and Intellectual Developments," explores the role of organized religion and its socio-historical effects on the formation of communities of the Fraser Valley. Biographies form the more appropriate genre to examine the role of religion in the history of Fraser Valley communities up to 1950.

Ron Dart explores the intellectual and religious mindset of one of Abbotsford's pioneers, Charles Hill-Tout. Dart examines the contributions that Hill-Tout made to the field of science (especially the evolutionist-creationist disputes) and the field of anthropology. In his discussion, Dart argues that the reader cannot understand Hill-Tout, the man, without taking into account his roots in the Church of England.

The social history of a particular community, the town of Yarrow, is examined through the lens of the Mennonite churches within the immigrant community. The churches functioned in various capacities: they provided places of refuge; they reinforced ethnic identity; they were active in the education of the immigrant community; and they functioned as institutions of social control.[2] Central to the development of Yarrow's Mennonite Brethren Church during the 1930s and 1940s, was Johannes Harder, the senior pastor for eighteen years. John Harder, the pastor's son, reflects on his father's life, character and legacy.

In Section Three, "Community and Family in Yarrow," the contributors explore aspects of family and community life in the ethnically homogeneous Mennonite community in the Fraser Valley. Marlene Epp addresses a knowledge deficit in the historical records of Mennonite history: the life of the immigrant women whom she names "yeowomen."[3] She asserts that the lives of these pioneer Mennonite women of the 1930s were characterized by incessant labour. She reports on the roles of maintaining the household, picking berry crops, harvesting hops, working as domestic maids in the cities in order to assist their economically distressed families, the labour of childbirth and the role of midwives. Epp contrasts the experiences of these pioneering women with those of the post-Word War II refugee families from Europe. The latter were often female-headed families who had to adjust to the Mennonite churches in Yarrow where women were officially silenced and their public demeanour carefully scrutinized. Both groups of women, Epp maintains, deserve a place of honour in the communities as "yeowomen."

Ruth Derksen Siemens' and Lora Sawatsky's study traces the patterns, habits, lifestyles, and choices of Yarrow residents over a span of four decades

(1930 to 1960). In examining the 149 responses to a questionnaire, they expose various factors that could have caused both the formation and dispersion of this community. Their research project is prompted by several questions: Why did the dispersion of Mennonite people from Yarrow begin so soon after the settlement and in such great numbers? Which factors contributed to the rapid decline? Which socio-cultural strata initiated these changes? Which stratified sampling most clearly delineates the nature of the decline and dispersion? How did the Mennonite *Russlaender* integrate into the surrounding Canadian society? Which generation was the first to become bicultural (Canadian and Russian Mennonite)? To what extent did education and employment opportunities affect individuals' decision to leave Yarrow? Did the early settlers' children choose their parents' vocations? If not, how much digression is evident?

Royden Loewen, using the twenty-eight memoirs and diaries in Len Neufeldt's, *Yarrow, British Columbia: Mennonite Promise,* reminds the readers that memoirs are deliberate "products of choice." The central concern for Loewen is the knowledge that the writers wished their subjects to realize. He observes that the writers emphasize that Yarrow was a specific place in a specific time, that its descendants "made good," that Yarrow represented a community with its network of church, family and street culture, and that it was a community with social boundaries, separating the settlers from their non-Mennonite neighbours. In short, the "Yarrow memoirs are the record of a people in an envisioned 'promised land.'"

Section Four provides a glimpse of both the arts and education within the Mennonite communities. While the arts enjoyed only a limited place in the early history of the Mennonite communities in the Fraser Valley, the muse was never entirely silenced. Increasing prosperity, as well as more educational opportunities following World War II, resulted in a renewed interest in music, literature and art. In her paper, "'Where berries grow and rivers run to sea': Memory and Metaphor in Leonard Neufeldt's *Raspberrying,*" Maryann Tjart Jantzen examines how these poems metaphorically explore the power of the past to inform the present through an impressionistic yet tactile recreation of the sensory and emotional ambiences of life in the small Fraser Valley village of Yarrow during the decades of the 1930s to the 1960s. Drawing on the often symbiotic relationship between poetry and memory, her paper argues that both can function as embodied history, not of facts and figures, but of emotional and sensory remembering. Thus, as these poems imaginatively reconstruct the past through recollections of lived experiences, they make a unique contribution to our understanding of a rich and transient historical moment.

Three articles in Section Four explore aspects of church sponsored educational institutions in the Fraser Valley. In "Planting the Cross in the Wilderness," Rev. Mark Dumont discusses the contribution of the Sisters of Saint Ann and the Oblates of Mary Immaculate in the establishment of Saint Mary's Indian Residential School in Mission. The Indian Residential Schools in Canada and the United States have been criticized for their deliberate policy (as one critic identifies it) of "deculturalization," namely "a process of stripping away the culture of a conquered people."[4] While Dumont does not discount this argument, in writing from the perspectives of the missionaries he maintains that schools like Saint Mary's, which represented the wisdom of their day, "made a welcome contribution to the lives of the children who attended them." Dumont in essence argues that historians need to exercise caution when judging past generations by contemporary standards.

In order to control the direction and pace of ethnic, including linguistic, and religious culturalization, the Mennonites who settled in the Fraser Valley, including Yarrow and Abbotsford during the 1930s and 1940s, established their own educational institutions. Beginning in the 1930s, Mennonite immigrants established several Bible Schools in Abbotsford and Yarrow. Historians of post secondary education have largely ignored the Bible School movement. Virginia Brereton (1990) and Bruce Guenther (2001) are two welcome exceptions. Guenther, while addressing criticisms leveled at these institutions, namely their low academic standards and their emphasis on indoctrination, argues that these schools had their roots, more often than not, within ethnic immigrant communities. He asserts that they were often "the most affordable and accessible religious training institutions possible for pioneering communities in western Canada." In providing instruction in English as well as in the German language, these schools formed a central influence in shaping several generations of young people from various immigrant communities and assisting in their adjustment to life in Canada.

Improved economic conditions in the 1940s resulted in an increased demand for secondary education. Two Mennonite high schools, one in Clearbrook and the other in Yarrow, were established during this time. Harvey Neufeldt analyzes the schools' mission as enunciated by the founders and the modification of their mission in the 1950s and 1960s, as the schools struggled to define their place within the ethnic community and the broader Canadian evangelical community.

In Section Five, John Redekop reflects on the impact of urbanization, religious dispersion and secularization on Fraser Valley Mennonites. He argues that increased economic opportunities following World War II, leading to geographic and, to an extent, religious dispersion, along with improved educational opportunities and secularization posed a challenge to the maintenance of distinctive ethnic, including religious, beliefs and practices. He presents four hypotheses that elucidate the Mennonite experience in the Fraser Valley: the Mennonites' emphasis on individualism rather than on community; their use of land as a "means to an end"; their tendency to place economic goals in a higher priority than the maintenance of the community; and their focus on future possibilities rather than on community traditions.

Endnotes

[1] While most papers are documented in MLA format, two previously published papers (Anne Doré's and Bob Smith's) use the Chicago Manual of Style.

[2] See Harvey Neufeldt, "Creating the Brotherhood: Status and Control in the Yarrow Mennonite Community, 1928-1960," *Canadian Papers in Rural History*, vol. 9, ed. Don Akenson (Gananoque, ON: Langdale Press, 1994), 211-38 and Harvey Neufeldt, "'You've Changed Too': The Education of the Yarrow Mennonite Community, 1928-1960," *Studies in Education* 7.1 (1995): 71-95.

[3] The silencing of the woman's voice in Mennonite history has begun to be addressed by authors such as Ruth Derksen Siemens (1999), in her study of the Vancouver Girls' Home and by Marlene Epp (2000) in her study of Mennonite women as World War II refugees.

[4] Joel Spring, *Deculturalization and the Struggle for Equality* (New York: McGraw Hill, 1994), xi.

Bibliography

Brereton, Virginia. *Training God's Army: The American Bible School Movement 1880- 1940*. Indianapolis: Indiana University Press, 1990.

Epp, Marlene. *Women without Men: Mennonite Refugees of the Second World War.* Toronto: University of Toronto Press, 2000.

Guenther, Bruce. "*Training for Service: The Bible School Movement in Western Canada.*" Ph.D. dissertation, McGill University, 2001.

Neufeldt, Leonard, Lora Sawatsky and Robert Martens, eds. *Yarrow, British Columbia: Mennonite Promise*. Vol. 1. *Before We Were the Land's*. Victoria, BC: TouchWood Editions, 2002.

———. *Yarrow British Columbia: Mennonite Promise*. Vol. 2. *Village of Unsettled Yearnings*. Victoria, BC: TouchWood Editions, 2002.

Neufeldt, Harvey. "Creating the Brotherhood: Status and Control in the Yarrow Mennonite Community, 1928-1960." *Canadian Papers in Rural History*. Vol. 9. Ed. Don Akenson. Gananoque, Ontario: Langdale Press, 1994.

———. "'You've Changed Too': The Education of the Yarrow Mennonite Community, 1928-1960." *Studies in Education* 7 No. 1 (1995).

Siemens, Ruth Derksen. Quilt asText and Text as Quilt: The Influence of Genre in the Mennonite Girls' Home of Vancouver (1930-1960)." *Journal of Mennonite Studies*, 17 (1999): 118-29.

Spring, Joel. *Deculturalization and the Struggle for Equality*. New York: McGraw Hill, 1994.

PART I

Pre-Settlement and Early Settlement

Reflections on First Nations' Settlements

A transcription of the opening address given
by Albert (Sonny) McHalsie
Thursday, June 5, 2003

O siyám el siyáye—Greetings, my friends.
["Oh respected leader(s), my friend(s)"]

That is the traditional way that we introduce ourselves when we speak in front of a gathering of our people. Literally, it translates "to respected leaders, friends, and relatives." First of all, I would like to introduce myself. I know many of you are probably wondering where I got my surname, McHalsie. I would like to share the history of this with you. My grandfather was *Nl'akapamuxw* which is the Thompson people. As a young boy he was known as *Bacupsh,* as he grew older he was known as *Naxexetsi* and as an elder he was known as *Meshk*. He was born in 1866 and when he was baptized by the early missionaries they gave him the name Antoine. Later, in the early 1900s, the Indian agent came to register his name on the Band List. The Indian Agent realized that the only Christian name my grandfather had was Antoine. So, the Indian Agent asked him, "What do you want for your surname? You need a surname." My grandfather responded by saying that he wanted his two adult names *Meshk* and *Naxexetsi*, so the Indian agent wrote down McHalsie. As a result many people tend to think I have Scottish ancestry due to the name Mc. It wouldn't be so bad if I didn't look so Scottish.

I am currently the Acting Executive Director of the Aboriginal Rights and Title Department at the *Stó:lō* Nation. I have worked in that department for the past eighteen years now. I began as a cultural researcher and eventually became the cultural advisor. I would like to thank you for inviting me here this evening and thank all the organizers for this conference and wish you well in the conference. I'd like to tell you a little bit more about my family background. I come from *Shxw'owhamel*, a place that you might know as Laidlaw. *Shxw'owhamel* translates as "where the river levels and widens." It's about ten kilometers to the west of Hope. I am married and have eight children, six sons and two daughters. I represent my family on the *Shxw'owhamel Siyám* council. My family lineage includes ancestry in both the *Stó:lō* and *Nl'akapamuxw* which is the *Stó:lō* and the Thompson. My mother was *Stó:lō* from *Chowethel* and my father was *Nl'ala/amuxw* from *Tuckkwiowhum* which is at Anderson Creek south of Boston Bar. My long family history goes right back to Captain Charlie of Yale and then to Semiahmoo and all the way over to Vancouver Island. There is a good description of this in a chapter in the book, *A Stó:lō Coast-Salish Historical Atlas*.

I would like to share a little about who the *Stó:lō* are. First of all the language that we speak is *Halq'emeylem* which consists of three main dialects. The upriver dialect, which is where I'm from, is pronounced *Halq'emeylem*, the down river dialect is known as *Hun'qumyi'num'* and then there's the island dialect which is known as *Hul'q'umin'um'*. Each of these dialects is subdivided into what linguists refer to as micro dialects or what anthropologists label "tribal divisions." Just to give you an example, the upriver dialect, or the *Halq'emeylem* dialect includes the *Tit*, which includes Seabird Island and Popkum and all the way up to Yale, the *St'qwompth* at the head of Harrison Lake, the *Sts'a'i:les* or Chehalis at the south end of Harrison Lake, the *Sq'ewlets* at the mouth of the Harrison River, *Ts'elxweyeqw* or the Chilliwack which is around the Chilliwack area, the *Sema:th* which is this area towards Kilgard, and also the *Leq'a:mel* which is on the other side of the river at Deroche. These are some of the micro dialects of the upriver area. The down river dialect and the island dialect are also subdivided into micro dialects. Those examples are just to give you an idea of how extensive our language is and a part of our history here.

The *Stó:lō* Nation territory or what we refer to as *S'olh Temexw* extends from just five miles on the other side of Yale all the way down to the mouth of the Fraser at *Musqueam*. The *Stó:lō* Nation political and service organization that is situated in Sardis, where I work right now. It represents eighteen of the Bands or First Nations from Langley up as far as Hope. Some of the Bands or First Nations within this area are not politically associated, but we still share the same family connections and common history. Some of the various resources that our people have shared include the Dry Rack Fishery up in the canyon and right down to the cranberry bogs in the *Musqueam* area. All of this was accessed through our family lineages. We accessed them through knowing our extended family, and also through what is commonly referred to as the "potlatch" or the give away.

We also have a rich history of our connections to the land which is also referenced in the atlas. When we look at our oral history, we have *Sxwôxwiyám* and *Sqwélqwel* which is the two main ways of sharing our oral history. *Sxwoxwiyám* is the origin stories that tell how the land was created. *Sxwôxwiyám* is also the word for the time period of these stories. The elders describe this as a time when the world was mixed up — when the world was not quite right. They say that back then animals and humans could talk to each other; animals and people could transform from one to the other. For instance, the mountain goats could take off their coat and be human underneath and put their coat back on to become a mountain goat again. So the world was quite mixed up.

In a story shared by George Chehalis, red-headed woodpecker lived in the mountains at the head of Harrison Lake. He had two wives, one was black bear and the other was grizzly bear. He had four children with black bear, three sons and one daughter, and none with grizzly bear. Grizzly Bear became jealous so she killed her husband and she herself was also killed. This left Black Bear as a widow and the four bear children as orphans. They were given special powers and the responsibility to travel through the territory to make the world right. They were known as *Xexa:ls* and they started at the head of Harrison Lake, made their way down to the Fraser, went up river toward the sunrise. Once they reached the sunrise they traveled through the sky down to the sunset and then came back up the river toward the sunrise and were never seen again.

All through their travels they did all kinds of different transformations, transforming some of our ancestors into some of the resources which we have today. For example, where I am from at *Shxw'ow'hamel*, the late Agnes Kelly shared a story about a famine when our people ran out of salmon during the winter months. One of the men was told by *Chíchelh Siyám*—the Creator (literally "respected leader") to go and stand by the edge of the river. The man dove into the river and was transformed into the sturgeon so we could have food in the winter months. His wife, she had missed her husband very much and *Chíchelh Siyám*, which is our word for the Great Spirit or the Creator, had told her to go stand by the edge of the river as well. She went down there and she had some deer meat wrapped around her wrist for her lunch and she got down to the river and her husband came in the form of a sturgeon and called her. She dove into the river and was transformed into the female sturgeon. Our elders tell us that because she had that brown deer meat wrapped around her wrist that today when you cut the head off a sturgeon, you see that brown piece of meat right behind the gills and it looks just like a piece of deer meat. That is because she had that brown deer meat tied to her wrist when she dove into the water.

So we look at these resources not only as resources but also as our ancestors. The spirit or the *shxwelí* is the word for the spirit or life force which remains in those resources and remains in the rocks and mountains that were once our ancestors who are now transformed. Our *shxweli* is what connects us to our land and resources.

There is another story. Some of you are probably quite familiar with Mt. Baker, as you have very good view of Mt. Baker from Abbotsford here. Mt. Baker was once a man who had a wife from up in Cheam. Some of you might have heard of Mt. Cheam. Originally it was called *Lhílheqey*. It's a long story so I won't go into all the details. She was transformed into a mountain up there. Her three daughters *Seyewot, Oyewot*, and *Xomo:th'iya* were also transformed into small mountain peaks right in front of her. Her husband was transformed into Mt. Baker. She also had three sons down south that were transformed into mountains. So we have all these different stories that connect us to the land, to the mountains and to the rocks.

Another example would be over in *Xa:ytem*, some of you might know it as Hatzic or Hatzic Rock. There's a story shared by the late Bertha Peters about how *Xexa:ls* came across these three leaders or *si:yá:m*, and he had given them the knowledge of the written language and asked them to share that with the rest of the people. They failed to do so. So *Xexa:ls* heaped them into a pile and transformed them into stone. There is a large rock there that represents those three *siyám*. It was at that time the elders told us that the *shxwelí* or the spirit or the life force of those *si:ya:m* are inside that rock.

A lot of the work that we're doing right now has a lot to do with our culture, history and spiritual revival. As I mentioned there are a number of publications that deal with those aspects: *You Are Asked To Witness* is a book that focuses on the grade 10, 11 and 12 curriculum; *I Am Stó:lō* is a book that incorporates the grade four curriculum; and then, the recent *A Stó:lō Coast Salish Historical Atlas* is directed to the general public, but is also a good reference for various resource agencies within government. It has also become very valuable for the different university departments including law, environment, history and anthropology.

So that is a little about who the *Stó:lō* people are as I don't have much time. Again, I would like to thank you for inviting me here this evening. On behalf of the *Stó:lō* Nation and on behalf of Chief Bea Silver from the Sumas First Nation and Chief Alice MacKay from the Matsqui First Nation, I would like to welcome you to *S'olh Temexw* traditional *Stó:lō* territory. And I wish you well in next few days. Based on the agenda it looks like there's going to be some very interesting topics here. So once again thank you for inviting me and I wish you all well in the next few days.

The Reclamation of the Sumas Lake Lands

Bob Smith

From prehistoric until modern times, the lands situated between Abbotsford and Chilliwack were periodically inundated by the Fraser River and by the numerous rivers and streams descending into the Sumas basin and lake from the northern slopes of the Cascades. The transformation of this natural landscape into hundreds of farms as well as into a transportation, energy transmission, and communications corridor linking the lower mainland with the interior was part of a larger process begun by Samuel Brighouse, who in 1864 initiated the dyking of Lulu Island. Eventually, the eight hundred square miles of lowlands from Agassiz to the Strait of Georgia would be insulated from flooding.

These dyking, drainage, and reclamation projects represented the imposition of the settlers' aspirations for new uses of these lowlands, ones very different from those nature intended. Between the 1870s and World War I, settlers in the Upper Fraser Valley supported one Sumas reclamation scheme after another in an attempt to protect their farms, roads, and bridges from the annual freshets of the Fraser, Chilliwack, and Sumas Rivers. The schemes failed because of insufficient local capital, bickering between east and west valley farmers, the lack of high risk, long-term investment from the private sector, and the provincial government's indifference or unwillingness to subsidize the cost.

With the election of the Liberal government in 1916 and the creation of the Land Settlement Board (LSB) in 1917, British Columbia's ambitious agricultural development projects to date, sprang up all over the province.[1] Included in these projects was the reclamation of the Sumas Lake lands, which Premier John Oliver, Minister of Agriculture E. D. Barrow, and the engineer F. N. Sinclair directed in the 1920s. The completion of the project depended upon the vigorous support of the state bureaucracy, led by politicians committed to the value of agricultural life and to less dependence on imported food. But even then the economic wisdom of the project remained in doubt. Its enormous costs had brought much provincial political criticism of Oliver's government as well as a great deal of local dissatisfaction among landowners who were expected to shoulder a totally unrealistic tax burden. However, in the end, the project made possible even more than it was originally designed to do; in one respect alone, it enabled local farmers to contribute more to the province's agricultural production than the scheme's proponents had ever envisioned.

Early Proposals

During the 1860s, a handful of settlers established farms covering several thousand acres east of Sumas Lake, which dominated the landscape from Abbotsford to Chilliwack between the Vedder and Sumas Mountains. Vegetables, beef, flour, butter, and fodder were produced in significant quantities for sale in communities up and down the Fraser River. From the start, cash crop farming was a promising enterprise, closely associated with the ambitions of merchants, property speculators, saw and grist mill operators, and other economic interests that benefited from a thriving agricultural economy. The major floods of 1876, 1882, and 1894 as well as frequent minor inundations ruined crops, bankrupted farmers, tore up roads and bridges, depressed property values, and reduced the profits of service businesses. Obviously, until the entire area was protected from the spring freshets, profitable farming operations would be restricted to the available high ground, although farmers could still graze their cattle on the extensive lowlands during the low water season.[2] By the early 1870s, it was apparent that dyking and drainage could make the 20,000 acres adjacent to Sumas Lake just as profitable as the high ground farms, and likely even more so, since the low lands were unforested, which would enable settlers to begin farming immediately without first facing costly and time-consuming land clearing. In 1873, the *Victoria Colonist* observed that dyking and drainage at Sumas were feasible and that the government could recoup part of the construction costs by selling 10,000 acres reclaimed from the lake and by levying assessments on adjacent occupied lands.[3] In addition, in 1873, several developers indicated to the Chief Commissioner of Lands and Works their interest in undertaking the project in return for the right to sell reclaimed land.[4] While settlers favoured the idea, the government did not act.[5]

The flood of 1876 inundated much of the valley. Sixty-nine farmers were reduced to accepting government handouts of seed in order to begin the 1877 season.[6] The Chadsey brothers complained to Victoria that flooding had twice forced them to relocate their mill and granary.[7] The provincial government instructed the engineer Edgar Dewdney to report on the feasibility of dyking the lands east of Sumas Lake where farmers had sustained the greatest damage. After several weeks of fieldwork, Dewdney recommended that a dyke be built between Chilliwack and Sumas Mountains and that a dam be constructed at the eastern base of Sumas Mountain. The dam would prevent the influx of the Fraser's waters in May and June and permit the drainage of the Sumas River which, conveniently, peaks earlier in the spring. Dewdney also recognized the problem created by the water descending from the Chilliwack Lake basin, which had created havoc on its course to the Fraser via the Luckakuck. He recommended the clearing, deepening and dyking of the Luckakuck in order to channel the waters directly and safely to the Fraser, thus preventing it from topping up Sumas Lake.

Dewdney had encountered a local sore point: lower Sumas farmers had purchased their land when the Chilliwack River flowed to the Luckakuck. However, after a time the Chilliwack began to enter Vedder Creek and flow their way, causing damage and raising the level of the lake. The Sardis and Chilliwack farmers, relieved at this trend, were even willing to facilitate it by felling trees in the area where the Chilliwack entered the Luckakuck, thereby giving nature a boost. As the historian, Imbert Orchard, put it, "What was good for Sardis was a disaster for Sumas, and vice versa." Dewdney's report included, among other matters, plans for dyke construction and estimates of the amount of earth to be moved. He stated that this plan would promote settlement and that it would protect the Yale Wagon Road and bridges from washout. Above all, Dewdney established the practicality of the scheme and laid the groundwork for a subsequent engineering survey, thus giving reclamation proponents the arguments and technical authority they required in the various schemes which they promoted.[8]

The distress caused by the flood of 1876, the Dewdney report, the Chadsey brothers' complaint, David W. Millers' letter to the *Colonist* requesting a government-guaranteed loan for dyking, as well as the general local sentiment calling for action no doubt all had their roles in the decision of the Minister of Finance and Agriculture, William Smith, to attend a meeting of Sumas farmers in November 1877. There he learned that farmers were willing to submit to a five dollar per acre tax to pay for the cost of dyking.[9] Consequently, in the winter of 1877-78, the provincial government reached an agreement with E. L. Derby, who had proposed to dyke the Fraser in return for 45,000 acres of unoccupied land and a five dollar per acre assessment on occupied land.[10] The government would thus kill two birds with one stone: it could appease local settlers and avoid committing itself financially.

The only problem was that Derby never built the dykes. There is considerable evidence that Derby was incompetent, of questionable character, and treated farmers shabbily. The dykes he had previously built in Matsqui were washed out.[11]

The provincial government seemed to have profited little from its experience with unsuccessful private developers. Though dyking legislation would change, locally-elected dyking commissioners would be empowered to enter into contracts with developers to undertake construction, and the provincial government would guarantee the interest on loans from the private sector to underwrite construction, the whole matter was needlessly complex and too dependent on investors.[12] Under these terms, the cooperation of several parties was required: local landowners, their dyking commissioners, the provincial government, construction companies, private investors, and the engineers. In 1892, John Lumsden and his associates had secured local approval, a provincial charter, conditional financing, and had a detailed survey by the Dutch engineer, Van Loben Sels, but Premier Theodore Davie refused to make good his initial promises to guarantee payment of interest on prospective loans.[13] In 1894, the provincial government again refused to back a project initiated by the Sumas Dyking Commissioners after they had already expended $18,000 and after tenders had been let and received.[14] In addition, the Dominion government had acquired the title to the lake bottom and reserved for itself the right to review all proposals. Since every project's financial viability depended on the sale of these lands, the Dominion government's approval was critical. In at least one case — the Lewis project of 1905 — Ottawa refused and the project collapsed after most of the other criteria had been satisfied.[15]

As a result of government inaction, the floodwaters of 1894 caused the greatest damage to date. The entire valley was flooded. As Imbert Orchard records in *Floodland and Forest*, crops as well as homes were destroyed. Rowboats became the best means of transportation and cattle had to be driven to high ground.[16] The government sent one of its own cabinet ministers, Colonel James Baker, to assist families to high ground, save livestock, and distribute fodder and seed. Col. Baker noted in his report the continuation of the "water wars" between the Sumas and Chilliwack forces over the course of the Chilliwack River/Vedder Creek:

> On arriving at Chilliwack . . . I was informed of a deputation of the inhabitants that some of the Sumas people were determined to blow up with dynamite the timber jam which prevented the waters from Vedder Creek flowing into the Luk-a-kuk, and that if this was permitted it would completely destroy some of the most valuable lands

in Chilliwack; that the Chilliwack . . . [people] were determined to resist it with force, if driven to do so, while the Sumas people were equally determined on the other side, as they suffered from the overflowing waters of Vedder Creek. I was informed that immediate action was imperative, as rifles were threatened to be used. [17]

Special constables were sworn in and dispatched to the site, and arrests were made. Judge Howay, however, dismissed the case against those charged.[18]

After 1894, the Chilliwack River increasingly drained into Sumas Lake, thus adding to the settlers' resentment. Understandably, several of the reclamation schemes proposed by Sumas landowners called for the rediversion of the Chilliwack River to the Luckakuck, which not surprisingly, the Sardis-Chilliwack settlers opposed. Since the Luckakuck falls 60 feet in only three miles, thus possessing enormous destructive potential, the farmers living near it were suspicious of any promises of security offered by engineers.[19] For example, directly after learning that the Rice project of 1911-12 specified a diversion of the Chilliwack through the Luckakuck, settlers met at Edenbank under the leadership of Henry Hulbert, a Sardis hopgrower, to draw up a petition of protest to be forwarded to the Dominion government. The settlers noted that they did not oppose reclamation, but only any project that involved this specific rediversion. The Lewis-Hill scheme of 1905 was opposed on the same grounds, even though the provincial government was prepared to offer Sardis-Chilliwack farmers some financial security in the event that the rediverted waters caused damage to their property.[20]

The Sumas reclamation proponents encountered additional opposition from, of all people, some Sumas farmers. It should be noted that between the 1870s and the 1920s, the majority of farmers in the lower and upper Sumas, the areas immediately east and west of the lake respectively, approved reclamation schemes. The province required their assent because a successful dyking and drainage project would enhance the value of their land, and they would therefore assume responsibility for part of the construction costs. However, there was also a vocal and significant minority of Sumas farm owners who voted against successive projects. As holders of the occasional high ground farms on the Sumas prairie, they resented the prospect of assessments to pay for flood protection they did not require. Also, they feared, quite correctly, that once the region was dyked and the lowlands reclaimed, sold, and fenced, their cattle would be denied access to the lands that by tradition and gentlemen's agreement served as grazing lands (and as a place to cut natural fodder) in the low water season.[21] Thus, in view of financing problems, government inaction, lack of cooperation between too many parties, opposition by the Sardis-Chilliwack farmers, and noisy dissent from some Sumas farmers, it is small wonder that the Sumas lands went unprotected and unreclaimed. The remedy for these problems awaited a timely change in government.

Political Breakthrough

By 1916, the McBride-Bowser Tory government was in trouble. The wartime reform sentiment stood in direct contrast to this regime's 13-year record of corruption and virtual give-away of public resources to big corporations. A solid group of labour representatives, clergy, feminists, prohibitionists, and farmers united under the Liberal Party and swept the Tories from power. The Tory regime had never done much for B.C. farmers in general, let alone Fraser Valley farmers in particular. This area's Conservative candidate, W. L. Macken, suffered as a result, and the political newcomer but established farmer E. D. Barrow was elected along with another farmer, John Oliver, from Delta.[22] This government, which also included a freshman member from Prince Rupert, T. D. Patullo, was committed to progressive agricultural and land management policies, and did not hesitate to involve government in some areas where private enterprise had failed. The province was woefully deficient in the production of foodstuffs: the reclamation of the Sumas Lands, among with numerous lands in the province, would constitute a step towards self-sufficiency. There were before 1916 at least seven major engineering surveys, all of which without exception had declared the Sumas reclamation project technically feasible. In order to transform the province's agricultural sector, the Liberals created the Land Settlement Board as an agency within the Department of Agriculture.

Minister of Lands Patullo recommended to the cabinet that broad powers be granted to the Board, that it take on the responsibility for the Sumas reclamation, depose the locally-elected dyking commissioners, and organize local support for this proposal.[23] Local landowners approved Patullo's plan and on 1 October 1917 the Sumas Dyking Commissioners turned over their papers and debt ($13,265) to the Land Settlement Board, which assumed all powers and responsibilities. However, the local settlers would be permitted to review the final survey and approve or reject it since they were expected to pay half the cost. In the spring of 1918, the board hired the engineers H. C. Brice and W. C. Smith to prepare preliminary surveys.[24] However, Sumas farmers grew restless because of the project's slow progress and the losses they incurred in the flood season of 1918. When the farmers began to consider a privately-financed dyking plan, the board presented them with the prospect of having to pay their full share of the government scheme in addition to any private one.[25] The board obviously wished to maintain overall control of the project. In 1919, the Brice-Smith survey was completed. It estimated that the project, expected to take three years to complete, would cost $1 500 000, half to be paid by the landowners, half to be raised from the sale of the lake lands

Entrance of F.N.Sinclair

When Brice took fatally ill, the board appointed F. N. Sinclair in his place. Friction developed between Smith and Sinclair, since they held different opinions on the survey.[27]

The board decided that each engineer would submit separate plans. Finally, in July of 1919, Sinclair's plan was chosen, and he was appointed engineer-in-chief.[28] Sinclair was an American who had worked for the Great Northern, the Victoria Vancouver and Eastern, and the BC Electric Railways, the City of New Westminster, and the Dominion government. Previously, in 1913, Sinclair had submitted a survey of the project to the dyking Commissioners, so he was well acquainted with the work.[29] His plan called for dyking the Fraser River between Chilliwack and Sumas Mountains and the building of a dam and pumping station at the eastern foot of Sumas Mountain. This dam would let the Sumas River, which would be channeled across the flood plain, out into the Fraser and also keep the Fraser from coming in. The dam's pumps would drain the lake.

Sinclair also hit upon the idea of diverting the Chilliwack River, not through the Luckakuck, but through a channel to be created, later known as the Vedder Canal. This innovation would gain the political support of the Sardis-Chilliwack farmers, who could be relied upon to oppose any rediversion of the Chilliwack River in their direction, and it would also avoid the technical problems that the precipitous descent of the Luckakuck presented. Sinclair estimated the cost at $1 500 000, half of which the landowners would pay according to a graduated-assessment schedule pegged to each farm's elevation; the lower the elevation, the higher the tax. This plan more or less satisfied the high ground farmers who did not wish to pay for flood protection they did not require. As will be concluded, the attraction of Sinclair's plan was as much political as technical. Premier Oliver, who attended the meeting, asserted flatly that while the government would lend the money required for construction, it did not accept any financial liability; the landowners, existing and potential, would have to pay the whole shot. The farmers approved the project by a vote of 86 percent.[30]

In January 1920, the Land Settlement Board invited bids from private construction firms. The lowest bid, by Marsh Bourne Construction Company, was substantially higher than the amount already approved. The board decided that the Sumas landowners would have to approve an additional $300 000. This they did by a vote of 102 to 6 on 27 March 1920.[31] This shortfall was the first in a long series of miscalculations on the project's cost. Events would prove that the estimate of $1 800 000 was nowhere near the amount required. As costs escalated, the Land Settlement Board decided against consulting the Sumas landowners, even though it still expected them to pay half the cost. Local resentment and political friction were in the making.[32]

The contract with Marsh Bourne was signed on 29 April 1920. The company agreed to complete the major earthwork, house and feed the construction crew, observe the province's labour laws, give preference to veteran-job-seekers, and exclude Orientals from any jobs. It was clear almost from the start that the board's decision to contract with Marsh Bourne was extremely ill-advised, perhaps even negligently so. The company was not prepared to proceed with construction. It did not possess the necessary equipment. By October 1920, it was virtually bankrupt. This crisis gave rise to numerous charges that Marsh Bourne Construction was a hastily arranged concern, only recently incorporated by Liberal Party favorites.[33] This on-paper-only entity proved totally unprepared for the work. Thus the Land Settlement Board had to inject additional funds, acquire necessary equipment, and retain professional supervisors below Sinclair's level. Although the board had every legal right to cancel the Marsh contract, it chose not to, thus lending credence to the charges of political favouritism. A government auditor reported that the company's executives had paid themselves unreasonably high salaries and had claimed unjustifiable personal and travel expenses. The auditor noted numerous "irregularities" in the company's books. Sinclair was infuriated by the delay in his construction schedule. About a year had been needlessly consumed.[34]

Construction

The major construction was completed between 1921 and 1923. Upwards of 150 men were employed during the peak periods of work. Giant electric-powered suction dredges were employed to cut out the Vedder Canal and build its dykes along a four-mile stretch from the Vedder Bridge to the foot of Sumas Mountain. From an engineering standpoint, the beauty of this new bed for the Chilliwack River was its gradual descent — only six feet over the distance. A greater descent would have given the water too much cutting power, especially where the canal turns west and north downstream from the Vedder Bridge. With the completion of the Fraser River Dyke between Sumas and Chilliwack Mountains, as well as the canal dykes, the eastern portion of

Sumas Prairie was protected. The pumping facility at the McGillivray Creek Dam then kept the eastern section dry enough to permit reclamation work. In the following year, 1923, a much larger pumping station and dam were built on the western side of the Vedder Canal at the foot of Sumas Mountain. The Sumas River was channeled to this point, several feet above the valley floor. At the dam, four 54-inch pumps capable of pumping 360,000 cubic feet of water per minute were installed. At the time, they constituted the largest pumping facility in Canada. (In the early 1960s, a fifth pump was added and the dam and station were completely replaced.) In the summer and fall of 1923, most of Sumas Lake was pumped dry. Then the Sumas Lake Drainage Canal, which runs from the south to the dam in the north, was dredged. With the addition of ditches running east and west into the drainage canal, excessive water could be removed. Sinclair's work proved equal to the 1924 freshets, but in December 1924 the ever troublesome Vedder River jumped its banks and flooded 1500 acres of the east prairie. Sinclair's plan had called for the construction of toe dykes, but due to escalating costs, only the toe dyke to the western side was completed.

Only two major breakdowns in the system have occurred since 1924. In the ice storm of 1935, ice and snow clogged channels and prevented the natural discharge of the Sumas River into the Fraser. The ice tore down the power lines to the pumping station, disabling the pumps. As a result, the Sumas River channel filled and overflowed into the lower-lying lakebed. Then, in 1948, the Fraser River breached the dyke protecting the prairie east of the Vedder Canal. Sinclair claimed that this occurred because the high-water level in 1948 exceeded the highest previous level, that of 1894. According to Sinclair's recollections, two boys who were asked to watch a weak point in the Fraser River dyke and give warning so that it could be reinforced with sandbags left for lunch, during which time the dyke broke.[35]

The Sumas project was done from start to finish by non-union labour, and it was not interrupted by a major dispute or strike, a virtually singular exception in the history of nineteenth and early-twentieth-century mega-projects in British Columbia, including the construction of the Canadian Pacific, Canadian Northern, Grand Trunk Pacific, and Kettle Valley Railways. In those cases, the employer could do as he pleased. He would offer only wretched bunkhouses and food, force workers to pay for medical services they never received, sell clothes and sundries at outrageously high prices in the company store, and even refuse to pay wages. Then, when workers went on strike, the employer responded by bringing in strike-breakers and weeding out strike leaders, thus forcing their followers back to work. These exploitative conditions in part explain the accumulation of incredible fortunes by men such as the railroad builders and financiers, William Mackenzie and Donald Mann, as well as the violent class warfare that legislative inquiries and scholars have repeatedly documented.[36]

Why was the Sumas construction not plagued by isolated strikes and work stoppages like many of the big projects? The workers were near towns, non-company stores, social amenities, friends and relatives, and other jobs. Following the brief post-World War I recession, the 1920s were boom times and unemployment was low. Thus, Marsh Bourne Construction was forced to keep these factors in mind when determining how it would treat its workers. Furthermore, the contract that Marsh Bourne Construction had signed with the Liberal government forced it to obey the provincial labour laws recently reformed by that same Liberal government. For example, the contract stipulated that the workers receive their wages every two weeks. They were protected by workmen's compensation.[37] Unskilled workers' wages approached the prevailing average wage for all construction workers in BC —about $25 per week. A skilled worker might earn $45 per week.[38] The work week was, however, long: ten hours per day, six days a week, and a half day every other Sunday.

Working conditions were far from ideal: the men had to slog around in the mud much of the time—and there was the rain, the snow, and the cold northeast wind. During the high water period, the men had to wear large straw hats with netting to ward off mosquitoes. On-site accommodations consisted of 12-by-20-foot tent cabins with wooden floors and four-foot wooden sides, each housing eight men. Coal stoves provided heat. The food was reportedly good, and there were shower rooms and toilet facilities.[39] However, several work related accidents caused injuries and death, including that of the construction company's president, J. R. Duncan, who was killed in an airplane crash on his way to the work site from Vancouver.[40]

Financing

The financial records of the reclamation project are lengthy and complicated, but one need not be an accountant or government auditor to establish several startling conclusions. The most important point of departure here is the government's position that it would refuse to accept any financial liability for the costs and, as the lender, fully expected to recoup its outlay by selling lake bottom land, by assessing taxes on occupied land, and by charging interest. The government did, however, pay the salaries and expenses of several officials from the Department of Agriculture and its Land Settlement Board who devoted a great deal of time to the Sumas project. Local landowners had agreed in 1919 to pay roughly one-half of the project's total cost of $1 500 000. Later they agreed to the revised figure of $1 800 000. Then, as costs mounted, mostly for legitimate reasons, the government, while no longer referring the matter to local assent, refused to retreat from its position that the landowners would have to pay their full share. By 1924, when the construction was more or less complete, the bill stood at $3 500 000. This figure continued to rise as the cost of reclamation work and interest was included. By the end of 1926, it stood at $4 000 000.[41] It did not take the local farmers long to realize that they might never be able to pay their share and they protested accordingly. In 1925, the west prairie landowners, acting through commissioners, claimed that the project had been illegally carried out.[42] The government quashed the suit by legislation that retroactively validated all governmental actions in the Sumas project, thus preventing any further legal action.[43]

The Sumas landowners pleaded for the creation of an impartial tribunal to adjudicate the dispute. They drew up a petition denouncing the provincial government's retroactive legislation as "tyrannical" and sent it to the Dominion Minister of Justice, Earnest Lapointe.[44] In 1925, witnesses before the Court of Revision, which had set the assessment in 1925, complained about dyke leakages, assessments on high-ground farmland, assessments that were too high, and the like. Charges of injustice, illegal and excessive construction costs, and an illegally-constituted Court of Revision pervaded the public testimony.[45] Farmers threatened to withhold their assessments, and rumours spread concerning the terms of the Minister of Agriculture E. D. Barrow's acquisition of property in the reclaimed east prairie.[46] There were other lawsuits. Matthew and Hannah Hall sued the board for $10 000, claiming that the project diverted water they required for their farm. They, however, lost their case. Engineer Sinclair, however, won his financial suit and settled out of court for $21 500.

The adjustment of the payment to the construction company dragged on for four years.[47] The government had long been sensitive to the various complaints, especially when it was called upon to defend itself in the legislature.[48] Barrow and the Land Settlement Board fought back through public speeches, government-sponsored tours of the project for businessmen from various boards of trade, and press releases, all touting the prospective benefits of the scheme.[49] The government's Court of Revision did examine each complaint. In 1924, just before the election, the legislature enacted a relief measure which scaled down or deferred in part the financial obligation of the landowners owning no more than 80 acres each.[50] This relief measure, however, obliged the government to stake its hopes of recovering costs on the sale of lake-bottom lands at prices that critics argued few could afford. The government throughout the 1920s and the 1930s continued to claim that the debt was a local responsibility.

Despite the sale of the new Sumas lands, the original costs mounted. By 1939, the bill stood at $7 600 000, double the original cost and quadruple the original amount approved by the landowners.[51] Eventually, the capital cost was forgiven and taken over by the senior levels of government, which have also more recently underwritten the costs of additional construction such as the new pump house and related works at the Sumas Mountain dam site. However, all district property holders, and not simply those on the flood plain, pay taxes annually for the maintenance of the dyking system, which in the 1983 fiscal year was budgeted at $357 000.[52]

Reclamation and Settlements

For decades, farmers, reclamation promoters, politicians, boards of trade, and newspaper editors had highly praised the agricultural potential of the lake lands. Working from these claims, student essayists in a competition sponsored by a local drugstore in 1922 described the project's benefits as "inestimable."[53] The claims seemed to be realistic because the adjacent lands in the Sumas basin had long been farmed. In order to make good these claims and thus be able to sell those 10 000 acres at a price sufficient to offset a large part of the government's construction costs, the government began experimental agricultural operations on the recently drained lake lands. In November 1923, the Land Settlement Board transferred Captain A. H. Rowberry from the board's development site at Crescent to supervise the work. Tractors were brought in and plowing and seeding commenced in 1924, much of the work being done on contract by local residents. Initially, over half the lake lands were seeded with fodder crops and some vegetables. With some exceptions, the crops did not fare well due to the nitrogen deficiency in the soil.[54] However the lake lands grew a beautiful crop of willows, the seeds of which had been well-distributed by the drainage process. The willows choked out much of the crops. This problem persisted through four summers. The experimentation, which included the cultivation of hemp and tobacco, gradually began to show good results, but this came at a great cost—$50 000 in 1924, and over $100 000 in 1928.[55] This cost was reduced by the sale of crops, but the substantial deficit was simply added to the farmers' bills.

At the same time that the lake lands were surveyed into lots, lateral ditches were cut across the lake lands to channel excessive water to the Sumas Lake Drainage Canal. Twenty barns were built, and an advertising campaign was launched to promote the sale of the lake lands. Under the direct supervision of E. D. Barrow, advertisements were placed in farm journals such as the

Grain Growers Guide and *The Washington Farmer*, and were distributed by dominion and provincial agents abroad, especially in the United Kingdom, Belgium, Holland and Scandinavia. Germany seems to have been omitted, perhaps because of the ill feeling that persisted following World War I. The provincial government, reflecting the racism of the day was adamant that lake lands not be sold to Orientals. In addition, samples of crops grown on the lake lands were exhibited at fairs. The advertisements, while including some unproven claims, could for the most part be characterized as truthful. They emphasized the region's mild climate, transportation services, proximity to markets, absence of drought (no exaggeration here!), legislation for farmers' cooperatives, low taxes, the improved condition of the land, and reasonable terms. E. D. Barrow even gave glowing personal testimonials, based on his 30 years of farming experience in the area and his position as Minister of Agriculture.[56]

Despite these efforts, to say the least, the sale of lake lands was not brisk. The reasons for this are clear. Against the advice of realtors, the Land Settlement Board required $200 per acre, with 15 percent down and the balance over 15 years at 6 percent per year. Eight thousand dollars for 40 acres was simply beyond the reach of most prospective buyers.[57] The board and ministry refused to change their minds and, as a result, 90 percent of the lake lands went unsold. Finally, in late 1929, and unfortunately before the impact of the coming Depression was clear, the Board reduced its price to $125 per acre for the remaining 8700 acres and liberalized its terms —10 percent down and the balance over 20 years at 6 percent.[58] The majority of the acreage sold quickly; later, in the middle of the Depression, the going price fluctuated between $40 and $90 per acre. Numerous farms, comprising about 25 percent of the lake land, reverted to the government on account of arrears in payments, and this despite every reasonable attempt by the Board to give farmers a chance to survive until better times.[59] Obviously, the Sumas lands offered little opportunity for the pioneer farmer, since only established farmers with substantial capital and larger corporate concerns such as Buckerfields, the Canadian Hop Growers, or the BC Tobacco Growers could buy in.

In the midst of the Depression, it did not appear that the cost of construction, development, and government overhead on the Sumas project constituted a good investment. However, just as World War II put the Canadian economy on an unprecedented strong footing after the aimless drift of almost a decade, the war pushed up the demand for foodstuffs, benefiting almost every farmer. The post-war economic boom, the expanding markets, and the government assumption of the original cost of construction combined with more consistent factors of climate, industrious farmers, and ready access to markets, to make good the original investment. Above all, the regulation of milk production (which strives to equalize output and demand and permits milk producers' returns to cover production costs as well as profits) ended the numerous disastrous aspects of the free enterprise system in this important Fraser Valley industry. The value of production created on 30 000 acres of land which were unproductive before 1924 was confirmed by Harold Imus in a land use study completed in 1948.[60] Additionally, less dependency on foreign foodstuffs and the development of a fairly secure transportation and energy (gas and hydropower) corridor linking the lower mainland with the interior accrued benefits to the province as a whole.

One benefit of the Sumas Reclamation scheme has gone unmentioned and, at first glance, may seem minor. In the sixty years of European settlement before the drainage of the lake, numerous observers attested to the extreme difficulties caused by mosquitoes for about a month each summer. The normal routines of life, labour, and leisure were significantly interrupted, forcing residents to take cumbersome protective measures such as burning smudge pots in their homes or even temporarily vacating the area. One settler remarked that mosquitoes had killed a baby on Sumas Prairie when it kicked the netting off its crib.[61] Readers of Charles Wilson's diary, *Mapping the Frontier,* will have noted that the Royal Engineers sent to survey the boundary were frequently reduced to inactivity by mosquito attacks. The Sumas reclamation and similar undertakings further down the valley did much to make the Fraser Valley more habitable than it had previously been.

The appearance of Sumas Prairie has been drastically changed from the Eden-like landscape that had impressed the Royal Engineer Charles Wilson and the naturalist John Keast Lord in the gold rush era. Significant alteration of the natural heritage has been a cost of the progress brought about by European and Canadian settlers. The drainage of the lake and adjacent marshes radically affected the habitat of birds and other wildlife that Canada's foremost naturalist-artist, Allan Brooks, had so patiently studied and elegantly rendered.[62] An eyewitness recounted significant changes:

> There was between ten and twelve thousand acres of . . . lake. . . .
> There was always fish in it. There was some quite large sturgeon
> taken out of Sumas Lake when they drained it. In the fall it was a
> sanctuary for ducks; there'd be duck on there by the million, and
> they would come in to feed on the marshes around the edge of the
> lake at night; and for an hour at dusk, why, a good shot would get
> anywhere from 20 to 40 ducks in an evening, just shooting them in
> flight. That has all been more or less forgotten about. Since the lake

was drained the ducks don't come this way anymore, and it was quite a hunter's paradise in those days.[63]

The drainage of the Sumas basin also eliminated the recreational activities of swimmers, beach walkers, picnickers, and pleasure-craft enthusiasts who frequented the lake and patronized area businesses.

The merits of the project should also be qualified by the commonplace but still important fact that the expensive system of flood protection does not offer absolute protection. The dyking system, incidentally, also denies the land of the nutrients that the Fraser River had naturally deposited over the flood plain for millennia. These deposits now remain in the river bed, gradually raising it, thus creating the need for dredging. And this system of flood control can break down, given optimum conditions such as deep snow packs in the north, early and fast run-off, high spring tides backing up the Fraser, and heavy rain, which together, even though monitored by government officials, could once again reproduce the massive floods that occurred in 1876, 1894, or 1948.

Endnotes

[1] Reuben Ware. "Land and a New Life," *British Columbia Historical News* 14.3 (Spring 1982): 13.

[2] H.R. Imus, "Land Utilization in the Sumas Lake District." (Masters thesis, University of Washington, 1948), 28-30.

[3] *Victoria Colonist*, 15 March 1873, 2.

[4] Edward Mohun, William Wolcox, and L.T. Dupont to Robert Beaven, Chief Commissioner of Lands and Works, 25 July, 1873, GR 868/1/6/1136, PABC.

[5] Henry Edmonds to the Ch. Com. of Lands and Works (hereafter cited as CCLW), 5 Sept. 1873, GR 868/1/6/1438/ PABC.

[6] Donna Cook, "Early Settlement in the Chilliwack Valley" (Master's thesis, University of British Columbia, 1978), 50-51.

[7] J.M. Murphy per Wm. Chadsey to CCLW,16 May 1876, GR 868/2/15/1063.

[8] Imbert Orchard, *Floodland and Forest: Memoirs of the Chilliwack Valley*, Sound Heritage Series, #37 (Victoria: Provincial Archives of British Columbia, 1983): 56; Edgar Dewdney to G. Vernon, CCLW, 27 Nov., 1876, in *Sessional Papers of British Columbia, 1876* (Victoria, 1877): 269-75.

[9] J.M. Murphy per Wm. Chadsey to CCLW, 16 May 1876, GR 868/2/15/1063; *Victoria Colonist*, 29 March 1877, 2 and 13 Nov. 1877, 3.

[10] The I' Sumas Dyking Act, 1878, 11 *B.C. Statutes*.

[11] J.A. Mahood to George Walkem, CCLM, 1 July 1878, GR 868/3/25/1466; J. Treatheway to Walkem, 31 March 1879, GR 868/3/27/380; W. S. Gore to Walkem, 17 June 1879, 868/3/28/850; D.M. McGuillivray, et al, to Walkem, 28, Oct. 1879, GR 868/3/29/1393; W.L. Gillanders to Walkem, 5 March 1880, GR 868/4/3/165; and *Victoria Colonist*, 1 June 1879, 3.

[12] J. L. MacDonald, "The History of Dykes and Drainage in B. C.," *Transactions of the 10th British Columbia Natural Resources Conference, 1957*(B.C. Natural Resources Conference, 1957): 75-78.

[13] J. A. Lumsden to Premier Davie, 21 Sept. and 5 Oct. 1892, Davie Papers, PABC, and Lumsden to Premier McBride, 6 Feb. and 5 March, 1907, GR 441/86/3/126.

[14] W. S. Latta, "Record of Events—Sumas," 3 and petition of the Sumas Dyking Commissioners to Edgar Dewdney, Lt. Gov. in the *Vancouver World*, Mar. 1896.

[15] "Record of Events," 27.

[16] Orchard, *Floodland and Forest*, 58-62.

[17] "Fraser River Relief: Report of Colonel, the Hon. James Baker," 10 October 1894, in *B.C. Sessional Papers*, 1894 (Victoria, 1894): 447-51.

[18] Orchard, *Floodland and Forest*, 63.

[19] Ibid., 56.

[20] A. Evans to Premier McBride, 25 March, 1905, GR 441/25/102; G. Salmon to W. J.Bowser, 19 Oct.1910, GR 429/18/2; *Progress*, 14 Feb.1912, 1.

[21] T. M. Hall to Premier McBride, 29 March 1907, GR 441/29/63, and 14 March 1910, GR 441/37/24; J. H. Collinson, et al, to Premier McBride, 15 Jan. 1905, GR 441/27/30; Collinson to McBride, 30 Nov. 1910, GR 441/40/642; and Orchard, *Floodland and Forrest*, 21.

[22] Bob Smith, "The Liquor Question and the 1916 Election in Chilliwack," *British Columbia Historical News* 15.3 (Spring 1982): 6-12.

[23] Pattullo to Oliver, 13 Dec. 1916, memo, GR 441/336/8; Pattullo to Barrow, 18 Aug.1917, GR 441/190/1126, and Pattullo to Brewster, 14 Sept. 1917, memo, GR 441/336/8.

[24] "Record of Events," 6-7.

[25] William Blatchford to H. M. Nelems, 5 Oct. 1918; Nelems to M. Smith, 8 Oct. 1918; E. D. Barrow to Brice and Smith, 16 Dec. 1918; C. St. George Yarwood to M. Smith, 16 Jan. 1919, and M. Smith to Blatchford, 4 Feb. 1919, GR 929/50/3.

[26] Sumas Advisory Board to the Land Settlement Board, 26 Feb. 1919, GR 929/50/4.

[27] Blatchford to Nelems, 28 June 1919, GR 929/50/5.

[28] Nelems to M. Smith and Nelems to Sinclair, 22 July 1919, GR 929/50/5, and "Record of Events," 8.

[29] Sumas, Early Engineering Reports, file 10-Sb-10-10; Inspectorate of Dykes, and Oliver Wells' Introduction to F.N. Sinclair, "A History of the Sumas Drainage, Dyking and Development District," 1961, typescript, Chilliwack Museum.

[30] Sinclair, "History; Record of Events," 8-9, and Minutes of the Sumas Dyking Meeting,"24 Nov. 1919, GR 929/50/8.

[31] "Record of Events," 10-12.

[32] Ibid., 13-14.

[33] C. C. Elridge to Oliver, 21 Oct. 1920, GR 441/208/8 and R. L. Maitland to J. W. Jones, 24 Jan. 1927, Jones Papers, 3/1/251-53, PABC.

[34] Sinclair, "History; Record of Events," 14-17; Sinclair to the Board, 21 Mar., and 22 July 1921, GR 929/49/2; C.E. Sonley to the Board, 16 July 1921, GR 929/49/2; and the Board to Barrow, 24 Aug. 1921, GR 929/49/2.

[35] Sinclair, "History."

[36] M. B. Cotsworth, *Railway Bungling (and Worse) in British Columbia* (Vancouver: Appleby, Appleby, 1918); *The Crisis in British Columbia* (The Lower Mainland Ministerial Association, 1916); Rolf Knight, *Stump Ranch Chronicles* (Van-

couver: New Star Books, 1977), and Jack Scott, *Plunderbund and Proletariat* (Vancouver: New Star Books, 1975).

[37] "Record of Events," 14.

[38] "Wage schedule," GR 929/49/2, and *The Labour Gazette*, 1923, vol. XXIII (Dept. of Labour, Ottawa, 1923): 881.

[39] "Marsh Construction Company: Sumas Reclamation Project," recollection by Arthur Van Meter, Dec. 1982, Chilliwack Museum.

[40] "Report on the Sumas Reclamation Project for the month of August, 1921, 11 GR 929/49/3; *Progress*, 30 August 1923, 1 and 4 June 1924, 1; "Record of Events," 19.

[41] "Balance Sheet," 31 Dec. 1926, 11, Sumas, Financial Statements.

[42] Land Settlement Board minutes, 1 July 1925, GR 929/49/9.

[43] *Progress*, 14 Oct. 1925, 1.

[44] Oliver Blatchford, Secretary of the Sumas Land Owners Association, to the Minister of Justice, Ottawa, 6 Feb. 1926, copy, Jones Papers, Add. Mss., 23, Vol. 3/1/191-93, PABC.

[45] Minutes of the Court of Revision, 29 and 30 January 1925, and 15 May 1925, GR 929/49/9.

[46] Oliver Blatchford to J. W. Jones, 17 and 21 Jan. 1927, Jones Papers, vol.3/1/240-43, 248-50.

[47] *Progress*, 8 June 1922, 6; Land Settlement Board Minutes, 27 Oct. 1925.

[48] *Progress*, 28 July 1921, 1, 7, and 17 Nov. 1921, 1.

[49] *Progress,* 20 April, 1922, 1; 11 May 1922, 1; 27 July 1922, 3; and 31 Aug. 1922, 1.

[50] H.A. Stewart to J.W. Jones, 10 March 1928 and enclosure, vol. 3/1/270ff.

[51] Sumas, Financial Statement, file 10-S6-3-0, Inspectorate of Dykes.

[52] Author's conversation with municipal officials, 12 May 1983.

[53] *Progress*, 14 Dec. 1922, 1.

[54] A. H. Rowberry to the Board, 8 Nov. 1924, GR 929/53/4; C. Rice to the Board, 28 April 1924, GR 929/53/1; and Minutes of the Commissioners, 26 Aug. 1924, GR 929/49/9.

[55] "Votes and Proceedings of the Legislative Assembly of British Columbia," 30 Nov.1928, GR 919/53/6.

[56] *Progress*, 29 June 1922, 1; R. D. Davies to J. W. de B. Farris, 11 June 1924,GR 929/53/2; "I' Sumas Reclamation project," GR 929/8/5; C.N. Reynolds to the Board, May 1924 enclosure, GR 929/55/1; A. Thorimbert to the Board, 16 June 1924, GR 929/55/1; and "Statement by the Honourable E. D. Barrow, Minister of Agriculture for British Columbia," n.d., GR 929/53/2.

[57] *"Votes and Proceedings of the Legislative Assembly of British Columbia,"* 30 Nov. 1925, Jones Papers, vol. 3 /1/10615, and Dixon to Board, 8 Feb. 1928, GR 919/53/6.

[58] *Progress,* 14 Nov. 1929, 1; 21 Nov. 1929, 6, and 20 March 1930.

[59] I' Sumas Land Sales, 1930-35, file 10-S6-7-4; and Minutes, Sumas Advisory Board, 1935, file 10-S6 -5, Inspectorate of dykes.

[60] Imus, "Land Utilization in the Sumas Lake District", 110-13.

[61] Orchard, *Floodland and Forest*, 22.

[62] Hamilton M. Laing, *Alan Brooks: Artist Naturalist*, British Columbia Provincial Museum Special Pub. #3 (Victoria: Provincial Museum, 1979).

[63] Orchard, *Floodland and Forest*, 21.

Transnational Communities: Japanese Communities of the Fraser Valley

Anne Doré

Introduction

From 1904 to 1942 Japanese Canadian families established unique transnational farming communities across British Columbia's Fraser Valley.[1] The history of these close-knit communities in general and their participation in the farmer's cooperative movement in particular illustrate the process of transnational community formation. In addition, racialization was a dynamic force in shaping, strengthening, and sustaining these distinct communities.

Since the 1980s the concept of racialization, including its role in the history of Japanese immigrants to both North America and South America in the first half of the twentieth century, has gained prominence in scholarly literature.[2] Canadian geographers Audrey Kobayashi and Peter Jackson examine racialization in their study of early Japanese Canadian settlers working in the sawmill industry in British Columbia. They describe it as the process by which some of the migrant's physical and cultural characteristics are assigned "political and ideological significance as a means of justifying negative, hostile reaction toward them."[3] The notions of the "social construction of race" and of the social construction of "natural difference" are basic to the process of racialization.[4]

Timothy Stanley demonstrates the racialization of Guangdong migrants, a group that was culturally distinct within China but that British and Anglo-Canadians saw as being no different from any other group of Chinese immigrants to Canada. By grouping ethnically distinct people under the broad label of "Chinamen," and by perceiving the Chinese as intrinsically alien, mainstream Anglo-Canadians relegated all Chinese to a subordinate role in society.[5] Similar categorization was imposed upon Japanese Canadians

38

whether they hailed, for example, from Hiroshima prefecture or from the island of Okinawa.

Sociologists Gillian Creese and Laurie Peterson show how newspapers, representing the White middle class, racialized Asian immigrants by portraying Chinese Canadians as "foreign and problematic newcomers, who did not share an equal right to shape a community in which many families have lived for generations."[6] Interestingly, the authors point out that, by doing this, the dominant White community was also racializing itself.[7]

With regard to Asian Americans, Yen Le Espiritu claims that, although it is partly imposed from above, groups can construct their own ethnicity "within the limits of their situation ... to advance their own political demands."[8] In the case of Japanese Canadians, "the limits of their situation" included things like segregated communities and receiving lower pay than Whites for performing equivalent jobs. Furthering their own political demands could be as simple as partaking in public education or as complex as winning the vote for Japanese Canadian First World War veterans, which occurred in 1931. In other words, ethnicity is multilayered and is characterized by "the continual creation and re-creation of culture."[9]

Even within the limits imposed by racialization, the culture of Japanese immigrants has never been static. In her study of Japanese Peruvians, Ayumi Takenaka found that they utilized their unique ethnic identity for their own benefit, thus implying that intent and agency play a role in the development and maintenance of ethnic identity.[10] She also examined the formation of transnational communities that had similarities with Japanese Canadian farming communities in the Fraser Valley.

Thus, while the racialization of an ethnic group imposes upon it limitations and restrictions, the group can, in turn, utilize aspects of the imposed categorization to further its own interests, to strengthen its solidarity, and to improve its image within the broader community. In other words, difference and otherness can be socially constructive for both the dominant group and for racialized minorities. The negative constructions of the former and the positive constructions of the latter intersect and are part of a dynamic recursive process. Furthermore, attitudes of superiority are not necessarily limited to the dominant group, even though it holds the psychological advantage of possessing greater power and influence. Minorities, too, can believe in their own superiority and use that belief to bolster, motivate, and empower their own communities.

At first glance, it may appear that the *Issei* (first-generation Japanese Canadians) farmers in British Columbia's Fraser Valley accepted the implied superiority of White Canadians and acquiesced to the racialization imposed upon them by White society. Closer examination, however, suggests that they were not interested in the pursuit of interiorization (full inclusion in mainstream Canadian society) and only appeared to have accepted the inferior status assigned to them. Their belief in the superiority of the Japanese spirit, or *yamato-domashii*, made their exteriorization from White society not only acceptable but also necessary to the preservation of their culture and ethnic identity. Just as Creese and Peterson point out that by racializing a minority group the White population racializes itself, so too the Japanese sense of moral and cultural superiority brought about internal (or self-) racialization long before the *Issei* settled in Canada. Japanese believing themselves to be naturally different from Whites is no less a form of racialization than is Whites believing themselves to be naturally different from Japanese. Interestingly, Japanese internal racialization was based on a positive interpretation of many of the same traits deemed negative by Euro-Canadians. These traits included respect for authority, highly structured family and community life, and a dedication to hard work and frugality. Furthermore, the function of Japanese self-racialization was internal in that it sustained and supported Japanese values and traditions without inflicting harm or imposing change upon mainstream society. This was not the case with White racialization, which was external, largely negative, and imposed restrictions and made demands upon the Japanese Canadian community.

While a degree of ethnic give-and-take is common to all immigrant groups, the *Issei* utilized such opportunities to maintain the essence of their culture, including language, family values, and community structure. Of course some change was inevitable, and the result was culturally distinct transnational communities. William Alonso defines transnational communities as "solidaristic communities in the host country."[11] These are often geographically concentrated and maintain bonds with their places of origin through remittances, visiting back and forth, sending the children back for education, and thinking about returning for retirement. By the early 1940s these Fraser Valley farming communities met Alonso's criteria and, with regard to their ethnic traditions, were neither fully Japanese nor fully Canadian but a unique blend of both. This was the result of the manipulation of both internal and external racialization through (1) the retention and evolution of many fundamental Japanese traditions and values, and (2) the acceptance of many aspects of Canadian culture.

Although Canada was heavily influenced by British culture, it was also shaped by multicultural influences within Canadian society. Furthermore, even if Japanese Canadians had not faced prejudice and discrimination, the experience of Japanese migrants in both Peru and Brazil suggests that, the

1942 expulsion aside,[12] they were not likely to have assimilated any faster than they did.[13] Moreover, Japanese Canadians did not pose a threat to Canada's security during the Second World War. Rather than maintaining their loyalty to a remote and distant Japan, they developed an allegiance both to their transnational Japanese Canadian communities and to Canada, whose "values of British fair play and democratic procedures"[14] guaranteed their rights and safety. Racialization on both sides contributed significantly to this process, allowing the *Issei* and their communities enough maneuverability to embrace much of what they saw as the best of both cultures. Although the *Issei* may have given the appearance of accepting the racialization imposed by the dominant society, they did not internalize either it or the inferiority it implied. Rather, racialization served to affirm their superiority, encouraging them to maintain their distinct ethnicity. Thus, within the limits imposed upon them, they manipulated their position to their best advantage and, in so doing, over a period of almost forty years created unique transnational communities that were both grateful and loyal to their host country. A very brief look at Japanese history and culture will help to establish both the richness and uniqueness of the Japanese Canadian community.

History and Culture

Most Japanese immigrants who settled in the Fraser Valley were born during Japan's Meiji Period (1867-1912). Ann Waswo explains that, although this period was characterized by the rapid and intense modernization and Westernization of Japan, most Japanese continued to adhere to many ancient *Samurai* traditions.[15] More appropriately referred to as the military tradition of *bushido*, or the way of the warrior,[16] these traditions included preserving the patriarchal family, holding collectivity above individuality, and maintaining discipline, loyalty, and service to authority. Reinforcing these values was a synthesized spirituality consisting of Buddhism, Confucianism, and Shintoism — a synthesis that is far too complex to be analyzed here. Suffice it to say that this synthesis promoted the important concepts of honour and pride.

Reginda Sumida explains that Buddhism recognizes the universal spiritual communion of all beings.[17] According to Adachi, Buddhism provided strength of character and personality; it "inculcated *yamato-damashii*, or Japanese spirit,"[18] among the people. They learned obedience to authority, parental dedication to the welfare of children, and filial devotion to parents. Confucianism instilled, among other things, a drive for self-improvement; and Shinto promoted loyalty through ancestor worship and the use of shrines in Japanese Canadian homes.

In addition, honour, based on proper behaviour and tied to a Buddhist/Confucian ethical code, also functioned as a guideline and control mechanism for each member of the Japanese Canadian family, whether within the local community or the larger White community. Moreover, the beliefs and practices of Buddhism, Confucianism, and Shintoism contributed to the Japanese immigrant's sense of pride and moral superiority.

At a grassroots level, and based on personal experience, Maryka Omatsu explains how mythology contributed to these feelings of superiority. Because Japanese immigrants believed that their native land was the offspring of the gods, they prided themselves as a chosen people. What Omatsu calls "indomitable pride" served as "a talisman" to help them through the difficulties they faced in North America.[19] Adachi discusses this "pride of race" as something so strong that no amount of racial prejudice could eliminate it.[20] Christopher Reichl asserts that a belief in Japanese superiority helped immigrants to preserve ethnic identity and to slow social assimilation. He shows that, in Brazil and Peru, discrimination and segregation were not imposed upon Japanese immigrants; rather, this form of exteriorization was initiated and maintained by the immigrants themselves.[21] Hence, it seems highly likely that Japanese Canadian pride and feelings of superiority limited their pursuit of assimilation and would have done so even if Euro-Canadians had been more welcoming. While prejudice and discrimination were clearly unjust and could not have been pleasant to bear, they facilitated a separation of White and Japanese immigrant communities that both groups desired and that both groups tested and altered over time. Thus religion, honour, and, perhaps most important, a sense of pride and superiority provided a seamless continuity between the individual, the patriarchal family, and the Japanese Canadian communities in British Columbia's Fraser Valley.

The 1901 census indicates that, of only 4,738 Japanese immigrants living in Canada, 97 per cent of them resided in British Columbia.[22] The total population of the province at the time was 178,657. But, as Thomas A. Berger points out, when the Chinese Canadian population of 14,885 was added to the Japanese Canadian numbers, it was clear that over 10 per cent of the population belonged to the visibly distinctive "Oriental" group:

> The competition for jobs was felt mainly by the working class but all classes in British Columbia felt that the burgeoning Oriental population represented a long-term threat to the White character of the province. They regarded the Orientals, few of whom could speak English, as unassimilable. Thus, they endangered the ideal of White homogeneity in British Columbia.[23]

This early example of clustering two distinctly different ethnic groups because of perceived similarities in physical appearance is what Espiritu refers to as ethnic "lumping."[24] It can also be seen as the beginnings of what might be called the pyrimidization[25] of racialization based on the previous racialization of two or more separate groups. However, because the various Asian groups did not share a common language, residential area, or work location in the first half of the twentieth century, they were unable to use this kind of ethnic lumping to their advantage by engaging in a form of panethnicity.[26] Therefore Japanese immigrants had to create and sustain their own unique support system not merely in order to survive but also in order to maximize the potential of their racialized position. That support system often emerged in a rudimentary form during the voyage to Canada or in the Canadian workplace.

Most early contact between Japanese Canadians and Whites occurred in the highly charged arena of competition for jobs. However, in the fishing, mining, railroad, and lumber industries, male Japanese Canadians were frequently segregated in work gangs headed be a "boss" who knew enough English to manage the work assignments and to maintain order.[27] While this clustering achieved the segregation desired by many employers and co-workers, it also fostered mutual support, the perpetuation of ethnic traits, and the formation of a communication network by which the *Issei* could share news of better opportunities. Through such networks, word of farming opportunities began to spread among the *Issei* during the early decades of the twentieth century. Tokutaro Tsuyuki bought a farm in the Maple Ridge area after a friend and pioneer farmer, Jiro Inouye, "encouraged him to acquire land and make his own living rather than depend on non-Japanese for jobs."[28] In 1928 Tanekichi Araki of Mission said, "After listening to several distinguished people from Japan, farming seems to be the best way for Japanese to settle down."[29] Farming presented an opportunity to convert work gangs and communication networks into permanent communities, to brace against unwanted cultural change, and to achieve a measure of distance from White criticism and discrimination. Moreover, in their country of origin, under the government of Meiji Japan, the *Issei* had seen agriculture as a highly honourable occupation; and under Confucian ideology, it was considered to be the foundation of society.[30]

Fraser Valley Settlement

The settlement of Japanese Canadians in the Fraser Valley progressed slowly and quietly. In 1904 four *Issei* took the first step in Mission, Pitt Meadows, and Haney, while the first *Issei* in Surrey and Mount Lehman arrived in

1907.[31] In 1917 Mission had only eighteen *Issei* farms, but by 1942 there were approximately 111 families, almost all of them farmers.[32] They established work patterns and a lifestyle similar to those they had known in Japan.

Farming not only distanced Japanese Canadians from the frustrations of the mainstream but it also allowed them to construct their communities in the tradition of the Japanese farming village, based on the cooperative spirit of the Japanese, who came together to support each other and to work for the common good.[33] While the cultural isolation of the community tended to decrease the need to learn English, it provided *Issei* farmers with invaluable social and economic support. Moreover, during the early decades of the twentieth century these communities highlighted the uniqueness of the inland, rural experience as opposed to the coastal experience.[34]

Discriminatory political and economic factors at work in fishing, mining, lumber mills, and railroad maintenance led many Japanese Canadians to seek stability and self-employment in farming.[35] As Kobayashi and Jackson point out, "resistance takes many forms," and because Japanese Canadians were denied their basic rights, including the right to vote, their resistance took subtle forms.[36] Changing jobs was one of them; striving to be hardworking, law abiding citizens was another.

Nevertheless, public outcry against Asian immigrants, partly fuelled by the fear of Japan's growing industrial and military strength but largely racist, led to the Vancouver Riot of 1907.[37] Chinatown was ransacked, but Japanese Canadians were forewarned and, although extensive damage was inflicted, they managed to defend their homes in the "Little Tokyo" of Powell Street until the angry mob turned back and dispersed. However, it appears that the District Council of Mission was far enough removed from the urban and coastal scene to take a different, albeit self-serving, look at the 1907 riot:

This council recognizes the fact that on account of the scarcity of cheap labour in this Province, clearing and other improvements on land cannot be carried out successfully and the development of the Agricultural [sic] resources of the Province is suffering on this account. We, therefore, wish to place ourselves on record as not being in sympathy with the uncivilized actions of those who took part in the recent demonstration at Vancouver against Orientals and we would further recommend that the government take some steps to supply the Province with cheap labour.[38]

As Patricia Roy points out, the early history of Japanese immigrants in British Columbia "demonstrates how racial antagonisms appear[ed] only *after* members of that race became an economic threat to white men."[39] Apparently the few Japanese Canadian farmers scattered throughout the

Fraser Valley in 1907 had not yet been categorized as an economic threat due to their work ethic or other "natural differences."

The 1920s marked the biggest and final wave of Japanese immigration and settlement in the Fraser Valley. In 1923, the revised gentlemen's agreement with Japan reduced immigration to 150 per year, but the influx of picture brides had already changed the structure of Japanese Canadian communities from one of single men to one of growing families.[40] Consequently, the racialization of Japanese Canadians was amended to include what Whites perceived as a predisposition to produce excessively large families and to promote child labour, particularly within farming families.[41] Nevertheless, farming in the Fraser Valley offered a relatively settled, stable, and independent livelihood. As Cole Harris observes of immigrants in general, farming "provided a niche, somewhat apart from the modern commercial economy, for families."[42] Moreover, in the specific case of Japanese Canadians, rural life offered the best opportunity for preserving ethnic identity and solidarity while assuring minimal outside interference and minimal cultural assimilation.

Growth of Farms, Families, and Communities

With dynamite and back-breaking labour, Japanese Canadian families cleared thousands of acres in the Fraser Valley from 1904 to 1942. As in the resource industries, the persistent industriousness of Japanese Canadian families did not go unnoticed. However, in agriculture there was an important difference. Whereas *Issei* and Whites had competed for the same jobs in the resource industries, the *Issei* farmers in the Fraser Valley initially sought land that no one else wanted. For example, in 1934 Sumida reports:

The district municipality of Maple Ridge has grown from an uninhabited section of land to a thriving farming area, mainly through the influence of the Japanese, who, in the last 30 years, have turned over three thousand acres of wasteland into fertile and productive farm lands.[43]

The fact that this land was not coveted, at least in its original state, by the White farmer put the individual *Issei* farmer in good stead with his new White neighbours. Moreover, Japanese Canadian settlers were said to be twice as fast at clearing land as were White settlers. In Port Hammond a White farmer reported, "I found out that this Japanese farmer in eighteen months had cleared four and one-half acres, an area which would take the average White farmer three years to clear."[44] Thus, among some Whites, the racialization of Japanese Canadians based on their work ethic generated a certain amount of respect and admiration. So even positive regard was rooted in a view of the Japanese immigrant as "naturally different" and unassimilable. Meanwhile, every success of the *Issei* reinforced their own sense of pride and solidarity as well as their positive view of themselves as "naturally different." This apparent juxtaposition of internal and external racialization constituted a narrow area of agreement between the two groups when it came to recognizing the "superiority" of the Japanese immigrant work ethic.

Although Japanese Canadians excelled in every type of work they had been allowed to pursue in British Columbia, it could be said that nothing tapped their industriousness and inventiveness as did farming their own land. Their farms were not particularly large, and so their choice of crops was crucial to their economic survival. For example, Sumida reports that in 1934 the average size of a farm in Mission was 12.1 acres.[45] In Maple Ridge the farms ranged from five to twenty acres.[46] From the beginning, strawberries and raspberries were the main crops of choice because they offered a high yield per acre and required only minimal capital outlay for equipment and machinery. The fact that the labour with berries was more intense than was the labour with most other local crops gave the *Issei* an opportunity to put their work ethic to full use. Their success not only sustained their families and communities but also surpassed that of their White neighbours and, thus, quietly demonstrated the Japanese immigrant's superiority. Although the berry industry was still dominated by White farmers in 1920, by 1934 Japanese Canadian farmers were producing approximately 85 per cent of the berries grown in the Fraser Valley.[47] Sumida claims that these farmers were "largely responsible for placing British Columbia strawberries and raspberries in all the larger cities of Canada, as far east as Toronto, and processed berries as far as England."[48]

In the *Issei* farming family the wife was just as involved in maintaining the farm as was the husband. Moreover, children would be initiated into farm chores as soon as they were old enough to begin working their way up from the easiest to the most difficult tasks. Not only was the participation of all family members essential to survival, but it was also the Japanese way. To some White farmers this constituted unfair competition, an abuse of women and children, and disrespect for the Sabbath. While their observations of Japanese Canadian families working together in their fields seven days a week may have been accurate, their interpretations of that work scene was racialized. Although *Issei* farmers and their families quietly carried on, members of the Japanese Canadian communities got together to attempt to liaise with the dominant White community in order to discuss problems and work out solutions.

The most prominent and accomplished of these people was Yasutaro Yamaga, who lived in Haney from 1908 to 1942.[49] Possessing a good understanding of both languages and cultures, Yamaga worked for decades to bridge the gap between the two communities. He spoke to women's groups and youth clubs in the Japanese Canadian community in order to help them understand Canadian culture and traditions. When local Whites complained about Japanese Canadian families dynamiting on Sundays, Yamaga explained the Lord's Day Act to the *Issei* and suggested alternative Sunday activities. He formed a Japanese Canadian PTA to deal with clashes and misunderstandings in the public schools. He also taught Sunday school at an inter-racial, inter-denominational Christian church in Haney. He was a man to whom the White community could relate: he was Christian, he was fluent in English, and he understood Canadian society and politics. While such individuals fostered better relations between the two cultures, these compromises fostered minimal rather than radical change.[50] For example, Sunday dynamiting, heard for miles around, could be replaced by quiet fieldwork that was only apparent to those who happened to pass within view of it. Thus liaisons not only helped achieve good relations with the White community, but they also helped to minimize change in the Japanese Canadian community and, thereby, maximize the preservation of tradition and autonomy.

Despite the usefulness of young people on the farm, *Issei* parents demanded that much of their children's time and energy be directed towards academic studies. A 1934 survey of BC schools evaluated the progress of *Nisei* (second-generation Japanese Canadian) students. The *Nisei* were generally seen as punctual, sincere, industrious, orderly, and disciplined. They were above average in most subjects but frequently showed some difficulty with English.[51] The greatest ease with English appeared to be among the students in Mission, where, at the request of the Japanese Canadian community, an English kindergarten had been established by Mrs. Barnett around 1918,[52] and in Haney, where Mr. Yamaga had helped to organize a similar kindergarten in 1927.[53] The keenness of the *Issei* to enrol their children in English kindergarten year after year underscores their commitment to academic success. Because academic success upheld the honour of the family and the community as a whole, it was expected to earn the respect of the broader White community as well.

Although the *Issei* encouraged a Canadian education, they were also anxious for the *Nisei* to retain proficiency in the Japanese language and to learn about Japanese history and culture. Because most *Issei* could not communicate well in English, the use of Japanese at home was essential. The Japanese language school was designed to meet this need and to serve as a buffer against public education, which, it was feared, might adversely affect *Nisei* attitudes. Therefore, several days a week most *Nisei* attended the language school as well as the public school.[54] While language schools strengthened Japanese language skills, they also provided one of many organized activities that forged links within the Japanese Canadian community and, under the umbrella of the *Nokai* (see following section), reinforced ethnicity.

The Centre of the Community

Like their counterparts in rural Japan, most Japanese Canadian farming communities formed a *Nokai* — literally, an agricultural society. The *Nokai*, however, being a complex social and economic association, was much more than an agricultural society. Outside of Japan the *Nokai* also became the institutional defender of cultural integrity. In the Fraser Valley it was adapted to meet the needs of Japanese Canadian farming families. However, this adaptation was as gradual and inconspicuous as was the movement to rural life.

Construction of a centrally located *Nokai* hall ensured that the *Nokai* and its activities were accessible to all and established it as the focal point of the community. Mission, Pitt Meadows, and Surrey each had at least one *Nokai*, while Maple Ridge had a Japanese Canadian population of sufficient size and geographic spread to establish four *Nokais*, each with its own hall.[55] Takata claims that there were even small loosely structured *Nokai*, of no more than twenty families each, at Mount Lehman, Clayburn, and Coghlan.[56]

The *Nokai* assumed two distinct roles within the farming community. The first was to serve as an economic grower cooperative to help regulate berry prices, provide a central depot for freshly picked berries, buy supplies and rent equipment in volume, provide a meeting place for farmers, and serve as a financial lending institution for its members. The second and more complex function was to serve as a benevolent society. To enable the *Nokai* to support both roles, Sumida explains that members, meaning *everyone* in the community, paid 10 per cent of their annual income to the association.[57]

When some Whites criticized the *Issei* for starting up separate farmers associations, their response focused on language barriers. In a letter to the editor of the *Fraser Valley Record*, S. Kuwakara defended the *Nokai* on the grounds that most of its members were "unable to command English language." He went on to offer reassurance of the members' commitment to Canada:

I'm sure all of us have a mind to live our lives here in this country, so that we are always striving to learn your manners, customs and education. Our children are attending to the public schools or higher one, while young boys study English at home or at private night schools.[58]

The *Nokai* helped to perpetuate the Japanese language, and the *Issei* no doubt saw this as a positive function. Nevertheless, the growing number of English-speaking leaders and liaisons within the *Nokai* worked around the language barrier to address the concerns of the larger White community while helping to maintain Japanese traditions in the smaller community. The *Nokai* was, therefore, fundamental to the development of unique transnational communities throughout the Fraser Valley because it offered significant resistance to both radical cultural change and to full assimilation. This is particularly apparent in the *Nokai*'s social and cultural functions.

As a benevolent society the *Nokai* was extremely diversified, supporting sports clubs, skill development, education, religious gatherings, and a variety of social services. Many of these activities (e.g., Sunday worship, the English kindergarten for pre-schoolers, and sports such as basketball and baseball) appeared to have a Canadian flavour. It is interesting to note that baseball was introduced to Japan in 1872 and that, within ten years, it was a standard sport in Japanese high schools.[59] In other words, baseball was already part of the Japanese immigrant's tradition and, contrary to appearances, did not constitute an adaptation to Canadian life. Likewise with the Buddhist Sunday worship: the *Issei* seem to have taken what they already practised within their community and made it fit the Canadian mould.

Although Buddhist temples were built in Mission and Port Haney by 1928, Buddhist services continued to be held in the *Nokai* hall of most communities.[60] In 1931 66.7 per cent of Japanese Canadians in British Columbia claimed to be Buddhist. *Issei* Senjiro Tonomura of Mission explains his long-standing Buddhist faith: "I hope that the teachings of Buddha will make the '*Nohkai*' run more smoothly and result in harmony amongst the farming community.[61] It should be pointed out, however, that the Buddhist faithful, such as Tonomura, allowed the gradual "Christianization" of their religion in Canada.

As Adachi tells us, Buddhist temples took the form of Christian churches, with hymnbooks, pews, and organs. Sunday services and Sunday school, whether in a *Nokai* hall or in a temple, were soon organized to resemble the Christian model. Even the conversion of Christian hymns to Buddhist versions — "Buddha loves me, this I know / For the Sutra tells me so" — demonstrate the influence of Christianity.[62] Perhaps they not only reflect the inherent adaptability of Buddhism but also the *Issei* desire to give the impression of embracing Euro-Canadian culture while quietly maintaining Shinto shrines in their homes and Buddhist values in their family and community life.

Not only did the *Nokai* support both the Buddhist and later the Christian religious interests of its membership, but it also reinforced the social hierarchy and expectations of the community. With regard to young people, the *Nokai* kept them occupied and focused on sports and cultural activities that reflected well on the community as a whole, often leaving them little time to socialize with White classmates and neighbours. The *Nokai* not only housed the Japanese language school, but it also contributed to its operating expenses and arranged for teachers to come from Japan. Space was offered for clubs (e.g., Judo and Kendo for boys; sewing, crafts, and dance for girls; and *Fujinkai*, a club geared towards the needs and roles of the farming wife, for women). Of all the members of the Japanese Canadian farming community, it was the women who were most restricted within the world of the *Nokai*.

Traditionally, Japanese women served their husbands and children within the confines of the home and their village. Midge Ayukawa explains that the picture bride was taught her subservient role both at home and in the Japanese school system. However, Ayukawa cautions us not to regard Japanese Canadian women as passive. Even in their narrow roles they were able to work to improve their lives and, in particular, the lives of their children.[63] In the Maple Ridge area, Kane Inouye, whose husband was less traditional than were most *Issei*, formed the first Japanese Canadian women's club in 1910; its purpose was to enable people to discuss mutual concerns, to learn to speak English, and to understand Canadian customs.[64] Little is known of the extent of its success. However, we do know that low status coupled with the language barrier tended to maintain an unbridgeable gap between *Issei* women and White women. Although Tami Nakamura claims her White neighbours were "nice," she also verifies the narrowness of her sphere of interaction: "We never had any white friends to meet with."[65] Spud Murphy of Abbotsford admits that, while he and his Japanese Canadian neighbours' children were the best of friends, their parents did not socialize together (telephone interview with author, 17 January 2000).

Although most *Issei* women had some involvement in women's clubs and social groups in the *Nokai* and within either the Buddhist or Christian churches, gendered roles were rigidly adhered to, leaving interaction with the White community firmly in the hands of the men. Machi Shinohara of Surrey seemed to enjoy a bit more mobility and socializing than did many *Issei* women. According to her son:

> One of her few *tanoshimis* (pleasures) was to be a member of the New Westminster Buddhist *Fujinkai* where each Sunday the ladies gathered to socialize. Another was to buy a *bakappe* (Chinese lot-

tery ticket), like all the ladies in the neighbourhood. There was a time when she won $47 and didn't know what to do with the money, because her *bakappe* buying was a secret from her husband.[66]

Even the more "worldly" Machi Shinohara worried about her husband's opinion and reaction, perhaps because she, like other picture brides, knew her place. With the help of the *Nokai*, segregation from the White community perpetuated not only the traditional position of the Japanese Canadian woman but also the language barrier between her and the white woman. This cultural isolation was instrumental in preserving Japanese tradition at its familial roots, and it serves as an example of ethnic practices resulting in more severe restrictions being placed on some of its own members than might have been imposed by the external racialization of the broader community.

In times of family hardship or tragedy, the *Nokai* became a social service agency. Read confirms that the association and its members provided every distraught or needy family with "whatever was necessary to get them through the difficult period."[67] This goes a long way to explaining why very few Japanese Canadians were dependent on government relief programs. Even in the depression year of 1934 "the percentage of Japanese on direct relief was less than one-third of the percentage of all groups on relief."[68] Haru Moriyama likens the Japanese Canadian community to a big family, adding, "No wonder the Japanese endured and survived so well no matter what misfortune befell them. They knew how to help each other."[69] The traditional Japanese ethic of mutual help served to minimize the intrusion of the dominant society's social service agencies. Furthermore, it fit well with the exteriorization of Japanese Canadians desired by both groups.

Throughout the Fraser Valley the *Nokai* hall was also used for various forms of ethnic-based entertainment, including Japanese films, *odori* (Japanese dance), *naniwabushi* (stylized Japanese folk singing), and various festivals and celebrations.[70] The *Nokai* organized work bees and building bees among its membership (interview with Mas Okamura, 19 July 1990).[71] Whether it was to build a road, a family home, or a chicken coop, the "bee" provided an occasion for sharing meals and conversation.

Although the *Nokai*-dominated structure of the Japanese Canadian community was based on life in Japan, it evolved in relation to the Fraser Valley setting, whose crops, climate, and terrain differed from those found in Japan. And, of course, there was the larger Euro-Canadian community. Cole Harris strongly suggests that the new environment inhabited by an immigrant group is a "motor of social change" that makes replication of the society from which it came impossible.[72] While total replication is indeed impossible, for

51

a number of reasons the Japanese Canadian community was able to replicate and preserve its heritage more fully than were most immigrant groups. These included the language barrier, the strength of *bushido* and Buddhist traditions, and, in particular, the belief in the superiority of the Japanese spirit. Another reason was the dominance of the *Nokai* in the community life of Japanese Canadians. The *Nokai* not only played an important role in maintaining the core of Japanese culture, but it also became a conduit for gestures of good will towards the dominant White community and for demonstrations of many pleasant aspects of Japanese culture.

Increasingly, through the *Nokai* the *Issei* organized activities that connected them in positive ways to the greater community but also minimized White involvement in their way of life and social structure. Essentially, the *Issei* protected their interests by revealing and sharing only what they wanted the dominant community to see. Because they sought the peaceful preservation of their communities and did not wish to lose them through banishment or assimilation, they painted a picture of Japanese Canadian life that would please their White neighbours. Just as Kurashige shows how one of the purposes of "Nisei Week" in 1930s Los Angeles was to "underscore the community's openness to white America," so Japanese Canadian contributions were designed to do the same in the 1930s Fraser Valley without actually throwing the doors wide open to White scrutiny and influence.[73]

For example, in both Mission and Maple Ridge the *Nokai* halls were often made available to the community at large for such mutually relevant gatherings as school concerts and graduations.[74] More commonly, the *Nokai* organized activities that took the *Issei* into the larger community. For instance, Yasutaro Yamaga tells us that, following the Armistice in November 1918, the Japanese Canadians of Haney joined in the community celebrations by staging a Japanese lantern parade, consisting of over 300 people with noisemakers and lighted paper lanterns waving up and down along the Trunk Road after dark.[75] In April 1925 the Mission Memorial Hospital thanked the Japanese Canadians "who so kindly came forward with help in the form of teams and labour ... in the matter of beautifying the grounds" of the hospital.[76] The *Nokai* in Mission entered a float in May Day celebrations, and *Nisei* school children participated in the maypole dance and other activities (interview with Beverley Mitchell, 21 January 2000).[77] Also in Mission, community celebrations of Empire Day in 1925 and George VI's coronation in 1937 featured *Nokai*-sponsored fireworks displays, which demonstrated a spectacular crowd-pleasing aspect of Japanese culture.[78] However, although the *Nokai* offered the *Issei* farmers the basic structure from which to pursue broader affiliations with the White community, it also isolated them.

Robert Miles stresses that the racialization of people involves "the processes in which they participate and the structures and institutions that result."[79] The *Nokai* functioned as an institution of external racialization by helping to maintain the segregation desired by the White community. The lack of White interference in the *Nokai* reinforces this theory since the White community made an effort neither to welcome Japanese Canadian membership in most Euro-Canadian organizations nor to prohibit or restrict the *Nokai*. For example, on 29 November 1929 Mission Village Council approved plans for the new Japanese Hall, and in March 1941 the Matsqui Municipal Council re-licensed the Clayburn Japanese Language School.[80]

On the other hand, by maintaining Japanese culture and social structure the *Nokai* was a highly effective tool of self-racialization. In Haney, Yamaga criticized the *Nokai* for isolating itself from the White community. He states that he always had to fight for Japanese Canadian participation in Haney community events.[81] In Whonnock, Harry Pullen recalls that Japanese Canadians "kept pretty well to themselves in the early days" but that, as time went on, they began mixing more with the White community (interview with Harry Pullen, 22 July 1985).[82] Nevertheless, the most significant overlap with the dominant community grew out of the shared economic base of farming: as the *Issei* farmers excelled in berry production, White farmers recognized advantages in establishing and maintaining economic ties with them.

It was only after White and Japanese Canadians joined economic forces that a significant bond was created between the two communities. That bond, however, did not lead to social and political integration, nor did it diminish the importance of the *Nokai*, which remained the primary organization of Japanese Canadian farming families and a central element in the evolution of their unique transnational communities. The growth of economic ties stemmed from the competitive nature of the marketplace rather than from any desire for assimilation on either side.

Like the Powell Street entrepreneurs in Vancouver, the success of the *Issei* farmers in the Fraser Valley often depended upon sound investment and business decisions. Unlike the Powell Street merchants, the *Issei* farmers' customers were not Japanese Canadians.[83] As can be seen from the berry production statistics (see above), the products of the Fraser Valley *Issei* farmer had become an important and integrated part of British Columbia's food production system. This integration was enhanced and strengthened by the growth of the cooperative movement; however, as the farming communities of the Fraser Valley grew, it became increasingly important for Japanese

Canadians and White farmers to join together in order to stabilize prices and to maximize profit.

Expansion and the Cooperative Movement

As the years passed, the *Issei* expanded their farms and diversified their products in order to ensure their survival. Both winter rhubarb grown in hothouses and spring strawberries grown in long, low greenhouses were Japanese Canadian innovations.[84] As a highly organized community tackling the day-to-day and season-to-season problems of farming, the *Issei* did well. However, as new crops and methods developed, overproduction often glutted the market, leading to price-slashing and financial loss. Dealing effectively with problems related to supply, pricing, and shipping necessitated connecting with the broader agricultural community. Small, specialized organizations, such as the Rhubarb Grower's Association established in 1925, began to bring Japanese Canadian and White farmers together.[85] While translators and liaisons like Yasutaro Yamaga partially bridged the language barrier affecting these business negotiations, one of Yamaga's greatest contributions to Fraser Valley farming communities proved to be his leadership skills within the cooperative union movement.

Yamaga's twofold purpose — to deal with marketing problems as well as anti-Japanese Canadian sentiment — was advanced when he drew Japanese Canadians and Whites together to form the Maple Ridge Berry Growers' Cooperative Exchange in 1927.[86] This co-op not only helped to stabilize market prices, but it also developed a packing plant, a processing plant, and storage facilities. Furthermore, it functioned successfully until the Second World War.[87] Also during 1927 Yamaga assisted in establishing a comparable co-op in Surrey.

Meanwhile, in Mission a similar movement was under way but took longer to come to fruition. In 1929 Taichiro Hattori wrote, "Of course, we would like to market in partnership with the white community. However hard we tried to date, it has ended with poor results."[88] No public record of meetings and dialogue related to this effort is known to exist. However, on 30 December 1932 the *Fraser Valley Record* announced the formation of the Pacific Cooperative Union (PCU), declaring that the initial membership of 120 growers "means the majority of the growers in the district are behind this organization."[89] While Cherrington credits only White farmer John B. Shimek with bringing about the formation of the PCU, he does acknowledge that the active participation of the Japanese Canadian growers was important to its success.[90] Small wonder, considering that in 1934 the membership of the

PCU was 75 per cent Japanese Canadian and 25 per cent White, while the produce handled was 90 per cent Japanese Canadian and 10 per cent White.[91]

Although the language barrier may have prevented some *Issei* from assuming positions on boards like the PCU directorate, they *were* represented. In both 1936 and 1939, for example, Teizo Nakashima served as vice-president, and four other *Issei* farmers sat on the directorate.[92] Furthermore, the PCU and other large agricultural groups (such as the Federated Coast Growers [FCG]) welcomed translators and interpreters to their meetings "to enable the Japanese members to follow the trend of the business."[93] The FCG is also reported to have issued and circulated Japanese translations of written materials related to its meetings about proposed changes in the provincial marketing act.[94]

A 1934 article in the *Record* attests to the success of the PCU — "it is the premier shipping organization in the lower mainland" — and discusses the union's connections with the Prairies and eastern Canada.[95] While the small local farmers associations (such as those in Whonnock, Ruskin, Mt. Lehman, and Coghlan) continued to serve local needs, their affiliation with the PCU addressed broader marketing concerns (interview with Harry Pullen, taped 22 July 1985. Whonnock Community Assoc., Box 2, Mission Community Archives.[96] The extensive reach of the PCU is demonstrated by its 1938 collaboration with the Mennonites of the Yarrow Growers' Cooperative. T.D. Regehr reveals that the two co-ops negotiated a contract to sell barrels of berries packed in sodium dioxide to British jobbers.[97] Thus the cooperative movement not only developed a complicated web of interdependency within and between neighbouring communities, but it also extended that web across regions of the province, the nation, and the world. Furthermore, the success of the PCU reflected well on its Japanese Canadian members and their communities, perhaps even giving them an overblown sense of security in relation to the broader community.

Neither the outbreak of the Second World War nor Japan's entrance into it in 1941 severed the economic bond between Japanese Canadians and the PCU. It would take the federal government's order for "evacuation" to inflict that fatal wound. However, life in the Fraser Valley was not immune from world events.

Shadows Cast by World Events

The First World War stimulated higher prices for berries and an expansion of cooperation between Japan and Britain, which had been initiated by the Anglo-Japanese Alliance of 1902. Both of these factors had a mellowing effect on public opinion towards Japanese Canadians. However, a series of economic downturns during the 1920s and the Great Depression of the 1930s repeatedly stimulated anti-Japanese sentiment. No doubt most Japanese Canadians learned neither to invest too much hope in the occasional periods of tolerance during economic upswings nor to venture too far from the protection of the *Nokai* and the Japanese Canadian community. Their pride in the Japanese spirit and way of life strengthened and sustained them. A close reading of the resources shows that they not only believed they could see their way through any crisis but that they also believed their good example as productive, law-abiding citizens would eventually win the respect and trust of White Canadians. Perhaps they did not anticipate the extent to which many White Canadians would link them to the imperialistic actions of Japan.

Throughout the years of rural settlement by Japanese Canadians, the country they had left behind was frequently in the news. Early newspaper articles highlighting Japan's modernization and success at international diplomacy were soon replaced by reports on the expanding Japanese war machine and military conquests in Asia.[98] Japan's withdrawal from the League of Nations in 1932, and its continued aggression in Asia, elevated public fears to the point that, when the Sino-Japanese War erupted in 1937, some British Columbians believed their province would be Japan's next conquest. Politicians and other community leaders could be heard to play upon this fear in order to push for harsh measures against Japanese Canadians. Irrational fears and hatred had always been there: now they could be justified by citing national and international crises. New calls for the exclusion of Japanese Canadians were heard throughout the province. Few voices cited the long-standing loyalty and respect of Japanese Canadians for Canadian authorities.

Maryka Omatsu explains *Issei* regard for authority and for the concept of *shikataga-nai*, or fatalistic resignation:

The overwhelming majority of the issei were traditionalists, who respected authority, whether it was the Emperor, his consul, or the government of Mackenzie King. Unless pushed into a corner that allowed no saving of face they were willing to accept their second-class status in Canada with Confucian fatalism — *shikataga-nai*.[99]

The *Issei* may have accepted the lower status assigned to them, but that does not mean that they believed in it. The protective structure of the *Nokai* community and family enabled the *Issei* to outwardly accept the status quo while inwardly embracing a spiritual and intellectual rejection of inferiority. Furthermore, the loyalty and respect of the community extended, as Omatsu says, to whomever the *Issei* perceived to be the ruling authority. In Canada that encompassed the existing political structure, from the municipal government right up to the office of the prime minister and even the British monarch. While Japanese Canadians may have expressed some pride in the military victories of Japan prior to the Second World War, this was essentially an extension of ethnic pride rather than a display of national loyalty. Just as Stanley demonstrates that Chinese Canadians believed a strong China would help earn them the respect of White Canadians, so too the *Issei* believed that Japan's growing strength and imperialism in the 1920s and 1930s would reflect well upon them.[100] Although they, like Stanley's subjects, may have wanted to maintain some ties to the homeland in case they were eventually expelled from Canada, their commitment to family and community in the Fraser Valley was extremely complex and was suggestive of a deep commitment to Canada itself. This commitment was most apparent as the children of the *Issei* matured and began to seek their place in Canadian society.

Throughout this time of growing international unease, the *Nisei* were maturing under the influence of two distinct cultures. Canadian citizens by birth, they were experiencing the same public education and peer group influence as were other Canadian children, while their home life continued to be shaped by the authoritarian, patriarchal, and honour-bound traditions of their parents and Japan. Over time, the Canadian values of individualism and egalitarianism began to challenge traditional Japanese values, creating stress and conflict between the *Nisei* and their parents. While the *Issei* wanted their children to understand and to embrace their Japanese heritage, they recognized that a degree of assimilation was necessary if they were to be accepted as Canadians with full rights and opportunities. But they also knew from experience that *Nisei* attempts at inclusion would not go unchallenged by the broader community. Only the Japanese Canadian community could provide the solidarity and support needed by the *Nisei*. It therefore became more important than ever to attempt to maintain ethnic values, customs, and institutions.[101]

Sumida asserts that in rural areas such as the Fraser Valley there was more mingling of *Nisei* with Whites, better relations between White and Japanese Canadian families, and less discrimination than was the case in the urban and coastal areas. He further suggests that this relative harmony was related to the *Issei*'s integration into commercial agriculture and the system of cooperatives.[102] Tami Nakamura speaks to this in relation to the Mission community:

> One reason there wasn't any discrimination in Mission was that whites and Japanese were in the same strawberry producers' association. Strawberries were all shipped out from the association at

the same price. So the races weren't likely to go up against each other on account of their interests.[103]

Whatever the reason, numerous examples of joint community efforts between Japanese Canadians and Euro-Canadians have been recorded.

In Mission, the Fraser Valley Record reported on two annual Christmas programs that Emma Barnett organized for the Mission community.[104] One was given by the Japanese Canadian English kindergarten and the other by the Japanese Canadian Girls Club. Both programs were in English. In both 1936 and 1937, Jujutsu and Judo exhibitions, including youth classes, were held at the Japanese Hall and were open to the Mission community.[105] In April 1937 the Fraser Valley Record reported on a joint meeting of men from the English-speaking St. Andrews United Church and the Japanese United Church in Mission.[106] There was a service, a social hour, and an English speaker whose talk was translated by Mr. Kudo for the Japanese-speaking guests. In Haney, Yamaga describes an annual community Thanksgiving dinner and music program for which Japanese Canadian women provided the main course and for which White women provided pastry and beverages. Yamaga observes that "there could not be seen a speck of racial hatred among the audience."[107] Spud Murphy reports that, as a youth in the Abbotsford area, he played basketball and competed in track on school-based teams that were made up of Japanese Canadians and Whites. They often visited other communities to compete. Of the Japanese Canadian friends and teammates of his youth he said, "You don't see colour. I've never seen colour" (telephone interview with author, 17 January 2000). Many White children who had Japanese Canadian neighbours report playing together and being friends.[108] Outside the Fraser Valley, Takata tells us that Nisei were often excluded from public places such as restaurants and swimming pools and that they were often segregated in theatres.[109] While this is an area that warrants further study, it does not appear to have been the case in the Fraser Valley. It is known, however, that in all communities, once the Nisei completed high school, they encountered many of the same types of job discrimination that their parents had faced decades earlier, before taking up farming. Education choices were also severely limited or led to dead ends in the job market. Violet Vachon (née Kujikawa) explained that she had wanted to take a commercial course after graduating from high school in 1938. However, knowing that she wouldn't get an office job because of her race, she abandoned the idea.[110] Teruko Hidaka of Whonnock was allowed to complete her teacher training but then was refused a teaching certificate.[111] Thus, Nisei dreams of economic and occupational advancement were dashed: the nation and society they had come to love and respect did not want them in the mainstream. For many Nisei in the Fraser Valley this meant remaining at home to work on the farm. While many did this begrudgingly, they did find solace in the transnational communities of their parents, where Japanese values and community spirit reinforced their ethnicity and self-esteem.

In spite of these challenges within the family, the Japanese Canadian farmers in the Fraser Valley found cause for optimism as the 1940s approached. Farming continued to diversify, offering new, promising opportunities. Fraser Valley newspapers tell us that by 1929 a hop farm of 640 acres was operating on the Sumas prairie and that within ten years PCU leaders were urging members to consider growing hops to check the overproduction of berries.[112]

Although the newspapers could also be counted on for periodic anti-Japanese Canadian ranting, the late 1930s produced some positive, supportive press for Japanese Canadians living in the Fraser Valley. On 14 April 1938 the *Maple Ridge Leader* ran two editorials in support of Japanese Canadians.[113] The first refers to Japanese aggression in Asia and urges: "Let us be fair in our dealings with our Japanese citizens, who have no voice or part in this war, and with whose country Canada is at peace and likely to remain so." The second writer thought there was too much agitating against the local Japanese Canadians, who are "good industrious law-abiding citizen(s)," and suggests that "a little more Christianity is the first stepping-stone." In 1938 the inception of the *New Canadian* newspaper in Vancouver gave voice to the concerns and opinions of the *Nisei*. Although somewhat removed from the Fraser Valley, the *New Canadian* was distributed there and frequently printed brief reports and articles from local *Nisei* organizations. Furthermore, articles from the *New Canadian* were reprinted in mainstream papers all over the country. In 1939 the *North Fraser Leader* ran one such article, which quoted Yasutaro Yamaga on the contributions of the Japanese Canadian farmers to the berry industry in Maple Ridge.[114] Because all of this positive press coverage preceded the war-induced economic upswing of the early 1940s, it cannot be linked to that phase of prosperity; rather, it likely signifies a gradual erosion of the external racialization of *Issei* farmers in the Fraser Valley. Unfortunately, that erosion was too late and too slow to save the Japanese Canadian farming communities.

Destruction of the Transnational Communities

Peter Ward's scholarly study of the half-century public campaign against Japanese Canadians in British Columbia concluded that their expulsion from their homes and property in 1942 was a result of broad-based racism stimulated by two major factors. The first was the "deeply irrational yearning" for a racially and socially homogeneous White British Columbia; the second was "white British Columbia's tendency to identify Japanese immigrants and their children with the expansionist foreign policy of Japan."[115] Although White fear and hatred may have waned periodically over the previous four decades, as international relations deteriorated calls for the removal of Japanese Canadians grew louder than ever.

It should be pointed out that almost all of the accusations and negative press against Japanese Canadians in British Columbia, particularly in the 1940s, originated in Vancouver, Victoria, and other coastal communities. Among the most vocal anti-Japanese Canadian politicians were A.W. Neill of Vancouver Island, Howard Green and Ian Mackenzie of Vancouver, Tom Reid of New Westminster, and the Vancouver City Council of the 1940s.[116] All anti-Asian leagues originated in Vancouver and Victoria.[117] Although very little organized public expression of anti-Japanese Canadian sentiment seems to have originated in the Fraser Valley, there was the occasional anti-Japanese Canadian editorial. In January 1942 a group of Fraser Valley farmers called on the provincial government to disallow any further purchasing or renting of farmland by Japanese Canadians.[118] However, this was mild compared to the calls for Japanese Canadian expulsion and deportation that, at the same time, were coming out of Vancouver. Two anti-Japanese voices in the Fraser Valley are worth noting. One was that of George Cruickshank, a Fraser Valley MP who advocated moving all Japanese Canadians "back east to Toronto."[119] The other was that of Reverend G.L. Collins of Mission, whose demands for keeping British Columbia "Christian and British"[120] led to at least one anti-Japanese Canadian community meeting in Mission in 1942.[121] Prior to the events of 1942 neither of these men's anti-Japanese Canadian sentiments appeared in Fraser Valley newspapers more than once or twice a year. Perhaps this infrequent appearance of anti-Japanese Canadian journalism is a reflection not only of the economic integration of the *Issei* farmers but also of a somewhat higher degree of social acceptance than existed along the coast of British Columbia.

Moreover, Fraser Valley newspapers occasionally printed letters and articles supportive of Japanese Canadians. On 18 December 1941, more than a week after the bombing of Pearl Harbor, a report on the annual meeting of the PCU, which at that time had over 600 members, summarized the closing remarks of John Shimek:

> The manager said that 28 different nationalities are sitting together in the hall, peacefully and amicably discussing their common problems and their business. When we as nations can do the same, we can truly say that at least we are cultured and civilized, such as we

claim to be. The Co-operative principal lends itself especially for this purpose and should and will be adopted more and more as common misery compells [sic] us more and more to do so.[122]

On 24 February 1942, PCU manager Shimek defended the co-op against Reverend Collins, who criticized it for its support of Japanese Canadian members:

These people affected have been loyal to us for many years, have helped to build this Union and we must try our best, without getting the jitters, to see them through this difficulty, with which they are confronted, through no fault of their own.[123]

Because the PCU stood alone in its support for Japanese Canadians, it seems to have had little influence on critics and hatemongers. However, the fact that it supported them to the bitter end says a great deal about the status and economic significance of the Japanese Canadian communities in the Fraser Valley.

Although Japanese Canadian farmers continued to maintain their separate communities and *Nokai,* their ties to Japan were virtually severed by the war. By 1942 both the *Issei* and the *Nisei* had not only created strong economic ties to Canada, but also strong ties of loyalty, gratitude, and trust. However, the Canadian government's decision to register, expel, and isolate Japanese Canadians made them, as Berger says, "a people without a country."[124] What no one seemed to recognize at the time was that Japanese Canadians had created unique transnational communities in the farmlands of the Fraser Valley. Although these communities were neither fully Japanese nor fully Canadian but combined the cultural traits of both, their success in agriculture and their social stability made them an asset rather than a threat to Canada. In spite of having achieved a significant degree of harmony and acceptance within their rural communities, the *Issei* and *Nisei* of the Fraser Valley were racialized, along with all other Japanese Canadians, because of the hatred, fear, and panic arising mainly from the province's coastal communities. Further, there is significant international evidence to indicate that these rural communities would have continued to thrive in peace and shared prosperity with their White neighbours if the government had protected them rather than having uprooted and scattered them.

For example, in Brazil, Makabe found that *Issei* pioneers chose exclusion from the mainstream even though they neither experienced significant discrimination during settlement nor mass expulsion during the Second World War.[125] In both Brazil and Peru, Christopher Reichl reports that Japanese immigrants assumed anti-assimilationist positions and maintained separate communities even though they were not restricted from living with the native population and often worked side by side with them. Reichl's description of Japanese Brazilian farming communities closely resembles the descriptions of those established in Canada's Fraser Valley.[126]

Takenaka shows that, by the 1990s, Peruvian Japanese were largely acculturated; that is, they were Spanish-speaking and Roman Catholic. However, they remained unassimilated, maintaining an ethnic identity as well as ethnic communities that were distinct from those of all other Peruvians. According to Takenaka, "it is values, or symbolic ideologies, rather than concrete knowledge about Japanese history, literature, or language that serve to bolster the [transnational] community."[127] We have seen that the movement by many Canadian *Nisei* towards Christianity and the use of the English language parallels the Japanese Peruvian move towards Roman Catholicism and the use of the Spanish language. In Canada, *Nisei* values and traditions were instilled by their parents and the *Nokai*, and were reinforced by *Nisei* organizations such as the Japanese Canadian Citizens League (with branches in Mission and Maple Ridge) and *Nisei* publications such as the *New Canadian*. Takenaka also demonstrates that the Japanese Peruvian formation of transnational communities has not only been instrumental in maintaining ethnic identity but that it has also been effective in maximizing economic benefits to the community and defending its members from ill treatment by outsiders. For Japanese Canadians, the transnational farming communities provided similar kinds of safeguards and, had they been protected and allowed to remain intact throughout the war, would have continued to do so.

Despite the domestic and international unrest of the early 1940s, Japanese Canadians of the Fraser Valley busied themselves with the essential routines of everyday life. Crops had to be planted, tended, and harvested. The growing and processing of hops was also well under way in Mission, and expansion of that industry was anticipated throughout the Fraser Valley.[128] Furthermore, the children continued to attend school. Annual activities such as kindergarten graduations, Christmas concerts, and sports competitions proceeded as usual for the enjoyment of both the Japanese Canadian and White communities.[129] Hence there was little time for deviating from the busy routine of rural life, much less for organizing subversive activity. For those who cared to notice, signs of Japanese Canadian allegiance to their chosen country were everywhere.

Wishing to demonstrate their loyalty, many *Nisei* attempted to join Canada's armed forces during the Second World War, but the Canadian government disallowed this in January 1941.[130] Spud Murphy of Abbotsford, who served in the Canadian Air Force, says that, had they been allowed, all his Japanese Canadian friends would have signed up (interview with author, 17

January 2000. In Maple Ridge, Doug Oike and his Japanese Canadian friends had tried to sign up for military service but were refused.[131] Even as Japanese Canadians were being refused at the recruitment offices, they were offering other kinds of support in the form of generous monetary and food donations,[132] and they were participating in such war-support activities as organizing V-bundles.[133]

Another example of cooperation typical of the Fraser Valley occurred in 1940 just after Japanese Canadians were prohibited, under wartime regulations, from handling ammunition and explosives. Yasutaro Yamaga attended a meeting of the Maple Ridge councillors to work out an arrangement that would enable Japanese Canadian farmers in the area to continue blasting to clear agricultural land. All agreed on the appointment of a "powder monkey"; that is, "a British subject who would have to give definite proof that the powder had been used in the specified time."[134] Although the special arrangements for explosives and the new registration were both carried out in case of Japan's entry into the war against the Allies, the timing and method of that entry caught everyone off guard.

When Japan bombed Pearl Harbor on 7 December 1941, Japanese Canadian farmers were as shocked as was everyone else. Within days the *Maple Ridge-Pitt Meadows Gazette* interviewed Yamaga.[135] He claimed the Japanese Canadian community was stunned but calm and "awaiting any instructions from the Canadian government." He added, "I trust the Canadian government to protect us, for we are doing our best as strawberry growers for the good of the community."

However, before any official instructions appeared, the PCU sent a letter to all Japanese Canadian members sympathizing with their situation and urging them to adopt a code of behaviour that would not attract attention or criticism.[136] The letter, published in the *Fraser Valley Record* on 16 December, asserted that the Japanese Canadian members were "unfortunate victims of existing circumstances, law abiding and anxious to do what is right." The tone of the letter is calm and supportive.

A month later the PCU sent another letter to all Japanese Canadian members complaining that they were not following its suggestions.[137] The second letter had an impatient and fearful tone, in one instance asserting that Japanese Canadians were "causing great annoyance and placing [themselves] in a precarious position," and labelling their behaviour as "downright antagonistic." It closed with, "if you wish to stay out of trouble, please cooperate with us at once and definitely." The letter also warned of the possibility of having vehicles confiscated, curfews established, and internment imposed. Both letters suggested that the White members of the PCU did not favour removing Japanese Canadians from their communities. Whether their objection was more economic or humanitarian is of little consequence. Less than six weeks later, the government began issuing plans for mass expulsion, using the euphemism "evacuation."[138]

On 26 February 1942 expulsion began along the north coast and Vancouver Island. No special consideration was to be given to Fraser Valley farmers as landowners, as an important link in the food production system of British Columbia, or as agricultural entrepreneurs in cooperative partnerships with Whites. No exception was made for them out of consideration for their distance from the coast: the regulations applied to all. The expulsion of most Fraser Valley farmers, however, was delayed until between April and June, by which time they had planted their crops.

In the Fraser Valley, as elsewhere in 1942, there appear to have been no mass expressions of outrage or protest against government policy regarding the treatment of Japanese Canadians. Nor is there much evidence of collective sympathy and support. An exception, however, is found once again in the PCU, with whom Japanese Canadian and White farmers shared a common economic interest. This support is further born out in the minutes of a meeting of PCU directors on 9 March 1942. Both Shingo Kunimoto and Teizo Nakashima of the Japanese Canadian community were present at this meeting. The discussion focused on exploring the legal possibility of Japanese Canadian members transferring the title of their property and vehicles to the PCU to hold in trust for them. While this would have protected the PCU "from loss on account of indebtedness of the members," and while it would have given the PCU the use of fifty-nine additional trucks, it also afforded "the best protection of Japanese members."[139] Considering that the return of Japanese Canadians to their homes in the Fraser Valley after the war was still anticipated at this time, the PCU's efforts to find a mutually satisfactory solution were admirable. No other organization matched its effort.

In conclusion, the history of Japanese Canadians in the Fraser Valley, from their voluntary arrival in 1904 to their forced removal in 1942, constitutes a unique chapter in BC history. While racialization by the White community brought about the exteriorization *Issei* farmers desired, it also pre-judged and categorized them, severely restricting their opportunities and contributing to the tragedy of the 1942 expulsion. The *Issei* belief in the strength and superiority of the Japanese spirit, values, and traditions sustained their dignity and productivity despite the discrimination they encountered.

Rural Japanese Canadians not only initiated many agricultural developments and improvements, but they also enriched the cultural landscape of the Fraser Valley. That the economic structure of these communities was integrated with that of the White farming communities through a network of farmers cooperatives suggests a significant step towards mutual acceptance. A separate but peaceful co-existence evolved and, along with it, unique transnational communities of Japanese Canadians. The degree of tolerance and cohesiveness achieved between the Japanese Canadian and White populations in the Fraser Valley appears to have exceeded that achieved between their counterparts in coastal and urban areas. This, in large part, was due to a shared economic base and a network of cooperative associations. And it was supported by newspaper articles related to Japanese Canadians, the community experiences shared by Whites and Japanese Canadians, and the testimony of both pre-Second World War scholars and individuals who resided in the Fraser Valley.

Many questions have yet to be addressed. A closer look at the experience of the Fraser Valley *Nisei* is needed, as is a greater understanding of the degree of acceptance and cohesiveness between the Japanese Canadian and White communities. This may be feasible if more attention can be given to the voices of those who lived in the Fraser Valley during the first half of the twentieth century. Memoirs, family histories, and other personal documents remain tucked away in the nation's attics and archives awaiting discovery and, in many cases, translation. Such documents provide the past with a human face and heartbeat.

Endnotes

[1] For the purposes of this paper, the name "Fraser Valley" applies to what John Mark Read calls "the Upper Fraser Delta." See Read, "The Pre-War Japanese Canadians of Maple Ridge: Landownership and the KEN-Tie" (MA thesis, University of British Columbia, 1975), 41. Included are the north and south sides of the Fraser River, beginning at Surrey in the west and stretching to Chilliwack in the east. The present-day communities in this area are Maple Ridge, Pitt Meadows, Mission, Surrey, Langley, Abbotsford, and Chilliwack. The Japanese Canadian community of Mission is cited most frequently, followed by that of Maple Ridge. While the latter had a larger Japanese Canadian population, the former has been more extensively documented, thanks to the efforts of Valerie Billesberger and her staff at Mission Community Archives.

[2] Robert Miles, *Racism and Labour Migration* (London: Routledge and Kegan Paul, 1982); and *Racism* (London: Routledge, 1989).

[3] Audrey Kobayashi and Peter Jackson, "Japanese Canadians and the Racialization of Labour in the British Columbia Sawmill Industry," *BC Studies* 103 (Fall 1994): 35.

[4] Ibid., 57-8. Regarding "natural difference" and the "race-making process," see also Bob Carter, Marci Green and Rick Halpern, "Immigration Policy and the Racialization of Migrant Labour: The Construction of National Identities in the USA and Britain," *Ethnic and Racial Studies* 19,1 (January 1996): 135-57.

[5] Timothy Stanley, "'Chinamen, Wherever We Go': Chinese Nationalism and Guangdong Merchants of British Columbia," *Canadian Historical Review* 77, 4 (December 1996): 485-8.

[6] Gillian Creese and Laurie Peterson, "Making the News: Racializing Chinese Canadians," *Studies in Political Economy* 51 (Fall 1996): 137.

[7] Ibid., 139. See also Ruth Frankenburg, "Whiteness and Americaness: Examining Constructions of Race, Culture and Nation in White Women's Life Narratives," in *Race*, ed. Steven Gregory and Roger Sanjek (New Brunswick, NJ: Rutgers University Press, 1994), 61-77. Although "whiteness" is normative in most American and Canadian communities, there is nevertheless a cultural specificity about it that sets it apart and categorizes it according to notions that presume a natural difference between Whites and non-Whites. The White racialization of ethnic groups endorses this "natural difference" and, hence, the racialization of Whites themselves.

[8] Yen Le Espiritu, *Asian American Panethnicity: Bridging Institutions and Ethnicity* (Philadelphia: Temple University Press, 1992) 133.

[9] Ibid., 5.

[10] Ayumi Takenaka, "Transnational Community and Its Ethnic Consequences," *American Behavioral Scientist* 42, 9 (June/July 1999): 1457-8.

[11] William Alonso, "Citizenship, Nationality and Other Identities," *Journal of International Affairs* 48, 2 (Winter 1995): 5.

[12] In agreement with Roy Miki, *Broken Entries* (Toronto: Mercury Press, 1998) 18, I use the term "expulsion" rather than the more commonly used "evacuation." As Miki points out, evacuation implies a *temporary* removal from danger and a return when the danger recedes. However, we now know that government authorities planned on the permanent relocation and dispersal of Japanese Canadians.

[13] See both Takenaka, "Transnational Community"; and Christopher A. Reichl, "Stages in the Historical Processes of Ethnicity: The Japanese in Brazil, 1908-1988," *Ethnohistory* 42, 1 (Winter 1995): 31-62. See also Tomoko Makabe, "The Theory of the Split Labour Market: A Comparison of the Japanese Experience in Brazil and Canada," *Social Forces* 29, 1 (March 1981): 786-809.

[14] Fumi Tamagi, "Evacuation Experiences of the Moriyama Family," *Coyote Flats*, vol. 2 (Coyote Flats Historical Society, 1972), n.p. Reproduced in "Rambling Reminiscences of Haru Moriyama," recorded and expanded by her daughter Fumi Tamagi (nee Moriyama) in Lethbridge, Alberta, 28 July 1982. Located in Mission Community Archives, box 185-11, Mission, BC (hereafter Moriyama, "Rambling Reminiscences") .

[15] Ann Waswo, *Modern Japanese Society: 1868-1994* (Oxford: University of Oxford Press, 1996) 22-30.

[16] See Carol Gluck, *Japan's Modern Myths: Ideology in the Late Meiji Period* (Princeton, NJ: Princeton University Press, 1985) 155, 180, 185-6, and 248.

[17] Reginda Sumida "The Japanese in British Columbia" (MA Thesis, University of British Columbia, 1935), 139-40.

[18] Ken Adachi, *The Enemy That Never Was* (Toronto: McClelland and Stewart, 1991) 113.

[19] Maryka Omatsu, *Bittersweet Passage* (Toronto: Between the Lines, 1992) 55.

[20] Adachi, The Enemy That Never Was, 109-10.

[21] Reichl, "Historical Processes of Ethnicity," 31-62.

[22] Charles H. Young and Helen R.Y. Reid, *The Japanese Canadians* (Toronto: University of Toronto Press, 1939) 6.

[23] Thomas R. Berger, "The Banished Canadians: Mackenzie King and the Japanese Canadians," *Fragile Freedoms: Human Rights and Dissent in Canada* (Toronto: Irwin, 1982) 95.

[24] Espiritu, *Asian American Panethnicity,* 7, 23, and 140.

[25] Here the term "pyrimidization of racialization" refers to the forced clustering of two or more distinctly different ethnic groups by a dominant group for its own purposes (e.g., segregation). However, the term may also be applied to the intentional coming together of two or more distinctly different ethnic groups for a common purpose, thus resulting in what Espiritu refers to as "panethnicity."

[26] Espiritu, *Asian American Panethnicity,* 25.

[27] Adachi, *The Enemy That Never Was,* 31.

[28] Family History of Tokutaro Tsuyuki, Maple Ridge Museum and Archives, file entitled "Japanese-People/Ethnic/General History," Maple Ridge, BC, 1.

[29] Juzo Suzuki, ed., "Farming by Japanese in Mission Area," in *Kanada Nohgyo Hatten Go: Development of Farming in Canada Issue*, Canada Nichinichi Shinbun, November 1929, trans. W.T. Hashizume, p. 19. Located in Mission Community Archives, Hashizume Fonds, Mission, BC.

[30] Gluck, *Japan's Modern Myths,* 34.

[31] Read, "The pre-War Japanese Canadians," 42; Sumida, "The Japanese in British Columbia," 290; Toyo Takata, *Nikkei Legacy: The Story of Japanese Canadians from Settlement to Today* (Toronto: NC Press, 1983), 70.

[32] Toyosaburo Nakamura, "Japanese Canadian Settlement in Mission: A Brief History," paper presented at 1980 reunion in Richmond, BC; and Chizu Uyemura, "Family History," 10. Both papers are located in the Mission Community Archives, Mission, BC.

[33] Read, "The Pre-War Japanese Canadians," 6-7.

[34] For several reasons, coastal fishing communities such as Steveston were more loosely constructed than were the farming buraku. The work in the former was seasonal and, therefore, the residents were transient and widely dispersed during the off-season. Adachi characterizes the Japanese Canadian section of Steveston in the early 1900s as "a rudimentary community." See Adachi, The Enemy That Never Was, 27, 47, and 58.

[35] While space does not allow for a detailed look at discriminatory legislation and workplace practices, these areas are thoroughly covered by Kobayashi and Jackson, "Japanese Canadians"; Adachi, *The Enemy That Never Was,* 26-35 and 50-1; and Patricia Roy, *A White Man's Province: British Columbia Politicians and Chinese and Japanese Immigrants, 1858-1914* (Vancouver: UBC Press, 1989), 81-8 and 244-58.

[36] Kobayashi and Jackson, "Japanese Canadians," 55.

[37] See Roy, *White Man's Province,* chap. 8.

[38] Mission District Council Minutes, 5 October 1907, Mission Community Archives, Mission, BC.

[39] Roy, White Man's Province, chap. 8

[40] For a detailed history of the series of gentlemen's agreements, see Adachi, *The Enemy That Never Was*, 81-3; Berger, "Banished Canadians," 98-100; and Young and Reid, *The Japanese Canadians*, 14-5.

[41] Young and Reid, *The Japanese Canadians*, 27; and Read, "Pre-War Japanese Canadians," 46.

[42] Cole Harris, *The Resettlement of British Columbia: Essays on Colonialism and Geographical Change* (Vancouver: UBC Press, 1997), 259.

[43] Sumida, "The Japanese in British Columbia," 299.

[44] Ibid., 315.

[45] Ibid., 308. This average is based upon eighty-one farmers who paid property taxes in 1934.

[46] Canadian Federation of University Women (CFUW), Maple Ridge Branch, *Maple Ridge: A History of Settlement* (Maple Ridge, BC: *Fraser Valley Record*, 1972), 16.

[47] Young and Reid, *Japanese Canadians*, 55-6.

[48] Sumida, "The Japanese in British Columbia," 299-300.

[49] Ibid., 311; and Gordon G. Nakayama, *Issei: Stories of Japanese Canadian Pioneers* (Toronto: NC Press, 1984), 50-5.

[50] Nakayama, *Issei*, 52; and Takata, *Nikkei Legacy*, 69.

[51] Sumida, "Japanese in British Columbia," 513-5.

[52] Barnett Family Fonds, 172, Mission Community Archives, Mission, BC.

[53] Yasutaro Yamaga Papers, University of British Columbia Library, Special Collections, Japanese Canadian Collection, box 20, pp. 9-10.

[54] Tomoko Makabe, "Mrs. Tami Nakamura," *Picture Brides: Japanese Women in Canada*, (Toronto: University of Toronto Press, 1995) 142-3; Moriyama, "Rambling Reminiscences," 27; Sumida, "Japanese in British Columbia," 524-7.

[55] Michael Hoshiko, ed., *Who was Who: Pioneer Japanese Families in Delta and Surrey* (Marceline, MO: Herff Jones, 1998), 214; and Read, "The Pre-War Japanese Canadians," 18, whose thesis takes a close look at the structure and function of the *Nokai* of the Maple Ridge communities of Haney, Hammond, Ruskin, Albion, and Whonnock.

[56] Takata, *Nikkei Legacy*, 70. *New Canadian* periodically reports on activities in the Coghlan Japanese Hall, including 16 January 1940, 3; and also 17 January 1941, 6

[57] Sumida, "Japanese in British Columbia," 303.

[58] *Fraser Valley Record*, 8 January 1920.

[59] Paul R. Spickard, *Japanese Americans* (New York: Twayne, 1996) 9.

[60] Sumida, "Japanese in British Columbia," 144.

[61] Suzuki, "Farming by Japanese," 5.

[62] Adachi, *The Enemy That Never Was*, 114.

[63] Midge Ayukawa, "Good Wives and Wise Mothers: Japanese Picture Brides in Early Twentieth Century British Columbia," *BC Studies* 105-6 (Spring/Summer 1995): 105-6, 112.

[64] Takata, *Nikkei Legacy*, 72.

[65] Makabe, *Picture Brides*, 141.

[66] Hoshiko, *Who Was Who*, 221.

[67] Read, "Pre-War Japanese Canadians," 12.

[68] Young and Reid, *Japanese Canadians*, 147-8.

[69] Moriyama, "Rambling Reminiscences," 22.

[70] Hoshiko, *Who Was Who*, 90, 93.

[71] Tape SMA 90.021-18, Surrey Archives, Surrey, BC.

[72] Harris, *Resettlement of British Columbia*, 254-5.

[73] Lon Kurashige, "The Problem of Biculturalism: Japanese American Identity and Festival before World War II," *Journal of American History* 86:4 (March 2000): 1647.

[74] CFUW, 19 and 6 May 1941, 2.

[75] Yamaga Papers, University of British Columbia Library, Special Collections, Japanese Canadian Collection, box 20, 3-4.

[76] *Fraser Valley Record*, 30 April 1925.

[77] Mitchell recalls taking part in May Day festivities with her schoolmates, White and Japanese alike. See also Beverley Mitchell, "Letter from Sakaye," *Fiddlehead* 99 (1973): 2-14, a short story based on Mitchell's childhood experiences in Mission during the late 1930s and early 1940s. A photo of the Japanese Canadian May Day float for 1936 is available through the Mission Community Archives, Mission, BC.

[78] "Empire Day Programme, 25 May 1925," *Fraser Valley Record,* Mission Community Archives, Mission, BC. and "Coronation Souvenir Programme in Honour of King George VI and Queen Elizabeth, 12 May 1937," *Fraser Valley Record*, Mission Community Archives, Mission, BC.

[79] Miles, *Racism*, 76.

[80] *Abbotsford, Sumas, Matsqui News*, 12 March 1941.

[81] Yamaga, Papers, 14.

[82] Taped interview located under Whonnock Community Association, Historical Project 1985, box 2, Mission Community Archives, Mission, BC.

[83] Hoshiko, *Who Was Who,* 214. Michael Hoshiko, son of a Surrey *Issei* farmer, makes this distinction in a short article on the Surrey Berry Co-op. Sumida, "Japanese in British Columbia," 280, verifies the need for Japanese firms involved in trade and business to find most of their customers among the Japanese.

[84] Suzuki, "Farming by Japanese," 20; CFUW, 18.

[85] Sumida, "Japanese in British Columbia," 311.

[86] Nakayama, *Issei,* 53-4; Sumida, "Japanese in British Columbia," 315-6.

[87] Nakayama, *Issei,* 54.

[88] Suzuki, "Farming by Japanese," 21.

[89] *Fraser Valley Record*, 30 December 1932.

[90] John Cherrington, *Mission on the Fraser* (Vancouver: Mitchell, 1974) 146-7.

[91] Sumida, "Japanese in British Columbia," 311-2.

[92] *Fraser Valley Record*, 31 December 1936; 9 February 1939.

[93] Ibid., 21 December 1934; 21 February 1935.

[94] Ibid., 28 February 1935.

[95] Ibid., 21 December 1934.

[96] See also *Chilliwack Progress*, 15 April 1942, 4.

[97] T. D. Regehr, *Mennonites in Canada, 1939-1970: A People Transformed* (Toronto: University of Toronto Press, 1996), 110.

[98] See *Chilliwack Progress*, Wednesday, 1 June 1904, 4, and 11 October 1905, for early reports of Japanese modernization and expansion. In the 1930s and

1940s almost all Fraser Valley newspapers ran articles reporting on Japanese imperialism and military conquests.

[99] Omatsu, *Bittersweet Passage,* 57.

[100] Stanley, "Chinamen," 502-3.

[101] A thorough look at Issei/Nisei relations can be found in Adachi's Chapter 7 entitled "Generations," 157-78.

[102] Sumida, "Japanese in British Columbia," 443 and 330.

[103] Makabe, *Picture Brides*, 142.

[104] *Fraser Valley Record*, 7 January 1932.

[105] *Fraser Valley Record*, 2 April 1936 and 25 February 1937.

[106] *Fraser Valley Record*, 15 April 1937.

[107] Yamaga, Papers, 8-9.

[108] Koazi Kujikawa interviewed by David Buss, March 1991. Tape at Mission Community Archives, Box 185-15; Sumida, "Japanese in British Columbia," 438. Also see Moriyama, "Rambling Reminiscences," 15, where she discusses her children's friendship with the children of their German neighbours.

[109] Takata, *Nikkei Legacy,* 23-4.

[110] Violet Vachon (nee Kujikawa) interviewed by David Buss, 15 March 1992. Tape #309, Box 185-15, Mission Community Archives, Mission, BC.

[111] Whonnock Community Association — Historical Project, 1985. Transcription of alphabetical card file by Fred Braches, January 1996, 15. Mission Community Archives, Mission, BC.

[112] *Abbotsford, Sumas, Matsqui News*, 17 April 1929 and 8 February 1939.

[113] *Maple Ridge Leader*, 14 April 1938.

[114] *North Fraser Leader*, 8 June 1939.

[115] Peter W. Ward, *White Canada Forever: Popular Attitudes and Public Policy toward Orientals in British Columbia* (Montreal: McGill-Queens University Press, 1978) 117.

[116] Patricia Roy, J.L. Granastein, Masako Lino and Hiroko Takamura, *Mutual Hostages: Canadians and Japanese during the Second World War* (Toronto: University of Toronto Press, 1990) 42; Adachi, *The Enemy That Never Was,* 189.

[117] Ward, *White Canada Forever,* 135-6, tells us that in the late 1920s four new "anti-Oriental leagues" formed in the province, one based in Victoria and the other three in Vancouver. It is interesting to note that none of these was based in rural communities and that, at that particular time, none of them thrived.

[118] *Abbotsford, Sumas and Matsqui News*, 7 January 1942, 8.

[119] *Maple Ridge-Pitt Meadows Gazette*, 14 March 1941; *Abbotsford, Sumas, Matsqui News*, 4 March 1942; and *Chilliwack Progress*, 6 May 1942.

[120] *Fraser Valley Record*, 18 and 25 February 1942. See also 5 March 1942.

[121] Ibid., March 1942, 1.

[122] Ibid., 23 December 1941.

[123] Ibid., 4 February 1942.

[124] Berger, "Banished Canadians," 114-5.

[125] Makabe, "Brazil and Canada," 789 and 808.

[126] Reichl, "Historical Processes," 41.

[127] Takenaka, "Transnational Community," 8.

[128] *Fraser Valley Record*, 2 September 1942.

[129] Ibid., 20 May 1941, 26 December 1940, 23 December 1941, and 30 May 1940.

[130] Thirty-five Nisei who enlisted in the Canadian armed forces prior to the attack on Pearl Harbor "were quietly allowed to remain in the services." Eventually a total of 150 Nisei were allowed to enlist, many being assigned to a special language unit of the Canadian Intelligence Corps. From the Japanese Canadian Centennial Project, *The Japanese Canadians, 1877-1977: A Dream of Riches* (Toronto: Gilcrist Wright, 1978) 103.

[131] "Forgotten Cultures," *Maple Ridge-Pitt Meadows Times*, 25 February 1996, 3.

[132] See articles describing donations in *Maple Ridge-Pitt Meadows Gazette*, 12 January 1940, 2 May 1941; *Fraser Valley Record*, 2 January 1942; and Roy, J.L Granastein, Masako Lino, and Hiroko Takamura, *Mutual Hostages*, 45.

[133] *Maple Ridge-Pitt Meadows Gazette*, 12 December 1941

[134] Ibid., 22 November 1940.

[135] Ibid., 12 December 1941.

[136] *Fraser Valley Record*, 16 December 1941.

[137] *Fraser Valley Record*, 15 January 1942.

[138] Ibid., 3 March 1942.

[139] PCU Minutes, 9 March 1942, Mission Community Archives, Mission, BC.

Sikh Immigration and Community in the Fraser Valley

Baljeet Dhaliwal

Introduction

Central to a people's identity are its key principles. Webster's New World College Dictionary defines the term principle as "a fundamental truth, law, doctrine, or motivation force upon which others are based." According to the Expo White Papers (2004), "...in any serious study of history—be it national or corporate—the reality and verity of such principles become obvious. These principles surface time and again, and the degree to which people in a society recognize and live in harmony with them moves them toward either survival and stability or disintegration and destruction." A people's inherent principles are often connected to a higher belief system. Guiding my explanation of how Sikh Canadians, a group once deemed to be undesirable by Canadian society, have become outstanding citizens participating in all sectors of Canadian life is my understanding of how the historical experiences of the Sikhs are related to their higher belief system.

The first and more comprehensive section of this paper presents historical and ideological background information; the second focuses on the narrative of one man's journey, providing one Sikh's perspective on what it means to become a Canadian. My paper will focus mainly on the pre-1960 Sikh community; thus, the post-1960 wave of immigration is beyond the scope of this paper.

My thesis is that the economic and cultural successes of Sikhs are connected to their historical minority/majority status in India as well as to key principles of their belief system. My examination of Sikhs' trials and triumphs in the central Fraser Valley and of the impact of Canadian immigration laws on Sikhs' emigrant/immigrant consciousness will provide the basis for my analysis of the adaptations made by these settlers as they became part of the larger Canadian society. As a minority group, pre-1960 Sikh settlers spent much time attempting to resolve social, economic, and political issues. I will argue that Sikh religious thought and experience provided them with the tenacity to persevere and to eventually thrive in the Fraser Valley and the rest of Canada.

Crucial to an understanding of this perseverance is the history of Sikhism as a minority community, particularly in India. From time to time Sikhs faced persecution and perceived themselves as being under threat of annihilation at the hands of the Mughal rulers in Delhi. An additional consideration is the fact that Sikhs were a colonized people within the British Empire. The realities of the permutations of colonization, the Sikh minority/majority status, and the Sikhs' struggle to maintain their religion in the face of persecution have all shaped an inescapable cultural tenacity that has assisted Sikhs in their immigrant experiences.

It should be noted that my interpretation of Sikh history and thought is heavily informed by what one might call a Tat Khalsa perspective, an important but not unique perspective from which one might interpret and understand Sikh history and thought.

Sikh Ideology

Historically, Sikhs resided in the state of India called Punjab, which came under Moslem rule during the Mughal Wars of the sixteenth century. Sikhism had its origin in the non-violent, pacifist teaching of Guru Nanak Dev (1469-1539), a former Hindu. Sikhism "propounds monotheism. . . . It also opposes the caste system and believes that all men are equal."[1] A morning prayer called Japji by Guru Nanak Dev provides an articulation of the premise upon which Sikhism is rooted.[2] Guru Nanak Dev preached pacifism during a period when his religion was under siege. Although the succession of gurus who succeeded him did their best to nurture the faith, repeated Muslim attempts to convert followers of Sikhism to the Islamic faith challenged their pacifist teachings.

There were occasions, especially during the time of the early gurus, where relations between Delhi and the Mughal rulers were not marked by violence and conflict. However, the growing power of the Sikhs in the Punjab was becoming a political threat to Mughal rule. During the years 1666 to 1708 the tenth guru, Gobind Singh, in his struggle for the survival of Sikhism, accelerated the shift from pacifism to an emphasis on militancy. In 1675, in response to the beheading of his father, Tegh Bahadur, by the Mughal leader, Aurangzeb, Guru Gobind assumed the task of avenging his father and of setting a new direction for Sikhism. Thus, he is the guru responsible for accelerating the modification of the originally pacifist character of Sikhism—a process that had already begun during the time of the sixth guru.

Developing a Sikh social organization proved to be a long and arduous process. Guru Gobind enjoined the Sikhs to elect an executive of five Beloved Ones from among themselves, and he promised to be present among them. Sarbat Khalsa was the name given to the whole commonwealth of the Sikhs, in whose name all prayers are offered and all public decisions made. Questions of Panthic, or public interest, were discussed in the plenary gatherings at the Akal Takht, the Sikh seat of power, to which all Sikhs had access. Questions of local interest were discussed in numerous local conclaves, or sangats. Even ordinary breaches of the rules of conduct were judged in such representative meetings, and no person, however highly placed, was above the jurisdiction of these conclaves.

It is significant that the Sikhs found it necessary to unite and distinguish themselves as a visible minority separate from the majority Indian population. By making themselves distinct, the Sikhs, while placing themselves in a vulnerable position, were becoming a strong self-identified community, a dynamic that would prepare them to remain united and committed to their ideology, both in India and abroad. This strong sense of cultural identity may account for the development of such distinctive Sikh values as pride, assertiveness and determination. Being unified into a cohesive people proved to be crucial for the Sikhs. However, at the same time, it also invited opposition from the Mughal- or Moslem-dominated government. The Sikhs' experiences as a minority religious group and later as a subjugated yet select class of people under the British Raj transformed their original Sikh ideal of moderation to a more dogmatic tradition.

Sikh symbols of identifications, ostensibly introduced by Gobind Singh in the formation of the Khalsa, include "the five k's" (the five k's conveniently refer to five Punjabi words that begin with the letter "k"). The first is "kes" or "kesh," meaning long hair, and symbolizing strength, courage and piety. The second is "kanga," the comb used to clean hair and to hold it in place. The third is "kacch," the short undergarment intended to remind Sikhs of chastity and moral restraint. The fourth is "kara," a steel bracelet denoting the unity within the divine and the cohesiveness of the community. The fifth is "kirpan," a dagger/sword symbolic of willingness to defend the faith and the ability to discern right from wrong. .

The concept of brotherhood or unity has proven to be an important principle in ensuring the survival of the Sikhs. As Magocsi (1148-63) points out, Sikhs have a strong sense of fraternity. An inherent type of trust uniquely shapes the way one Sikh relates to another. Fraternalism has proved beneficial, particularly when Sikhs have found themselves persecuted for their religion or struggling to survive as a distinct Indian ethnic minority. While attempting to secure their religion during the Mughal wars, Sikhs increasingly clarified what it meant to become a secure enclave. During this time, the Sikhs reaffirmed their commitment to principles such as loyalty, evidenced in the way they supported one another in living and working together. It is this very need to survive that explains the renewed sense of belonging central to the Sikhs' immigrant consciousness.

Sikh ideology and social organization promoted a strong sense of identity for Sikhs, both as a subjugated people in India under the control of the British Raj and as minorities abroad. Sikhs in Mexico and Panama did not experience the same problems as their Canadian counterparts, reinforcing my thesis that the major problems faced by the Sikhs in Canada were rooted in legal and social discrimination. For example, the Canadian law of 1875 that denied the franchise to immigrants from India or China[3] affected the Sikhs' ideological consciousness. However, their minority role, both earlier in India and later as immigrants to Canada, combined with their ideology assisted them to become successful twentieth-century emigrants. Thus,

> Sikhs, faced with the perils of discrimination, have gone through a major perceptual shift. Though a once colonized people, hence victims of power, they were valued also for their capabilities as warriors, disciplinarians, and hard working people. As a result of having two distinctive roles, one resulting from being a colonized people, the other stemming from their ideology, Sikhs dealt with a unique construct of reality (Dhaliwal 41).

Emigration Consciousness: Why did Sikhs immigrate to the Central Fraser Valley?

Sikh immigration to Canada can be divided into several periods: 1794 to 1850, a period characterized by non-discriminatory laws; 1850-1920, a time marked by the passage of laws curtailing Asian immigration; and the next fifteen years, from 1920 to 1935, a period when lower numbers of people of Indian origin emigrated due to the immigration regulations imposed during World War I. As a result of fewer immigrants to Canada, generally the hostility in Canada that existed toward South Asians decreased, and, in the Fraser Valley, their economic security increased.

Two major factors accounted for Sikh emigration from India during the early-twentieth century. The first was the Sikh custom of land inheritance; the second was Great Britain's colonization of India. According to Sikh tradition, the eldest son inherited the family's land; consequently, the other sons often traveled abroad to earn money. In addition, the British system of administration led to increased employment opportunities for Sikhs both in India and abroad, in places such as Hong Kong, Fiji, the Middle East, Uganda, and, later, North America, England and elsewhere. For example, Macauliffe indicates that many Sikhs went abroad as part of British regiments sent to "Fiji, China, the Middle East, and parts of Uganda. Sixty to seventy percent of the posts assigned to Sikhs during their posting in these countries were clerical in nature. This held true for the majority of Sikhs who immigrated to Canada in 1904 as well" (Macauliffe 22). British colonial policy aimed at cultivating buffer systems between the British and the inhabitants of a colonized country. For instance, in India, Parsees from Iran served as buffers between the British and the Indians.

British Columbia, including Vancouver, was a dominantly white European society in the late-nineteenth century. In 1898, representatives from various countries of the Empire traveled to England to join in the celebration of Queen Victoria's Diamond Jubilee. Similarly, Indian troops also traveled to London to celebrate the coronation of Edward VII. In 1902, a small contingent of eighty-three Sikh officers and servicemen from the Crown Colony of Hong Kong traveled through Canada on the way to and from London. They arrived in Vancouver on June 3, 1902, on the Empress of Japan. As members of a British regiment, these men created quite a stir among the people of Vancouver. As Buchignani, Indra and Srivstiva state, "The Punjabi contingent attracted the most attention, for by Vancouver standards they were the most novel" (6).

While Sikhs would later be viewed more negatively in Canada, in 1900 they were not deemed to be a threat. As British military representatives, Sikhs were held in high regard. The press captured the pervasive positive attitude; a news story stated, "TURBANED MEN EXCITE INTEREST/ Awe inspiring men from India held the crowd" (Buchignani 231). As a result of their travels to London via Canada, and particularly via Vancouver, some Sikhs from Hong Kong began to emigrate; however, not until 1905 did Sikhs begin to arrive directly from the Indian subcontinent.

Some Sikhs were unaware of the degree to which a colonized "victimized" mentality had scarred their sense of self. Sikhs who immigrated to Canada from Hong Kong saw themselves as respectable British subjects, but still experienced discrimination in Canada. Their experiences of discrimination might well have become overwhelming had it not been for the temples that served as communal gathering places, where Sikhs were able to find comfort and gain a sense of security. Were it not for the discriminatory laws and practices in Canada, the Sikhs might well have assimilated with ease into

the dominant society. During their initial settlement period, Sikhs participated in many societal events. However, while assimilation in external areas
such as clothing styles was taking place, deeper issues of cultural blending
were not yet being worked out. Sikh immigrants to Canada have endured a
long history of changes within the socio-political climate, with both the host
country and the immigrant community having undergone periods of transition and adjustment.

During the 1940s, powerful colonial countries allowed less powerful
subjugated nations to reclaim their own identity and freedom as it became
evident that keeping a people in subjection was not a positive sign of power.
Thus, Sikhs, too, began to question their status in Canada. Although they
viewed themselves as British subjects, Canadian immigration laws had made
it apparent to the Sikhs that they had little or no status:

> This contradictory state left some Sikhs with very unsettled and
> resentful feelings. . . . Some said that it was not until they had lived in
> Vancouver for a few years that they realized that they viewed them-
> selves as inferior to the whites, that is, as having the colonized men-
> tality of a subjugated class of people (Dhaliwal 21).

Moving from Emigration to Immigration Consciousness: the Role of Education

It soon became obvious to the early settlers that educating their children was
necessary to ensure the survival of their culture. Jagpal states, "For the Sikhs,
one of the advantages of coming to Canada was the opportunity for their
children to get an education. Many Sikh parents, realizing the importance of
learning English, sent their children to school for this reason alone" (86).
Education provided hope for future prosperity. The crucial role education
would play in their children's future soon became self-evident, since "the
children are the future."

However, several factors limited the Sikhs' attempts to educate their
children. Although the importance of education was recognized, the struggle
for economic survival took precedence at times. In addition, "What further
diminished the value of education was that the Sikhs lacked the provincial,
municipal and federal franchise. As a consequence, many jobs and professions were not open to them" (Jagpal 88). Also, Sikhs faced sending older
non-English speaking children to schools in a system that lacked the knowledge necessary to accommodate them. For example, teenager Gurdave S.
Billan was forced to start in a grade one class at Henry Hudson School in
Vancouver. He soon left to sell wood with his uncle. Children in similar
situations did not stay in school for long; instead, they dropped out to go to

work. Educational experiences in the Fraser Valley were similar to those in the Victoria and Vancouver areas.

New legislation helped bring about more favourable conditions. When educators and education policy integrated new pedagogy and curricula to accommodate non-English speaking students into their schools, children found schooling to be more enjoyable. However, many Sikh students had attended school before these necessary changes took effect. Yet, all the while, Sikhs understood that their personal and national freedom was dependent on getting their children educated.

Politically, the Sikhs lacked political power to affect decision-making at the federal, provincial and municipal levels. In fact, they were not even recognized as a legally constituted part of the population. Laws greatly determined the extent to which Sikhs were or were not able to participate in education and in society. For instance, educated Sikhs emigrated from India only to discover that their degrees had little value and that they were unable to secure employment due to racially motivated laws and regulations. While instances of racism and intolerance continue to this day, Sikhs are continuing to integrate into the dominant society, as policies and directions designed to bring about a greater understanding between ethnic groups enable them to participate in new careers.

Injustice and Policy Making: The Emergence of the Immigrant Consciousness

The overt cases of mistreatment and discrimination which the Sikhs experienced upon immigrating to Canada forced them to realize that their expectations of being treated fairly as British subjects had little credibility. Newspaper articles dated as early as 1920 referred to South Asian immigrants as Hindoos (sic). This term revealed a lack of ethnic, cultural and political understanding amongst the dominant white community, for whom the Sikhs constituted an unknown entity. Sikhs, then called Hindoos (sic), East Indians, or Orientals, were simply lumped together with other Asian groups. For almost thirty years, they were not identified by their ethnic name. In the early-twentieth century, all Asians were considered undesirable and inferior to white people. The ideological intent of the Canadian government was to keep Canada "white"; thus, it barred any "Oriental," a term then used to refer to the Japanese, Chinese and Sikhs, from voting and from exercising any legal rights. "Oriental" people were vulnerable to discrimination because they were a racially visible minority and considered unsuitable for the Canadian way of life. The instability endured by Sikhs during this period required that they develop community strategies to ensure survival and success. These strategies were internal community support and greater participation within the dominant society

Racial tension increased sharply following the initial non-discriminatory years. The colour of skin and the type of dress worn by Sikhs created a furor within the dominant population, motivating the government to take drastic measures in order to ensure that British Columbia would remain white. Discrimination against Sikhs was based on racial, economic, and political reasons. White society's ignorance about and fear of foreigners led to unfair regulations. Drastic as well as subtle forms of discrimination prohibited Sikh participation in society, with the intent of discouraging these "brown-skinned people" from remaining in Canada. For example, on January 8, 1908, the Government of Canada issued an Order-in-Council requiring that any immigrant arriving at a Canadian port must have come on a continuous journey from their country. This continuous journey legislation targeted primarily the Japanese and South Asians.

This discrimination aided in creating a community of Sikhs who in their external lifestyle did their best to adopt the lifestyle of white society. While in some cases, integration and at times assimilation included acquiring many western values, at the same time, longstanding Sikh principles were so deeply rooted that in the home language was maintained and religious ceremonies remained part of everyday life. During the earlier years, these discriminatory practices forced the immigrant groups to strengthen their group cultural identity by bonding closely as they began the process of acculturation, integration and/or assimilation.

It was not until 1930 that Sikhs began to integrate with more ease into Canadian society. With time, greater participation by Sikhs in every sector of the dominant society gained momentum. In 1947, Sikhs gained franchise rights for the first time. As a result of the multicultural policies of the 1960s, Sikhs and all people of Indian ethnicity acquired the label "Indo-Canadian." This term suggests the emergence of a new and different social process involving peoples of Indian origin who may have differing ethnic and religious beliefs but are distinguishable by skin colour. The term suggests the rise of collective thought, perhaps a new ideology. A collective allegiance among a series of cultural groups provides a base from which they can voice their concerns.

However, contemporary use of the term Indo-Canadian can be seen as having both a positive and a negative connotation. On one hand, the term does not distinguish between groups of Indian background, thereby lumping all "brown-skinned persons" together, conveniently setting them apart from non-brown-skinned people. On the other hand, the term is positive since people of Indian origin are recognized along with white members of society as being Canadian.

Discrimination became a catalyst for change. It brought together younger individuals from differing Indian backgrounds to unite as Indo-Canadians in order to combat racism and to struggle against political, social, and economic hardships. Individuals such as Paul, the pioneer whose story is told in the postscript, maintained a strong allegiance to their Sikh community although also participating comfortably within the dominant society. The pioneer Sikhs balanced their two cultures, while today's Sikhs appear to be integrated at all levels of society. Not surprisingly, alignment among the younger generation is increasingly along class lines, which is competing with ethnicity as the focal point of identification among Sikhs today.

The integration of Sikhs into contemporary Canadian society is evident at various levels. This integration is a recent phenomenon of the past twenty years; before this time, Sikhs remained in a closed ethnic enclave. The long period endured by Sikhs as less valued people explains their lower level of participation in the dominant society's industries, businesses, and education. Laws regulated their participation in dominant society. The municipal franchise was granted to "East Indians" in British Columbia in 1948, thus nullifying the earlier law of 1875. Individuals were now able to teach and vote, thus obtaining greater influence and hopefully able to make a difference. The Sikhs' principles, ideology, history, and culture molded them and prepared them, as an immigrant community, with the necessary means to become active agents in forging their identity in the central Fraser Valley.

Postscript

On Becoming Canadian and an Integral Part of the Fabric of the Fraser Valley

The story of my father, Paul Singh Dhaliwal, illustrates what it meant to be an Indo-Canadian living in the Fraser Valley, first in Mission and later in Abbotsford, during the twentieth century. In his situation, as in most cases, emigration was connected with the Indian family's socialization process. According to Magocsi:

> The oldest Sikh families in Canada invariably can trace their histories to one of the men who emigrated in the first few years of the twentieth century. These men came by train from Punjab to Calcutta, by open-deck steamer from Calcutta to Hong Kong, and then in steerage on Canadian Pacific liner from Hong Kong to Victoria and Vancouver.... Emigration, however, was determined first within

the Punjabi family system. The elders of a young man's extended family or his immediate household had a final say on whether or not he could leave. If his labour was needed or if he was required to manage family property and family affairs, he would have to stay. Only a family with spare adult males could sanction emigration. And emigration was so exceptional for women that the 1911 census showed only three percent women out of a total South Asian population of 2,000 in British Columbia (Magocsi 1151).

Paul explains, "My dad came to Canada in 1908. He and his cousin Bugwahn came together on ship from Hong Kong" (Dhaliwal, Paul. Interview). Paul's father was unique since he had served in the British police force and attended the Gamma school of wrestling. (Wrestling is a sport popular among Sikhs.) Dhillon states that "During the British and the post-independence periods, the Jats (the term Jat refers to a caste of Punjabi Sikhs) from South Asia have settled in various parts of the world. Overseas travel of many Jats, in the service of the British Empire as soldiers or policemen began prior to the 1880s" (Dhillon 331). During his stay in British Columbia, Paul's father and his cousin found a home in Abbotsford. Friends of his uncle described the building of the Sikh temple. A mill stood at the southwest end of Mill Lake; it was from here that Sikh men carried timber, on foot, for building the temple, since hiring a truck was too costly. Doing service for God was central to the doctrine of Sikhism. The Temple or Gurdwara was built in 1911; it affirmed the tenets of benevolence and devotion. The Abbotsford Sikh Temple created a place for Central Fraser Valley pioneer Sikhs to gather for both religious and social occasions.

Around 1912, both Paul's father and his cousin went back to India. Paul was born in the state of Punjab in India in 1914. He explained that "My dad stayed back in India. His cousin came back to Canada. My dad got the plague and died. Before he died, he asked Bugwahn Singh to take me to Canada. So he did" (Dhaliwal, Paul. Interview).

During the years of 1912 to 1914, the continuous journey laws influenced travel opportunities for Sikh immigrants. The nature of Bugwahn's journey back to Canada was determined by governmental regulations. The continuous journey legislation enacted by the Canadian government prior to 1914 led to the infamous Komogata Maru incident of 1914 in Vancouver harbour, where "only twenty-two Sikhs, all former residents of Canada, were allowed to land" (Jagpal 33) and the rest were refused admission to Canada. Although Bugwahn was not a passenger on the Komogata, he traveled to Canada during this period of heightened discrimination. Of great importance for him was the law stating that the men who had remained in Canada and the twenty-two men from the Komogata who had earlier resided in Canada had the legal right to bring their sons to Canada.

Fulfilling his promise to his cousin, Bugwahn Singh Dhaliwal arranged for my father, Paul Singh Dhaliwal, to come as his son. Paul's warm words express his gratitude: "My uncle treated me like his son" (Interview, Paul). Paul's family expected that his only and elder brother would remain in India to care for the land and family, while Paul, the second eldest, would travel abroad and make money. The money was then either to be sent home or to be brought back to the family.

Paul Singh Dhaliwal began his journey in 1930 to Canada from Chananwal, his village in Punjab. The journey from Chananwal to Calcutta took twenty-two days. Traveling alone and mostly on foot, Paul remembers well the hardships of the journey—hardships which symbolized much of Paul's life to come. Paul sadly states, "The wait for a ship took weeks and sometimes months. When I was in Hong Kong I stayed at the Sikh temple" (Dhaliwal, Paul. Interview) Temples have always played a key role in the journeys of Sikh immigrants. People he met along the way assisted him as if he were a family member. He recalls that, after arriving in Hong Kong, "I stayed for two weeks waiting a CPR ship. The kind of ship that moves things from one country to another. The ships made trips between Japan and Canada."

Today a ninety-year-old Abbotsford resident, he remembers the difficult early emigrant/immigrant years. He vividly recalls, "I walked many miles not just to come to Canada but in Canada too. One time I walked all the way from Abbotsford to Chilliwack to sell a cow. I walked back home and it was a long walk. I worked hard in mills and driving truck." As an immigrant, Paul spent many years making adjustments to the dominant society. He overcame many challenges, both of the heart and of the land, as he forged his own Canadian identity as a resident of the Lower Mainland and the Fraser River Valley.

In 1930, at the age of sixteen, Paul arrived in Victoria and then made his way to Vancouver. He brought with him from India a tin trunk, an Indian-mattress and a quilt. Arriving in Vancouver, he and another man, Lal Singh, "left the CPR dock at the foot of Granville Street in Vancouver and walked to the 1500 block of West Second Street. We found the Sikh temple on Second Street. I was too tired, we walked all the way from the dock to Second Street, you know in Vancouver." Like the Sikh temple in Hong Kong, this temple served as a meeting place as well as a religious centre. Following in the steps of other immigrants, the weary travelers Paul and Lal knew that the temple would provide a sanctuary where they could eat and rest. It provided an opportunity for Paul to prepare himself to travel to his uncle's home in Abbotsford.

His uncle Bugwahn was awaiting his arrival in Abbotsford, BC. Paul further explains, "I arrived one week early. Lal's friend had a truck. 'No,' I said, 'no.' I was too scared to travel in the truck. But Lal's friend said come, it is safe." Reluctantly, Paul agreed to travel in the truck and arrived safely in Abbotsford. Here he lived for six weeks in a house located on the present site of Blackwood Lumber next to the new Sikh temple on South Fraser Way.

In 1934-35, earlier Sikh pioneers such as Mayo and Kapoor had established themselves as entrepreneurs in the wood business. They, along with other Sikh partnerships, operated sawmills and logging camps; however, it was not until the late 1950s that a significant number of Sikh settlers began to work in the agricultural sector. In addition, it was not until after World War II that Sikhs were represented in professional careers.

Although only a youth, Paul joined his fellow Sikhs working in the lumber industry. He moved to Greenlake to take up a job that his uncle had procured for him. Placed on a train to Pemberton, Paul carried with him a piece of paper on which one word was written: "Greenlake." At each stop, he would show this paper, until he arrived at his destination and was told to leave the train. He also had with him a piece of paper on which was written the English alphabet. Paul studied the letters and eventually began to make sounds to form words. He lived in the bunkhouse at the Parksville Lumber Company near Whistler, some forty-two miles from Squamish. He worked here for a few years, and in the winter, due to his young age, was assigned the task of stoking the fire. Paul recounts, "I found the winters very cold. I did not know where to get warm and because I was the young one, I stayed up the night to keep the fire burning. Life was tough in Canada." He returned for a stay with his uncle in Abbotsford before he took another job at the Hillcrest Company on Vancouver Island, working a fifty-hour week for ten cents per hour. Paul had heard about this job possibility from his cousin Hari who was working at the mill. Paul stayed in the cookhouse/bunkhouse until 1934. In 1935, he came to Vancouver to celebrate New Years' at the Second Avenue Gudwara. He remembers:

> I know the address 1863 Second Avenue. I stayed here and one day Mayo called and said the mill burned. So, I stayed in Vancouver, no reason to go back. I began work on Sixth Avenue in Vancouver at another sawmill. You know where False Creek is. I stayed ten months and Mayo said come back to work. I did and worked there until the end of 1939. World War II started on September 9, 1939. So in 1939, I come over to Vancouver for Christmas and stayed with a

friend, Soyn, and began to drive truck for Soyn and Brothers Trucking. I stayed during 1940 and 1941 with this company but I quit because the pay was poor. In 1942, I worked for Cedar in Port Moody during the winter months of January, February, March and April. In June, a fellow named Narangen Grewal and his partner Sadahar Singh asked if I would haul sawdust from their mill. I was happy working in the Port Moody mill. But no, Narangen said, come we will give shares in the mill. I was thinking, asked my friends, and made a decision. Okay but I said to Narangen on my terms, no shares. I will buy my own truck.

In 1942, Paul purchased a truck with his savings and established his own business in Mission. He recalls that in 1942 there were about four or five people of Indian origin living in Mission, including Inder Singh Gill, Mayo Manhus, and Narangen Grewal. Since during these years mills shut down in the winter, Paul would then go to Vancouver to train as a wrestler. At two hundred and ten pounds, he soon developed a reputation. Promoters from the United States approached him about employment in their shows.

In 1945, Ted Thia, a promoter from Portland Oregon, made appropriate immigration arrangements for Paul to cross the border into the United States. Paul recalls, "I had a six-month visa. I wrestled in Seattle and Portland and then moved to San Francisco. After six-months of wrestling in the States, I came back to go to the wedding of Phungan Singh." Upon Paul's arrival in Abbotsford, two significant events occurred: First, a promoter from Salt Lake City offered him a contract for five wrestling matches. He recalls that he was offered a substantial fee. The second event was a letter from his mother asking that he return to India; it was unlike any other letter he had received from her previously. He sought counsel from the men who had become his family. "I called these men together, said here I have the letter from my mom and the telegraph from the promoter. They said, listen, go home to your mother." Again, claims of loyalty to family prevailed. After telegraphing the promoter in Salt Lake City to inform him that he would not be able to fulfill the contract, Paul left for India in 1947. He married there in 1949 before returning to Canada in May of 1950.

Paul's return to Canada had several implications. It meant that he would now be sponsoring his wife, who followed him to Canada in October 1950. In addition, this meant he would be planning to make a life in Canada. In contrast, during "the 1950's, many Sikhs still looked at Canada as a place to work rather than a country in which to settle. The immigrants that Canadian Sikhs chose to sponsor under the new quota system were generally male relatives destined for the unskilled labour force" (Magocsi 158). Paul resumed his sawdust delivery service, working for a number of years in the Mission area. In 1957, he had a trucking business called Paul Brothers. He hauled lumber from Whonnock Mill and later owned Mission Fuel Ltd. During the following year, he expanded his business to include a fleet of trucks for hauling lumber and logs. Today he is retired, living on a blueberry farm in the Matsqui/Abbotsford area.

Paul observes that as immigration from India increased, Mission lost "the old time feeling." By this "old time feeling," Paul means the trust and ease that existed as the white and immigrant communities worked together in harmony. New immigrants from unrelated backgrounds began to become part of a community that once had been comprised of Sikhs who had learned how to blend in with the dominant white society. Magocsi observes that

> The immigration of professional people from all parts of India increased many times after 1962, when Canada dropped the quota system and began to emphasize education, training, and job qualifications. For Punjabi Sikhs, however, a more significant change in immigration policy came when in 1967 Asian residents acquired the same rights as other residents to sponsor or nominate more distant relatives (Magocsi 1162).

This influx of people of Indian ethnicity after 1962 marks the beginning of a third wave of immigrants important because of their greater numbers. Their story, however, lies beyond the scope of this paper.

Conclusion

This brief exposition, with its insights gained from the story of one individual, aids in developing an understanding of who Sikhs are as a people. This story provides insight into the immigration and settlement of Sikhs during the early-twentieth century. This does, not however, suggest that all integration of Sikhs into the dominant society follows this pattern of immigration and settlement. However different the individual journeys of Sikhs may have been, the ethnic ideology that united them served as a foundation for the community. The commitments made by pioneer Sikh settlers in the central Fraser Valley have left a legacy that has touched the hearts of both dominant and minority people of the region.

Endnotes

[1] M. Khatri, http://www.indianchild.com/guru_nanak.htm/.
[2] Japji
There is One God.
He is the supreme truth.

He, the Creator,
Is without fear and without hate.
He, the Omnipresent, Pervades the universe.
He is not born,
Nor does He die to be born again.
By His grace shalt thou worship Him.
Before time itself
There was truth.
When time began to run its course He was the truth.
Even now, He is the truth. And evermore shall truth prevail.

[3] Provisions of the 1875 law, "Relating to Qualification and Registration of Voters," included:

No Chinaman or Indian shall have his name placed on the Register of Voters for any Electoral District, or be entitled to vote at any election of a Member to serve in the Legislative Assembly of this Province. Any Collector of any Electoral District or Polling Division thereof, who shall insert the name of any Chinaman or Indian in any such Register, shall, upon conviction thereof before any Justice of the Peace, be liable to be punished by a fine not exceeding fifty dollars, or to be imprisoned for any period not exceeding one month.

In every Electoral District or Polling Division thereof, the Collector therefore shall, on or before the first day of June, 1875, strike off the name of every Chinaman now on the List of Voters for his District or Polling Division thereof; and any Collector who shall neglect or refuse to strike off any such name, or shall insert the name of any Chinaman or Indian in any such Register, shall upon conviction thereof before any Justice of the Peace, be liable to be punished by a fine not exceeding fifty dollars, or to be imprisoned for any period not exceeding one month.

A brief overview of the role of discrimination and its relation to human relations is found in "The Official Memorandum of the United Nations." Among the forms of discrimination officially practiced in various parts of the world, the United Nations lists the following:

- Unequal recognition before the law (general denial rights to particular groups)
- Inequality of personal security (interferences, arrest, disparagement because of group membership)
- Inequality in freedom of movement and residence (ghettoes, forbidden travel, prohibited areas, curfew restrictions)
- Inequality in protection of freedom of thought, conscience, religion
- Inequality in the enjoyment of free communication
- Inequality in the right of peaceful association
- Inequality in treatment of those born out of wedlock
- Inequality in the enjoyment of the right to marry and found a family
- Inequality in the regulation and treatment of ownership
- Inequality in the protection of authorship
- Inequality of opportunity for education or the development of ability or talent
- Inequality of opportunity for sharing the benefits of culture
- Inequality in services rendered (health protection, recreational facilities, housing)

- Inequality in the enjoyment of the right to nationality
- Inequality in the right to participate in government. Inequality in access to public office

Bibliography

Adams, S., "The Komogatu Maru Incident," *Last Post* 5:3 (February, 1976): 34.

Buchignani, Norman and Doreen M. Indra with Ram Srivastiva, *Continuous Journey: A Social History of South Asians in Canada.* Toronto: McClelland and Stewart Limited, 1985).

Campbell, J., J. R. Hollingsworth and Leon Lindberg, eds. "Theory 46:360 Weber, M. briefe," *British Journal of Sociology, 1906-1908.* www./se.ac.um/serials/bjs/90-90bks.hum-72.

Clarke, Colin, Ceri Peach and Steven Vertovec, *South Asians Overseas.* New York: Cambridge University Press, 1990.

Dhaliwal, B. "Certain Sikh Views of Education in the Vancouver Region." Master of Arts Thesis, Simon Fraser University, 1985.

—— . Interview with Paul Singh Dhaliwal. Abbotsford, BC, 14 May 2004.

Dhillon, D. *Sikhism: Origin and Development.* New Delhi: Atlantic Publishers and Distributors, 1988.

Expo White Papers. *Moral Compassing.* Covey Publications, 2004.

Jagpal, S. *Becoming Canadian.* Madeira Park, BC: Harbour Publishing, 1986.

Khatri, M. http://www.indianchild.com/guru_nanak.htm/

Magocsi, P. "The Sikhs." *Encyclopedia of Canadian Peoples*, ed. P. Magosci. Toronto: University of Toronto Press/Muticultural History Society of Ontario, 2001.

Macauliffe, M. *The Sikh Religion: How the Sikhs Became a Militant Race.* Calcutta: S. Gupta, 1958.

Peking, Siege. http://www.earnshaw.corn/shanghai-ed-india/tales/library/pott/pott/16.htm

Singh, K. *A History of the Sikhs.* 2 Vols. New Delhi, India: Mohan Makhigani at RekhaPrinters/ Oxford University Press, 1963.

Ujimoto, K. and G. Hirabayashi, *Visible Minorities and Multiculuralism: Asians in Canada.* Toronto: Butterworth and Company Ltd., 1980.

"Relating to Qualification and Registration of Voters." Victoria, BC: Richard Wolfenden, Government Printing Office, 1875.

Webster's New World College Dictionary. 3rd. ed. New York: Simon and Schuster, 1988.

Interview

Dhaliwal, Paul Singh. Personal Interview. 14 May 2004.

The Settlement of the North Shore

Catherine Marcellus

For a number of reasons, the history of the north shore of the Fraser Valley is notably different from that of the Chilliwack-Abbotsford area. Perhaps the most important factor is the terrain next to the Fraser River, the hillside rising to mountain passes within two or three hundred feet of the shore. This geography has made the land far more difficult to settle, but compared to the south shore, the view is more spectacular. The broad sweep of the river stretches east and west as far as the eye can see, and the distant stunning beauty of Mount Baker dominates the landscape. This view undoubtedly attracted settlers from many different lands.

The river has been both friend and foe to settlers. It was a means of transportation for the First Nations' people who traveled from the east in search of a home. They settled just beyond a great bend of the river where today stands the village of Hatzic.[1] Some five thousand years ago they built their pit-houses near the Fraser, which provided a plentiful food supply with the annual migration of salmon. Several centuries later, in 1808, a European arrived, Simon Fraser, who worked for the North West Company and had crossed the entire continent before encountering this river. The river took his name, and partly as a result of his exploration the northern part of North America became British territory.

Midway through the nineteenth century, settlers began arriving in great numbers from the south and west. They were the fortune seekers who came from Europe, the United States and Asia, having heard about the gold strike on the Fraser. A few of them settled on the rich pasture land of Nicomen Island[2] where in a few years the first Post Office in rural British Columbia was established. In 1860, more canoes arrived, bearing the French Oblate priest, Father Fouquet, who was searching for a place to establish a mission. His twelve paddlers brought him up the river from New Westminster and landed the canoes below a steep bank covered with blackberries. On the top of this bank was a large level piece of land which looked eminently suitable for agriculture once it had been cleared. For the time being, however, Father Fouquet had his mission built near the shore. Here he intended to teach aboriginal children about Christianity and about European skills. When construction of the Canadian Pacific Railroad began in 1883, the Catholic fathers were forced to relocate their mission up the hill to the level land, where they built the residential school named St. Mary's. The community that sprang up around it became known as Mission. Today the Fraser River Heritage Park, a centre for community activities, with a stunning view of the valley, is located on the place where St. Mary's once stood.

Another group of settlers arriving with the building of the CPR were Chinese immigrants. Due to the racism of the day, these segregated Asians established a Chinatown on the Mission flatlands which was thought to have been the second largest of its kind in the province. A disastrous fire in 1929 brought an end to the Chinese settlement as its inhabitants drifted away. No doubt the overt bigotry of the European majority had an effect on their unwillingness to stay.

By 1890, the Gold Rush was over and many of the adventurers were ready to settle on the fertile agricultural land nearby. Numerous French-Canadian Catholics, attracted by the mission and its church, settled on Hatzic Prairie as well as on the eastern end of Nicomen Island, and established the community soon to be known as Deroche. As a result of the increase in population, a general store and nursing home were built below the mission. Meanwhile, logging, which was to become the area's major industry, was developing on the hills to the north.

In 1890, the CPR publicized its plans to build a rail line to Bellingham in Washington State. This entailed creating a junction a short distance west of Mission and then building a bridge across the Fraser River. Enterprising businessmen seized the opportunity to develop plans for a community. One of these developers, James Welton Horne, organized a large auction sale of lots. Although the auction was a great success, not many individuals came to live in the new town at this time. Rather, settlers seemed to be primarily interested in farming and logging operations.

In 1894, European pioneers discovered to their regret that the river could indeed be an enemy. Had they been aware of this, they might not have settled on the low-lying land beside the river that had become known as the "Mission flats." Aboriginals were familiar with the floods that periodically devastated the valley and even had a name for them: *Ta Couchi*. The '94 flood, while devastating, did teach the newcomers some important lessons —

most notably that consideration should be given to constructing a proper dyke and building the town farther up the hill.

Stave River, about seven miles west of Mission, played a significant role in the settlement of the area. Several Hudson's Bay employees at Fort Langley hoped to make barrels for shipping salted salmon to the Hawaiian Islands. In the late 1850s, a resourceful explorer discovered a stand of pine, ideal for making barrel staves, in the area of the present-day Stave Valley. Thus, a river received its name and a new business began. The seven-mile Stave River, which drains Stave Lake into the Fraser River, drops approximately eighty-two feet between the lake and the Fraser. Before long, enterprising entrepreneurs sensed the economic possibilities this geological phenomenon could provide, and in 1899 a group of Vancouver financiers incorporated the Stave Lake Power Company. It was not until 1912, however, following a change of ownership, that the power dam was completed and electricity delivered to both Bellingham and Mission.

In the meantime, unique communities developed on both sides of the Stave River. To the west was a cooperative venture based on the concepts of John Ruskin, the nineteenth-century British socialist. Especially vital to this endeavour was a cooperative sawmill which sold its products to E. A. Heaps & Co., a manufacturing business located in the village of Ruskin. In the 1880s, Italian immigrants began settling on the eastern side of the Stave and eventually began a community named Silverdale. They logged the huge first-growth trees on the land and sold them to the CPR, which subsequently utilized them in the construction of the Mission Bridge. These Italian settlers also planted grapes, made wine, and built a small Catholic church. Curiously, most of them later left the Catholic Church and joined an evangelical group that was called the Glad Tidings Tabernacle.

About three miles north of Silverdale, rising to the east and sloping down to the river, a community called Silver Hill was established in 1910. Five Swedish men purchased the land from an individual named Carl Wolf. Unbeknownst to them, Wolf, who arrived in 1908, had sold them the land but not the timber rights. Despite this, they stayed on and succeeded in attracting numerous others to join them. In order to celebrate and maintain their traditions, they built a hall where they could gather for community events. Recently, the development company Genstar has accumulated land on the hill and is planning to build a new community in this location. This will likely be the next area for intense population growth east of the Stave River.

Over the years, the Stave River constituted the greatest barrier between the eastern and western valleys. The major route around this barrier, the

Dewdney Trunk Road, ran from Haney across the dam at Stave Falls, then wound downhill for a long distance, finally emerging into the valley of Hatzic about three miles east of Mission. Although passable, this road did not turn out to be the primary transportation route to Vancouver. Rather, the majority of settlers used either steamboat or train to reach the city. Even after 1935, when the Lougheed Highway, which was built parallel to the railroad, became the most direct route to Vancouver, many people preferred to cross the Mission Bridge and use the highways south of the Fraser River.

Settlement between the Stave River and the western edge of Mission remained sparse. Beginning in the first decade of the twentieth century, however, hillsides adjacent to Cedar Valley Road were gradually brought under berry cultivation. With the arrival of Japanese settlers, along with a few Doukhobor families who settled in Cedar Valley area of Mission in the 1930s, a major berry industry developed, including two fruit processing plants in Mission. The forced evacuation of the Japanese in 1942 dealt a severe economic blow to the community, and the berry industry did not recover for years. The Japanese contributed much to the development of the community. One Japanese woman remarked that they had been attracted to Mission by the view of Mount Baker which reminded them of Mount Fujiyama and their former home. Beautiful trees and shrubs planted by these immigrants are still standing as a memorial to them.

The Japanese evacuation is just one example of intrusive decisions made outside the region that have adversely affected the history of the north shore. Problems that bedevilled the community often resulted from decisions made by outsiders. As early as 1909, plans for routing the BC Electric Railway along Dewdney Trunk Road and down Cedar Valley Road, which had been under discussion for some time, were changed in favour of a new route on the south side of the Fraser River. This decision immediately opened up the city market to farmers from the Chilliwack and Abbotsford areas and helped stimulate the development of a major dairy industry. Both the berry growers and milk producers of the Mission area used the CPR for shipping their produce and transportation to the city of Vancouver. For residents of Mission, the CPR provided efficient conveyance for their goods, but to the south, the BC Electric opened up whole new lands for competition.

After the 1890s, following the construction of the Mission Bridge, the commercial settlement of Mission developed on the flats surrounding Horne Avenue. The flood of 1894 was a major catastrophe that taught local residents to be watchful. It inundated Nicomen Island, destroyed farms and railroad tracks, and eventually ruined all the lowlands of Mission. The town was changed forever and started to take the shape it has today, with its main thoroughfare shifting from Horne Avenue, running north and south, to Washington Street, running east and west. Washington Street, known as First Avenue today, is now part of the busy Lougheed Highway.

The need for more and better dykes on both sides of the Fraser River remained a paramount issue. Dykes were expensive, however, and it would be some time before the eastern valley had sufficient political influence to persuade the federal and provincial governments that constructing them was worth the cost, despite years of intermittent flooding. It required a major disaster, the Great Flood of 1948, to finally convince federal and provincial authorities of the need for a rational plan for flood control. As the Mission area population increased, so did government efforts to improve and maintain the dykes. Consequently, even in years where the waters have been high, damage has been minimal. The Fraser, however, was still not totally tamed. In 1956, just as the community was beginning to recover from the Flood of '48, the south end of the old bridge collapsed, and for over a year the only link between the two sides of the river was a small ferry. Mission's merchants suffered greatly, and this lack of effective transportation doomed the town's attempts to attract business from across the Fraser. As it turned out, this disaster was the beginning of the end of Mission's attempts to attract business from customers living on the other side of the river.

The early years of the twentieth century marked the arrival of the first Indo-Canadians to this area. The potential of the lumber industry was a great attraction and by the middle of the century, several Indo-Canadians had become owners of some of the largest mills. Shortly thereafter they became engaged in politics with Naranjan Grewal being elected a member of the Village Commissioners in the early 1950s, thus becoming the very first Indo-Canadian to be elected to public office in the province.

Between 1894 and 1972, Mission City and the District of Mission became the centre of population and commerce on the north shore of the Fraser River. Main Street became the major commercial area, which by the late 1960s included three banks. In the mid-sixties, a maximum security prison was built in the district, bringing with it both economic spin-offs and social problems. Development was being hampered, however, by split administration, with one governing council representing the district and the other the town of Mission. The townsfolk feared the tax burden arising from the upkeep of the miles of roads in the district, while district citizens were apprehensive of costs incurred by the upkeep of city streets and institutions. However in 1969, a new mayor, Neville Cox, promoted a referendum which successfully amalgamated the two governments. A new city hall was built up the hill near the prison and away from the centre of town. Old animosities were soon forgotten.

Although Mission experienced progress, by the early 1970s it lagged behind developments south of the Fraser. A major reason for this was the construction of Highway 1, the Trans-Canada Highway, a route south of the river providing direct road access into Vancouver in the west and to the rest of the province in the east. Abbotsford was suddenly the perceived centre of the region. Many government services were quietly removed from Mission to the Abbotsford area. Mission's own courthouse was threatened, Canada Manpower was closed, and Mission was not included in the plans for a new college in the Fraser Valley. Hard-working activists in Mission—a community now viewing itself as victimized—were successful in saving some services in the town. These, however, never rose to the level of their counterparts across the river.

Mission served as a regional health care centre for some seventy-five years. Begun in 1920 by a volunteer organization, a debt-free hospital was donated to the city of Mission in 1925. In spite of many problems, additions were made to the hospital even during the Great Depression, and then again shortly after the Second World War. Nevertheless, in 1955, a new government in Victoria threatened to close it. A citizens' rebellion saved it, and finally in 1965 a new edifice was built on Hurd Road. In 2004, this hospital now finds itself once again under threat. Most Mission citizens support the concept of a community hospital to which they have contributed, feeling that disastrous decisions have been made by outsiders without knowledge of the community.

While the people of Mission welcomed the opening of a new bridge over the Fraser River in 1972, they unfortunately did not foresee all of its consequences. As some residents later stated: "All the business went south and problems came north." This proved to be an apt description of the community's struggles over the next three decades. Mission residents had become used to going to Abbotsford for special shopping just as they once went to Vancouver. However, while community pride was not evident in local shopping establishments, it was generated through local artists and cultural groups. Most notable was the establishment of the Mission Folk Festival in 1988 which built on a long tradition of community cultural events dating back to May Day celebrations and Strawberry Festivals. The creativity of Mission's potters and painters was enhanced by the wooded lots high on the hills, and the opening of the Clarke Foundation Theatre in 1996 inspired interest in the performing arts. It was not until the late 1990s, however, that commerce started to revive with the construction of a new shopping area appropriately called "The Junction."

Undoubtedly one of the most beautiful sites in the Fraser Valley, the Benedictine Monastery atop Mount Mary Ann, continues to attract large numbers of pilgrims each year. The building faces east, overlooking Hatzic Prairie and Dewdney, and from below its stunning bell tower can be seen for miles. The Benedictine monks came to Mission in 1958 to found the Seminary of Christ the King, which trains priests and educates Catholic boys. The beautiful church with its wonderful sculptures, rendering a graceful interpretation of early-Christian themes, attracts thousands of visitors each year.

Settlement in the village of Hatzic, situated below the monastery and stretching down to Highway 7 (the Lougheed Highway), began in the early-twentieth century. With its lovely private and commercial gardens, Hatzic remains one of the most desirable residential areas in the Mission area. Below the highway and along the river front is a booming-ground and centre for tugboat operators, a reminder that the logging industry continues to be vital to the economy of the Mission area. Between Hatzic Lake and Dewdney Mountain lie the farmlands of the north shore, through which gold seekers passed on their way to the Cariboo after the gold strike of 1858. At the base of the mountain, a road leads north through Hatzic Prairie. This prairie, settled over a hundred years ago by French and English Canadians, today contains an attractive residential area, many small neighbourly farms, a large greenhouse development and even a movie industry.

The Lougheed highway bends south at Dewdney Mountain, crosses a bridge, and passes onto Nicomen Island before turning east again. The land between the river and highway is called Dewdney and was incorporated as a municipality in 1892, shortly after the District of Mission itself was incorporated. Dewdney has remained a farming area. It was here that the Associated Milk Producers, one of the earliest cooperative ventures in the province, was established in the early 1930s. Its creation was not without conflict—on one occasion angry producers gathered on the road and overturned the truck of an independent dairy.

A short bridge connects Nicomen Slough to Nicomen Island, which extends for fifteen kilometers in the middle of the Fraser River. All of the land east of Hatzic Island no longer belongs to the District of Mission, but is part of the Fraser River Regional District. Although Nicomen Island was not incorporated as a municipality until 1892, the history of its population can be traced back to the time of the Gold Rush and the disbanding of the Royal Engineers. Its fertile soil attracted settlers who found farm life to be more stable and appealing than searching for gold. The eastern end of the island and the area on the mainland known as Deroche were almost entirely settled at first by French-Canadians, who developed large dairy farms. The coming of the CPR brought with it settlers from various ethnic groups, such as Dutch immigrants, who established themselves as farmers there after World War II. Over the years the islanders have suffered greatly from periodic flooding, but in recent times better dyking has made farming more reliable and effective.

In summary, the north shore of the Fraser River has been settled by different ethnic groups for different reasons. In earlier years, the main drawing card was natural resources such as the land, logging, and salmon, which still serve as an attraction for its inhabitants today. Over the years, vastly diverse cultures have emigrated here and in most cases have blended together to create a viable community. Life has often been hard and nature unkind, but the inhabitants' way of coping has been a typically Canadian one of co-operation. Separated from other communities by river and mountain, and finding that dependence on regional resources has frequently proven to be disappointing, the inhabitants of the north shore have realized that their future depends on building a strong sense of community purpose.

The various ethnic groups of Mission generally co-exist very well. Many have their own meeting places in halls or churches but join with neighbours when political or community decisions are made. For example, the Mission District Council is noticeably multi-cultural, but its members have been elected on the basis of ability rather than ethnic background. They seem to work well together, especially on issues such as community events and recreation. Throughout the region, historically, cultural events such as the Soap Box Derby, the Strawberry Festival, the Pow Wow, the Folk Festival, the Fall Fair and the Santa Claus Parade have revealed the community at its best. Despite changing times and rapid population growth, events such as these continue to energize Mission's citizens and unite them in their struggles with the outside.

Notes

[1] Hatzic is a lovely residential area just on the bend of the Fraser River. Its location is reflected in its name. The community stretches from the Highway up the mountain and faces both the river on the south and Hatzic Prairie on the east. It is well known for its beautiful gardens, both residential and commercial. It is about 1 ½ miles east of Mission, but politically is part of the district of Mission.

[2] Nicomen Island lies in the middle of the Fraser River and stretches from the area known as Dewdney (about 5 miles east of Mission) to Deroche. It is about 6 ½ miles long and 4½ miles wide. The Lougheed Highway runs along the middle of the island.

PART II

Early Religious and Intellectual Developments

Charles Hill-Tout, 1895-1944:
Visionary of the Fraser Valley

Ron Dart

Introduction

A great flurry of interest surrounding Charles Hill-Tout sprang up in the 1970s. The UBC-MA thesis, by Judith Banks, *Comparative Biographies of Two British Columbia Anthropologists: Charles Hill-Tout and James Teit* (1970) was followed by James Hill-Tout's *The Abbotsford Hill-Touts* (1976). The collection of many of Hill-Tout's major essays, in four volumes by Ralph Maud, and published as *The Salish People* (1978), deepened and furthered interest in Charles Hill-Tout. But since Maud's *The Salish People*, there has been little ongoing research on Hill-Tout. He was very much a visionary of the valley, and this short essay explores why we need to return to Hill-Tout and, by doing so, learn much about the early years of the Fraser Valley.

When Charles Hill-Tout was in the high noon of his life, he was generously quoted by such well known academics as Sigmund Freud, Emile Durkheim, James Fraser, and, on a more popular level, Thor Heyerdahl (of Kon Tiki fame). Hill-Tout corresponded with such luminaries as Max Muller, Franz Boas and one of the leading British folklorists and mythographers, Sidney Hartland. Hill-Tout has been called the father of Canadian anthropology.[1] His approach to the study of the Coast Salish offered a solid and sustained criticism of the leading American anthropologist of the time, Franz Boas. Hill-Tout also questioned many missionary attitudes and practices such as Robert Duncan towards First Nations people. Hill-Tout was at the centre of the creation-evolution debate in the nineteenth and early-twentieth centuries. He was a gifted poet, educator, founder of two colleges on the west coast anticipating UBC, popular lecturer and commentator. Hill-Tout was also a prosperous businessman, and he used his wealth to further study and research.

Charles Hill-Tout and his highly creative and hospitable wife, Edith, were co-founders of St. Matthew's Anglican parish, the oldest church in Abbotsford, and whenever St. Matthew's struggled financially, the Hill-Touts were quick and generous to bail out the fledgling parish. The Hill-Touts' home in Abbotsford, between 1905 and 1920, became a sort of intellectual salon in which all the hot button issues of the day were held up for debate and discussion, as well as some fine rounds of tennis. Hill-Tout Street in Abbotsford was named after Charles and Edith Hill-Tout, and to this day a biography is waiting to be written on this pioneering couple who in many ways were decades ahead of their time.

Hill-Tout: The Early Years (1858-1896)

Charles Hill-Tout was born on September 28, 1858 in the county of Somerset in England. His Church of England connections were quite strong, and in his teens it seemed he was headed for the priesthood. Hill-Tout attended Oxford University, and while there, he became quite involved with the monastic and contemplative order of St. John the Evangelist, otherwise known as the Cowley Fathers.[2] The Cowley Fathers, to whom young Hill-Tout was drawn, were children of the Oxford Movement (or Tractarians) of the early part of the nineteenth century. The Oxford Movement went the extra mile to call the Anglican tradition back to her catholic roots. This movement had been shaped and formed by the High Romantics such as Samuel Taylor Coleridge, William Wordsworth and Robert Southey.[3]

Both the High Romantics and the Oxford Movement had a passion for the wisdom of the past (tradition), an abiding commitment to community (against the corrosive nature of individualism), an attachment to the earth and rural life (as an antidote to the city and the frenetic pace of industrialization), and a mystical, mythic, intuitive and poetic way of knowing (as opposed to a dogmatic, creedal and propositional way of knowing and doing theology). Hill-Tout, as a young man, would have internalized all of these tendencies in his involvement with the Cowley Fathers.

The creation-evolution debate was very much on front stage at the time, and the more conservative Cowley Fathers would have sided more with the creationists. Darwin's *The Origin of Species* had been published in 1859, and *The Descent of Man* in 1871. Thomas Huxley was doing his rounds at the time, and as he lectured from place to place, he pointed out that religion after Darwin had best heed the insights of science. Science, for many, was becoming the new religion. Religion, so it seemed, could not compete with the commitment of science to hard, clean and cool empirical facts. The debate, in short, tended to pit science against religion, but Hill-Tout was not convinced, even at this early age, that the science-religion or evolution-creation debate could and should be reduced to such simplistic either-or positions. Some have suggested that Hill-Tout's growing differences with the Cowley Fathers led to his decision not to be priested and to move to Canada. We will return to this question later in the paper, and to Hill-Tout's more mature reflections, lectures and writings on this issue.

Whatever the reasons for leaving England, and however complex, Hill-Tout left behind the Cowley Fathers and headed across the ocean. Charles had married Edith Stothert in 1882, and the couple had spent a few years in England, but they were soon in the new world. The Hill-Touts moved to Toronto about 1885 and remained there until about 1889. Hill-Tout was well connected with Dr. Daniel Wilson at the time, and Wilson, although a professor of English Literature and History at the University of Toronto, was at the forefront of the new discipline of anthropology in Canada.

Hill-Tout taught in Toronto for a few years at an Anglican school, bought some land in Port Credit and did some farming. The teaching was not as lucrative as anticipated, and an investor made Hill-Tout a generous offer for his farm. Hill-Tout used the money to return to England, and assuming that his years in the colony were over, prepared to settle down and raise his children in an environment and place he knew well and loved.

But life in merry old England was not to be for the Hill-Touts. Charles and Edith only stayed in England from 1889-1891. Hill-Tout was soon back in Canada, but by this time, at the age of thirty-two, he moved with his family and six children to Vancouver. He was keen to unpack his interests, gifts and abilities in a fuller way and manner. The lure of the West Coast and the emerging anthropological work on First Nations worked its wonders on Hill-Tout.

Vancouver had a population of about 3000 at the time of the Hill-Touts' arrival. Their old friend from Oxford, Finnes Clinton, was the rector and priest in charge of St. James (a High Church parish) and a key player in education in Vancouver at the time. Hill-Tout's Anglican connections in England, Toronto and Vancouver opened up many paths and possibilities for this man whose interests were on the cutting edge of intellectual thought at the time. Clinton offered Hill-Tout the position of housemaster at St. James Boys School, and he was also offered a position at Whetham College which he accepted.

The demands of being involved with two schools took their toll on Hill-Tout, and he gladly welcomed the opportunity of becoming the principal at the new Anglican Diocesan College, Trinity College. The desirable position was offered to Hill-Tout by Bishop Sillitoe, but he soon locked horns with the good bishop on a variety of contentious issues and was on the street again. Hill-Tout started Buckland College about 1895. Buckland College was one of the main institutions of higher learning in Vancouver and BC until McGill College of British Columbia (which became UBC) started in 1905. Hill-Tout was clearly front and centre at the time of many of the major religious and educational issues.

Hill-Tout had bought land in Abbotsford in the early 1890s, and it was just a matter of time before he moved eastward and pursued his career and vocation in a more firm and focused way. It seems that the Hill-Tout family moved to Abbotsford about 1896, and it was here, initially from their log cabin and then their much larger Victorian home and manor, that Hill-Tout forged the path he was to walk for the next two decades.

Hill-Tout: The Middle Years (1896-1920)

Charles Hill-Tout was almost forty when he moved with his wife and family to Abbotsford in 1896. It would not be long before he was thoroughly involved in the life of this small but growing village. There are four areas to be briefly touched on in Charles Hill-Tout's middle years: 1) Hill-Tout and St. Matthew's Anglican parish, 2) Hill-Tout the successful businessman, 3) Hill-Tout the pioneering anthropologist and 4) Hill-Tout the aspiring poet.

First, as mentioned previously, Hill-Tout was very much a member of the Anglican tradition. As a young man he became involved with the Cowley Fathers in England. When he lived in Toronto, he taught in a Low Church Anglican school. Later upon moving to Vancouver, he taught at St. James and became the first principal of the diocesan College, Trinity College (modeled after Trinity College in Toronto). It is impossible to ignore or omit this aspect of Hill-Tout's life, although most commentators on Hill-Tout have tended to play down his Anglican connections.

It is quite understandable, therefore, that when the Hill-Touts moved to Abbotsford they would become involved with an Anglican parish. Abbotsford was still quite young at the time, and even though there was a slow but growing population, no Anglican church building as yet existed. In fact, no Christian churches of any denomination had been built in Abbotsford by 1896 when the Hill-Touts arrived. A small English community, however, was beginning to establish itself. It was just a matter of time before a decision would be made to build a small Anglican building. The Hill-Tout family became quite involved in both the planning and construction of what became St. Matthew's Anglican Parish, the first and oldest church in Abbotsford.[4]

As previously mentioned, Hill-Tout's Anglican heritage is often minimized in the telling of his life, but in many important ways, it was his

Anglicanism that constituted the deepest part of his soul. When scholars miss this part of him, they miss most of him. Ralph Maud, in his important collection of Hill-Tout's work on the First Nations, *The Salish People* (1978), alludes to but never truly probes Hill-Tout's Anglicanism, and James Hill-Tout's, *The Abbotsford Hill-Touts* (1976), ignores this important aspect of his father's life. Edith Hill-Tout played the organ at St. Matthew's, and in my many conversations with Margaret Weir before her death (the oral keeper of the Abbotsford archives and a good friend of the Hill-Tout family), she often mentioned the way Charles and Edith Hill-Tout were active and committed to the life of the small, young-but-growing St. Matthew's Anglican parish.

Hill-Tout was also a successful and active businessman in the early years in Abbotsford. He did not separate his increasing scholarly interests from his keen sense of business. There were no colleges or universities to fund scholars like Hill-Tout; consequently he had to fund many of his own intellectual interests. Hill-Tout had nine children, and open mouths and growing bodies demand their due. He had purchased, while in Vancouver, a substantial amount of land in Abbotsford. When the family moved out to Abbotsford in 1896, Hill-Tout contracted with a lumber company and the Canadian Pacific Railroad to sell CPR, initially, 50 000 ties. There were tensions between the tie cutters and lumberjacks, but the conflicts were resolved. Hill-Tout had a thriving contract with the CPR, and he started a lucrative sawmill on the shore of Abbotsford Lake. The Hill-Touts' hard work and increasing prosperity meant that it was just a matter of time before the log cabin would be outgrown and left behind for a larger and better place to tend and care for family, kith and kin. The move was made about 1905, and the large Victorian manor that the Hill-Tout family moved into became the centre (turrets aplenty, wooden tennis court in place, a fine lawn for English high tea and spacious rooms for books, company and hospitality) of Abbotsford life for many. In the midst of the dense forest and pioneering way of life, the Hill-Touts had carved out a spot of civilized England in the Fraser Valley in the early years of the twentieth century.

The land was farmed and the family prospered. The Hill-Tout children and various hired hands worked the land and contributed to the growth of the farm. The children, in the early years, were taught by a governess, but transferred to the public schools once they opened in the area. Hill-Tout's contracts with the CPR, the sawmill and the growing farm provided much of the needed funding for Hill-Tout's other and more substantive interests. Hill-Tout was doing quite well by 1912—he bought a Napier touring car (at an estimated cost of $ 10,000). It is interesting to note that until 1922, those who lived in British Columbia, following the English custom, drove on the left side of the road. Hill-Tout's new Napier did just that on his many trips about the Fraser Valley's still rather scarce road network and across the border into the USA to visit friends.

Third, Hill-Tout, although doing well at a financial level, had other interests that were much closer to his core concerns. He was one of the most important Canadian anthropologists in his time, but his approach to studying First Nations had to be clarified in the midst of a methodological and academic struggle. Hill-Tout, as mentioned above, had in his early years, come under the influence of the Oxford Movement, and the English High Romantic movement that had done much to shape and inform the Tractarians. The High Romantics often turned to the country, the land, nature, the worker, the peasant and labourer as sign and symbol of a form of humanity uncorrupted by the modern world, capitalism and industrialization. It is understandable, therefore, that when someone like Hill-Tout moved to Canada and British Columbia an interest in First Nations and their disappearing way of life would absorb his attention.

There were three ways, in a broad and general sense, of viewing and interpreting the First Nations and other indigenous peoples in the nineteenth and early-twentieth centuries both in Canada and much of the western world.

The first approach was to see the First Nations as primitive, savage, undeveloped and barbaric people who needed to be civilized and Christianized. The various theories of evolution at the time tended to pit the advanced and evolved civilizations of Europe over and against other cultures and nations that did not mirror such a stage of human development. The burden of the white man was to aid the progress of other nations and races, either through revolutionary or evolutionary means, to the heights of the European peaks. This way of thinking led, in practical terms, to residential schools, reservations and much missionary work.

The classic example, within the Anglican tradition, of this model being worked out was the missionary work in Northern British Columbia of William Duncan of the Church Missionary Society (CMS). Duncan (1832-1918) came to the West Coast in the 1850s, and began missionary work amongst the Tsimshian people in Metlakatla on the northwest coast. Duncan had a profound impact on the Tsimshian people, and within a few years (1874), St. Paul's church was built. St. Paul's could seat 1200, and it often did. The Tsimshian were converted and dressed like the English in the Victorian era. Many came from all parts of the world to see, first hand, this seemingly successful experiment in conversion. William Duncan was hailed by many for his pioneering and successful work in northern British Columbia. But Duncan's more Low Church and evangelical model of conversion clashed with his bishop, George Hills. It was just a matter of time before a clash would occur. By 1887 the conflict had become intense, and Duncan headed north to Alaska with about 800 members of the Tsimshian band. Their plan was to start another utopian settlement there. Metlakatla became a symbol to many of what not to do and be when dealing with First Nations, and Hill-Tout was well aware of this tragic model.[5]

If the first paradigm was a western conversionist model, the second and opposite approach, can be seen as the romantic attitude towards First Nations. The romantic paradigm tended to reverse and take the opposite approach to the conversionist model. First Nations were seen as the last bastion of all that was good, true and beautiful. The noble savage stood against the ravages of civilization, lived near soil and land and reflected what it truly meant to be human. If Duncan and Metlakatla can be seen as the extreme of the imperial and conversionist model, then Grey Owl can be seen as the apex of the romantic model. Grey Owl was an Englishman who came to Canada, assimilated into the First Nations way of life, and convinced many he was one with such a noble people. The appeal of John Richardson's poem, *Tecumseh* (1828), his novel, *Wacousta* (1832) and Charles Mair's *Tecumseh: A Drama* (1886) did much, like Grey Owl, to hold high the myth of the noble First Nations warrior. There were many romantics who viewed the First Nations in this way. Tecumseh and Joseph Brant, Pauline Johnson, Emily Carr and Longfellow's Hiawatha stood within such a lineage.

Where did Hill-Tout find himself in all this? Hill-Tout, like many Anglicans at the time, sought to find a middle way, a *via media*, between the imperial-conversionist model and the romantic-idealized paradigm of First Nations. The Anglican mainstream approach to First Nations, from which Hill-Tout dipped his bucket, can be found in Tony Hall and Splitting the Sky's excellent article, "Red Tories, Red Power: The Protection of Indian Rights and the Security of the Canadas."[6] As an anthropologist, Hill-Tout had to deal with two issues. First, there was the question of methodology, and second the attitude about and towards First Nations and their place within the evolutionary stage of things. Hill-Tout, unlike Franz Boas (who tended to dominate the anthropological world of his day) spent a great deal of time with the Coast Salish people. Boas, on the other hand, would flit in, do some field research and be gone. Boas followed a certain scientific model that elevated distance, objectivity and hard, cold facts. Hill-Tout was more prone to linger with the people, hear the inner spirit of the tales told, speculate on ways of reading the First Nations history and write his reports in a less formal manner. His approach was more intuitive and poetic than was that of Boas, and this method bore different fruit.

Ralph Maud's collection in four volumes of many of Hill-Tout's articles, *The Coast Salish* (1978), tells its own convincing tale of both Hill-Tout's approach, his elusive writing style and what he saw and learned by such an approach. *The Coast Salish* covers the Thompson, Okanagan, Squamish, Lillooet, Mainland Halkomelem, Sechelt and South-Eastern Tribes. The stories recorded allow chiefs and people from various tribes to speak from their place, time and history. There was much that Hill-Tout netted in his many essays from an oral culture that would be lost to us today if his hard, persistent and demanding fieldwork had not been done between 1896 and1906. Hill-Tout's participant-observer model greatly anticipated a way of studying other peoples that has become more accepted today. Greater emphasis has been placed on this aspect than on other areas—and there is much more that could be said—for the simple reason that, as a pioneering anthropologist, he forged a more creative way of doing First Nations studies. He also charted a middle way between the conversionist and romantic way of viewing First Nations.

The fourth salient feature of Hill-Tout's middle years was his role as a poet. University College of the Fraser Valley (UCFV) now has, in its Special Collections, the corpus of Hill-Tout's poetry. Most of the poems, in a collection entitled *Echoes of Days that have Flown,* were written between the 1880s and the 1930s. There are about forty-five poems in *Echoes,* and there is much editing, writing and rewriting of a variety of poems. Some of the poems are handwritten, whereas others have been typed out. Most are love poems, and there is a tension in these poems between the deeper meaning of love, lust and flirtation (at a more sophisticated level) with experimental relationships. Needless to say, Hill-Tout had sides to him that only came out in his poetry. Hill-Tout was very much the late-Victorian romantic: in many of his poems he used nature and metaphors drawn from the natural world to explore and examine the subtle and complex nature of male-female relationships. Some of the poems do slip into the sentimental and silly, but most rise above a self-indulgent and superficial pose and posture. The greater part of *Echoes of Days that have Flown* ponders, as the title indicates, things done in the past, for good or ill, and what such accumulated memories mean for the waning and twilight years. The days had flown, much had been seen and learned, the autumn years were upon Hill-Tout, and he reflected on such a journey. The minor themes in the volume are more philosophical and theological. The hard issues of the day are faced, such as science and religion, higher and lower Biblical criticism and the undermining of the Christian way. Hill-Tout uses both free verse and sonnet as means and form to express his reflections, but there is no doubt what the core of *Echoes* is about. All is

106

but a faint and fading echo as the journey is taken closer towards the river one and all must cross. This loosely collected book of poetry tells us much about the personal and inner life of Hill-Tout, and about the times and places in which he lived. I suspect a close reading and study of *Echoes of Days that have Flown* might reveal a side of Hill-Tout that has been ignored, by his biographers, because of the excessive attention paid to him as a leading anthropologist.

Hill-Tout: The Final Years 1920-1944

The end of World War I in 1919 brought with it a shift in Hill-Tout's life and direction. James Hill-Tout said of his father, regarding the farm, "My father's contribution to the endless chores were, to be frank, minimal."[7] James goes on to say:

> When Willie returned from the War, his father (Charles) turned over the farm to him completely, and our parents and Lillian moved to Vancouver. The Professor as my father was commonly called, now devoted all his time to his scholarly interests, particularly as an active member of the Art, Historical and Scientific Association— the body that really ran the old City Museum, at Hastings and Main— of which he had been a member since 1894.[8]

Charles and Edith Hill-Tout, just before Sumas Lake was about to be drained, left Abbotsford, handed their prosperous farm to their children and moved back to Vancouver. There were many trips back to Abbotsford, of course, but much work remained for Charles to do, and Vancouver had the resources he needed to continue his scholarly labours. Two issues came to dominate the thinking and imagination of Hill-Tout from 1920 until his death in 1944: the creation-evolution debate and synthesizing his final thoughts.

Hill-Tout was, as I previously mentioned, interested in the evolution-creation debate from an early age. The heated discussions in England in the nineteenth century between Darwin-Huxley (the evolutionist school) and the religious creationist tradition (embodied by Bishop Ussher) frequently seemed to generate more heat than light but nevertheless dominated public discussion. Need it be a case, though, of evolution or creation? Was there a mediating, middle way between such stark and opposing positions? Was a rerun and repeat of Copernicus and Galileo really needed? Just as Hill-Tout found a middle path in the First Nations issue between the conversionist and romantic extremes, in the creation-evolution debate he did much the same. Furthermore, he attempted to do this in an empirical manner.

The issue was brought to the forefront in the United States in 1925 with the famous Scopes Trial often dubbed the "Monkey Trial," in Dayton, Tennessee. Scopes, a biology teacher, was fired from his job for teaching the theory of evolution to his young students. Clarence Darrow, a well-known Chicago defense lawyer, offered his services to Scopes. William Jennings Bryan, a former presidential candidate, came to the defense of the creationists. The Monkey Trial stirred intense interest, was most controversial, and initiated a lively debate in North America. Hill-Tout stepped into the fray in 1925, travellling about North America in his efforts to articulate a middle way in this debate. Hill-Tout's lectures and various publications on the topic soon became a best-selling book, *Man and His Ancestors in the Light of Organic Evolution* (1925). Hill-Tout argued that it was possible, in the light of archeological research, to bring together both the creationist and evolutionary perspectives. Creation, he argued, was done in an organic and evolutionary way. The argument for organic creation offered a way out of the impasse, but such a position offended the hard liners on both sides. Hill-Tout, although assailed by both factions, held his ground.

Hill-Tout also sought to synthesize some of his ideas in his final years. He continued to write, publish and lecture widely in North America on First Nations, the age of the earth, trends in anthropology, fossil beds, Indian masks, totemism, the Great Fraser Midden, prehistoric burial grounds, Native carvings and Vancouver's early years. He raised the question as to whether the mind of the indigenous peoples of North America and around the world differed from that of the savant and "civilized." All in all, Hill-Tout published about fifty-five articles in his productive life, but by the late 1930s the well was drying up.

Although the Hill-Touts lived in Vancouver, Charles was often gone away on lecture tours. His publications between 1920 and 1938 never thinned out, but by 1938, the last article had reached the press. The tree, once laden with much fruit, lacked the sap and inner life to produce any more abundant harvests. Hill-Tout was quick and eager to share his bountiful harvest with one and all in his early and middle years, but time was demanding its predictable due. Edith Hill-Tout died in 1931. Of her, *The Abbotsford News* said in part, "the late Mrs. Hill-Tout was a very artistic accompanist on the piano and in the pioneering years about Abbotsford her services were often in request. Naturally very hospitable and kindly, she was greatly esteemed by many friends both in the country and in Vancouver."

Hill-Tout's name was put forward to the UBC Senate in 1935 for a LLD (Hon.), but no action was taken. In 1941, at 82, Hill-Tout remarried, and *The Vancouver Sun* chronicled the event in an article on March 7, 1941, entitled,

"Romance that Began at Picnic in Park." Hill-Tout died June 30, 1944 at the age of eighty-five, a much loved and respected citizen of both Vancouver and Abbotsford.

Charles Hill-Tout: Visionary of the Valley

Charles Hill-Tout was very much a pioneer and visionary of the Fraser Valley. Charles and Edith assisted in the founding of St. Matthew's Anglican parish in Abbotsford. The Hill-Tout home was a centre and source of much hospitality and cutting-edge intellectual thought. Hill-Tout had a keen eye for business, and he never separated the role of business and wise investing from the role of thinker and scholar. Hill-Tout's work on the Coast Salish remains an important source of information on the Salish culture. Hill-Tout's poetry takes the curious reader into the mind of a man that was often torn and pulled in a variety of directions, but it is the work of a sensitive mind and imagination. Hill-Tout's engagement with the creation-evolution debate is as timely and timeless as when he dealt with the issues in the 1920s.

There is a need for a well researched biography on Charles and Edith Hill-Tout, and such a biography could unpack how both of them, in their different ways, were very much pioneers and visionaries of the Fraser Valley. The work done in the 1970s by Judith Banks, James Hill-Tout and Ralph Maud now needs to be deepened, updated and fleshed out in much more revealing detail. When this is done, a more comprehensive picture will emerge of the Hill-Touts, the early years of Vancouver, the Fraser Valley and of Abbotsford.

Endnotes

[1] Coley, 33-45.

[2] The renewal of monastic orders in England, within the Church of England, has been well tracked by A.M. Allchin, in his groundbreaking book, *The Silent Rebellion: Anglican Communities: 1845-1900* (1958).

[3] The close intellectual affinities between the English High Romantics and the Oxford Movement has been ably and nimbly traced by Stephen Prickett in his fine book, *Romanticism and Religion: The Tradition of Coleridge and Wordsworth in the Victorian Church* (1976).

[4] This story has been well told and recounted in an early history of St. Matthew's, *St. Matthew's Anglican Church: 1900-1980*, then in the fuller and more developed centennial history, *St. Matthew's Anglican Church: A People's History: 1900-2000* (2001).

[5] Scott, Andrew, *The Promise of Paradise: Utopian Communities in B.C.* (Vancouver: Whitecap Books, 1997), 18-41 and Peake, 51-66.

[6] Tony Hall and Splitting the Sky's, "Red Tories, Red Power: The Protection of Indian Rights and the Security of the Canadas," in *Searching for Canada: The Red Tory Journey* (n. p., 2001).

[7] James Hill-Tout, *The Abbotsford Hill-Touts* (Abbotsford: Privately Published, 1976), 21.

[8] Ibid., 30.

Bibliography

Banks, Judith. *Comparative Biographies of Two British Columbia Anthropologists: Charles Hill-Tout and James A. Teit.* M.A. thesis, University of British Columbia, 1970.

Cole, D. "The Origins of Canadian Anthropology: 1850-1910." *Journal of Canadian Studies* 8 (February 1973): 33-45.

Dart, Ron. *St Matthew's Anglican Church: A People's History (1900-2000).* Ed. Ron Dart. Abbotsford: Synaxis Press, 2001.

Grove, Lyndon. *Pacific Pilgrims.* Vancouver: Fforbez Publications, 1979.

Hill-Tout, Charles. *Echoes of Days that have Flown.* Unpublished: Special Collections, University College of the Fraser Valley.

Hill-Tout, James. *The Abbotsford Hill-Touts.* Abbotsford: Privately Published, 1976.

Maud, Ralph. Introduction. *The Salish People: The Local Contributions of Charles Hill-Tout.* Vol. 1.*The Thompson and the Okanagan.* Vancouver: Talon Books, 1978.

——. Introduction. *The Salish People: The Local Contributions of Charles Hill-Tout.* Vol. 2. *The Squamish and the Lillooet.* Vancouver: Talon Books, 1978.

——. Introduction. *The Salish People: The Local Contributions of Charles Hill-Tout.* Vol. 3. *The Mainland Halkomelem.* Vancouver: Talon Books, 1978.

——. Introduction. *The Salish People: The Local Contributions of Charles Hill-Tout.* Vol. 4. *The Sechelt and the South-Eastern Tribes of Vancouver Island.* Vancouver: Talon Books, 1978.

Peake, Frank. *The Anglican Church in British Columbia.* Vancouver: Mitchell Press, 1959.

Prickett, Stephen. *Romanticism and Religion: The Tradition of Coleridge and Wordsworth in the Victorian Church.* Cambridge: Cambridge University Press, 1976.

Riggins, Loretta, ed. *The Heart of the Fraser Valley: Memories of an Era Past.* Abbotsford, BC: Abbotsford Printing Inc., 1991.

The Life and Work of John A. Harder: Some Reflections

John Harder

Introduction

As I reflected on the life of my father, Johannes (John) Harder, I realized that it would be difficult to compartmentalize my father's life, that is, to separate his public life—his work in the church and community—from his private life, from Johannes Harder the man, whose identity was shaped in part by his youthful experiences in Russia. My challenge is to integrate these two aspects in a meaningful way. My discussion of my father's life is based on my personal impressions, recollections and experiences. Although Johannes Harder's influence extended far beyond the local community to other Mennonite settlements in BC, the rest of Canada, the United States, Western Europe and parts of South America, I intend to focus on the man I knew while I was growing up in Yarrow. My discussion will also be informed by the material my siblings and I have collected in preparation for writing a biography on the life of my father.

Reflections on the Life and Legacy of John Harder

I will begin with a brief chronological account of my father's life, weaving into it some of my own impressions gained from my eighteen years growing up in my parental home. I am the oldest of six children, three boys and three girls. I was conceived in Russia, survived the rough ocean crossing to Canada and saw the light of day shortly after my parents' arrival in Ontario in 1924.

My father, Johannes Harder, was born in Russia in 1897. His parents, Abram A. and Justina Harder, were founders and directors of the Grossweide Orphanage. This orphanage was entirely a work of faith, with no church or government support. Reading my grandfather's journal, I was amazed to see how often and how regularly the specific needs of the orphanage were met following prayers by the staff. Undoubtedly, my grandparents' example influenced my father to generously practice Christian charity throughout his life.

Marriage proved to be an important factor in shaping the man my father was to become. In 1922 he married Tina Rempel, the matron of the orphanage, who was seven years his senior, and popularly known as "Tante Tina" (literally, "Aunt Tina"). It is my impression that she was instrumental in influencing his decision-making in various matters, particularly those pertaining to issues of morality and discipline. Mother seems to have had a rigid conscience, on occasion even a punishing one, which plagued her throughout her lifetime. I believe that this moral certainty, along with her age, explains my father's willingness to heed her advice.

Arriving in Canada with no visible means of support, my parents explored employment opportunities, first in Ontario and then in every western province, before coming to the Fraser Valley, "the land of milk and honey" — at least so they thought. In January 1930 they arrived in Yarrow. Unfortunately, because of his minimal command of the English language and because of the severe ongoing economic depression, my father found jobs to be few and far between. These early years proved to be a financial disaster for the struggling immigrant communities of British Columbia, not only for our family, but for others as well. While employment opportunities did come along from time to time, the meager income from these was not nearly enough to sustain a growing family. Thus, our family barely survived those difficult years. My parents did not believe that one should rely on public assistance, or "relief," as it was called; instead father believed that he should provide for his family through his own hard work. He was not afraid to tackle any task, no matter how physically and mentally challenging it was. He seemed to possess a tremendous capacity for work. I credit my father for keeping our family alive during this difficult period, when his time and efforts were also being shared with the fledgling Yarrow Mennonite Brethren (MB) Church, the leadership of which he had reluctantly assumed.

During their five itinerant years prior to their arrival in Yarrow, my parents had diligently sought but rarely found the type of Christian fellowship they desired. When they did find meaningful fellowship, father would often find himself thrust into leadership roles such as directing Bible studies, group worship or house fellowship groups. His leadership skills and gifts were quickly recognized wherever he went, and Yarrow was no exception. In September 1930 he was appointed clerk (secretary) of the small congregation, and a few months later, in December of the same year, he was elected senior pastor, a position that he held for eighteen years. When he resigned as

112

pastor in 1948, the congregation numbered just under 1000 members, by far the largest Mennonite congregation at that time in the Fraser Valley.

My father's commitment to the church and the ensuing responsibilities dominated his life. As far as I know, he had no formal theological training, his qualifications being largely based upon personal attributes such as integrity, leadership skills, commitment and biblical knowledge. His formal education in Russia consisted roughly of what we would classify as high school completion, followed by a medical or pre-medical course of study at the University of Kharkov. The Russian Revolution and its aftermath ended his university studies, since the orphanage desperately needed his services. Father's knowledge of the scriptures seems to have been acquired largely through self-study and parental teaching, reinforced by his parents' lifestyle. He developed leadership qualities at an early age. Not only did father instruct and supervise the youth in the orphanage; as a young man, being proficient in both languages, he also frequently preached to Russian and German congregations. During the pre-emigration period, one MB congregation had planned to ordain him, only to cancel the ceremony when it was discovered that his wife had not been baptized in an MB Church. This obstacle to his ordination was removed when mother was subsequently baptized by immersion in Alberta a few years later. The Yarrow congregation arranged for his ordination in July 1931, shortly after it elected him as leader.

Ordination began a stressful period in my father's life because of the many responsibilities that came with the position. But it is my personal opinion that the stress was also accentuated by the non-Christian attitudes and behaviours of some of the lay leaders who engaged in power struggles, seeking to increase their influence and visibility. The stress was further compounded by our family's economic difficulties. Ministers in MB churches were expected to serve without compensation. My father received no stipend or salary throughout his eighteen years of service. However, the personal generosity of certain church members, especially of Mr. J. Derksen, Yarrow's first and for a time its only merchant, helped ease the financial burden somewhat. Our family obtained the bare necessities of life, such as flour, sugar, rice, and rolled oats, on credit (of course, without the use of credit cards). During these very difficult years, Derksen would cancel any outstanding balance and present our family with a statement to that effect, usually for Christmas.

My father had a passion for knowledge and a deep desire that the community provide learning opportunities for Mennonite youth which would integrate spiritual nurture with academic knowledge. Throughout his lifetime, he promoted, supported and participated in various educational initiatives, including German schools, Bible schools, Sunday schools, and especially, the establishment of a Christian high school in 1945. I was enrolled in the latter school during 1946-47, in order to complete my university entrance program after my discharge from the wartime army. Father enabled all his children to pursue a post-secondary education; consequently, all six of us were able to acquire what mother used to call "respectable professions." Three of my siblings entered medical professions, while three of us entered educational fields.

While growing up in Yarrow, I became increasingly aware of my father's public life, gradually learning about his responsibilities and his struggles as well as his character. He was a person of principles and strong convictions. His life was congruent; he practised what he believed in the home, in the community, at work and in the church. My sense was—an impression corroborated by others—that he was somewhat severe in countenance and a strict disciplinarian, both at home and in the church. And yet, there were occasions when we children would see glimpses of a gentle man with a fun-loving disposition. And as Jacob Loewen, former translation consultant with the United Bible Society, reports, even church discipline was exercised in an atmosphere of love, compassion and justice.

A situation that occurred early in father's leadership in the Yarrow church illustrates above all else his emphasis on integrity in financial dealings. Despite the financial hardships experienced by my parents during their early years in Canada, they had managed to repay in full within five years their *Reiseschuld*, their indebtedness to the Canadian Pacific Railway (CPR) for their travel costs. I recall that paying off the *Reiseschuld* was not an equally high priority for everyone, a factor that over the years created some hard feelings in the Yarrow MB Church. Father felt strongly that church members in particular should do everything in their power to settle their accounts with the CPR as soon as possible. I seem to recall that this was a recurring church issue during the early years—I can still remember names of alleged delinquent members during the early years of the church.

My father was not without his weaknesses. As family we were aware of his temper that on rare occasions would be vented on us, probably because we deserved it. But to his credit, father was very aware of this weakness and would readily apologize. Although this meant that he had to "humble himself," he was prepared to do so in order to make amends and restore harmony. Apparently, my father's willingness to "humble himself" and confess his errors was common knowledge, both in the Church congregation and the *Vorberat* (the church council). He would often seek advice and encouragement from his closest friend, Peter Loewen, Yarrow's longtime Sunday school superintendent, who would be honest with him and not inclined to minimize the "sin" or excuse my father's behaviour. I believe his willingness to admit his mistakes and to confess them publicly endeared him to his congregation and the governing body of the church and sent a strong message to both the church and to his family.

In addition to his commitment to the church, father was a lover of nature, who on occasion arranged outdoor excursions for the family. I recall outings to Harrison Hot Springs and Cultus Lake (with gender-segregated swimming, of course), a bicycle excursion to Ryder Lake, and a climb up Vedder Mountain with all six children. He also encouraged us to keep in good physical condition. One of my father's first construction projects after moving to a new house was to erect an exercise bar on which he would demonstrate his prowess. In my middle teen years, I subscribed to a fitness program designed by Charles Atlas (a former self-proclaimed 97-lb weakling), which included large black and white photos of his nearly nude physique, bulging muscles, etc. When my father saw those photos, he bragged to me that in his prime he could have posed for similar photos. I recall seeing my father in the nude, when he, my brother and I went swimming together — none of us owned any swimwear. I recall thinking that father's comments concerning his physique were not idle boasting.

Father had little regard for man-made monuments; instead he loved to explore and admire natural beauty. Not infrequently, he would drive down an unfamiliar road in order to discover its destination and to marvel at the hidden scenic treasures of nature along the way. God's creation was more important to him than man's achievements. Not having developed an appreciation for excellence in music and art, he didn't hesitate to share his views with the congregation. Instrumental performances without any lyrics had little meaning for him. On occasion, this led to conflict with Mr. George Reimer, the church's music director. Consequently, during the early years of the Yarrow settlement, the basis for the selection of music for religious services and for special occasions such as weddings was the content of the lyrics rather than the musical scores. He did not approve of wedding marches. Nor for that matter was he impressed by elaborate flower arrangements. On one occasion, before officiating at a wedding, he personally came down from the pulpit to move a flower arrangement because it obstructed his view of the bridal party. In the process, he announced that he did not like speaking through the flowers: "*Ich mag nicht durch die Blumen sprechen.*"

At home Johannes Harder attempted, to the best of his ability, to instill his values and his biblical understanding in his children. Morning devotions and evening prayers were practised regularly. When home, Father usually read scripture in the morning and followed this with a short meditation. In the evening, the family assembled for prayer in which we were expected to participate. At the time, I didn't fully realize the benefits of this practice, but in retrospect I appreciate the biblical knowledge and understanding we children received at home from these teachings. I have often marveled at my father's grasp of theological concepts and principles. I always considered my father's teaching and preaching to be much above the average, especially when compared to that of the self-appointed ministers who insisted on being heard.

As evidence of their love and acceptance of my father's ministry, the Yarrow congregation planned a special celebration for my parents' twenty-fifth wedding anniversary in May of 1947. In addition to the special service in the church, our parents were presented with numerous personal greetings and with several rather extravagant gifts. The latter included a complete twelve-piece dinner set for mother and a specially designed office desk and a multi-volume biblical concordance for father. Needless to say, my parents were not only surprised, they were overwhelmed with the love and generosity of the congregation.

During World War II, German was still the dominant language of instruction in Bible school and church worship. According to Jacob Loewen, the use of German created quite a stir in the local English-speaking population, which, especially after Pearl Harbor, regarded this practice with suspicion. One Bible school teacher reported that local government officials and law enforcement agents paid several visits to Yarrow to interrogate the Bible school faculty and other community leaders in order to ascertain whether or not a subversive element was present in the school.

Father, along with other residents of Yarrow, resisted the acculturation process, hoping to maintain the social system as well as the cultural norms and practices of the "old country." It is my belief that our parents were unaware of the tensions that we children experienced in our attempts to integrate into the school in Chilliwack. Language, especially, proved to be a source of tension. At home we were expected to speak German, but at school, especially during the war years, we did not wish to be identified as German immigrants. The school's dress code for girls proved to be yet another contentious issue. Our parents did not readily accept the school's dress code, especially for girls in physical education, deeming it to be immodest if not immoral. I was mortified one day when I saw my father, along with several church leaders in the school hallway, conferring with the principal. I knew very well why they were there. I remember attempting to escape from the scene as quickly as possible. I certainly did not want to be identified or associated with this delegation.

As mentioned previously, my mother had considerable influence on Father. She dutifully supported him spiritually and emotionally, especially in his pastoral ministry. It has become obvious to me that she adopted the role of enforcing moral standards, especially as they pertained to the younger women in the church and to my sisters in the home. Her efforts to correct or admonish female transgressors seen wearing makeup or immodest dresses that exposed the thighs or upper arms may have succeeded for a time. But what our parents didn't seem to realize was that change is inevitable.

In our family it was Mother who interrogated us after a night out, which more often than not simply involved attending junior choir practice, by asking questions such as: "Who did you walk home with?" "Who else was in the car?" "Where did she sit?" My parents were very concerned that their family set an example for the church and community. Thus, there was much ado about gender relationships, engagements and marriage. It seems to me that my father had a problem handling issues related to sexuality. It is not surprising, therefore, that he gladly relegated the role of enforcing sexual standards to Mother.

When it came to Bible School students, our parents' sexual conduct code forbade any fraternization such as couples pairing off in public prior to the church officially announcing the couple's engagement. It was also expected that marriage plans would be made soon after a couple's engagement. My father's policy in this respect was well known in the church and community. I became acquainted with my future wife mostly through correspondence. My intentions were for us to gradually establish a mutual friendship, but when my parents learned about our interest in each other, they insisted on an early engagement, hopefully to be soon followed by a wedding. On one occasion, Mrs. Kaethler, my father's sister, invited our family, along with our cousin, for a Sunday afternoon visit. It just so happened that Laura, my fiancée, and my cousin were best of friends; consequently, my aunt had invited Laura as well. Upon arrival at the Kaethlers, my mother created quite a scene. Laura and my cousin had to leave and visit elsewhere for the afternoon. However, we were not deterred. Laura and I are still happily married after fifty-five years.

On another occasion, our family decided to go to the circus in Chilliwack. Unlike us children, my mother did not appreciate such an outing nor did she enjoy the performance. When the trapeze artists made their first appearance in their scanty costumes, mother was horrified. She and the younger children left in protest. As far as I can recall, my father, my brother and I stayed to the end of the performance.

In my opinion, my father experienced many inner conflicts brought on by matters of church discipline and behavioural expectations largely dictated by the church membership. Consequently, he suffered from stress-related symptoms such as recurring migraine headaches, bouts of respiratory and asthmatic attacks and rheumatoid arthritis. He also developed a cardiovascular condition, which, I believe, caused his premature death at age sixty-seven.

PART III
Community
and Family in Yarrow

Yeowomen of Yarrow: Raising Families and Creating Community in a Land of Promise

Marlene Epp

Mennonites have often conceptualized their historical self-definition in terms of who is "inside" and who is "outside" the ethno-religious boundaries of their communities. This conceptualization is especially relevant when one considers the story of the mid-twentieth-century settlement at Yarrow, British Columbia. For the Mennonite immigrants from the Soviet Union, who had historically often felt like outsiders in their own history, the Fraser Valley of BC may well have felt like the promised land, even like a possible utopia. Both those arriving as early settlers at Yarrow, beginning in 1928, and those who later arrived as displaced persons from the Ukraine after the Second World War had experienced economic decline, religious repression, and waves of terror, violence, disease, and starvation. Many of the Mennonite refugees who had settled first on the prairies quickly became disillusioned by their harsh initial experience of Canada. So the magnificent mountains and the lush green valley with its life-giving rivers seemed to promise a utopia where these wandering people could build a perfect community. Bounded by steep mountainsides and quick-flowing rivers, the village of Yarrow became both a physical and psychological enclave of protection from Machno's bandits, Stalin's secret police, and even from dry prairie winds.

For those who succeeded economically, socially and spiritually, Yarrow was indeed the promised land. But not everyone achieved this kind of success or was even recognized for his or her contributions. For them Yarrow may well have been, as Leonard Neufeldt has so poetically phrased it, a "village of unsettled yearnings."[1] Some Yarrow residents yearned for economic success but never achieved it. Some yearned for demanding and unattainable salvation. Some yearned for social acceptance but always remained on the fringes of the community. Some like the many yeowomen of Yarrow, worked hard to build their community and played a crucial part in its social and economic success, but were never officially recognized as significant participants.

Both men and women may have felt "unsettled" in Yarrow; this essay will focus on women's contributions to building the community. When the term "yeowomen" was suggested to me, I chuckled at the too obvious play on words. Yet when I investigated the word's meaning, I knew it was appropriate for describing the historic experience of women in Yarrow. The term yeoman is defined as "a person attending or assisting another" or "one that performs great and laborious services." Historically, women in Mennonite communities have been portrayed mainly in gendered terms as functioning to provide assistance, labour, and service. Of course, undoubtedly, men were also driven by gender expectations of being economically successful and of providing for their families, a significant challenge for those who had already confronted failure on the prairies. My emphasis here is not meant to negate the unique settlement experience of men but to emphasize the often unrecognized contributions of women.

My choice to focus on the women is in part because of the traditional invisibility of women's worlds in much of the published historical record. Though women's lives and labour have been crucial and central in the building of settlement communities, history books, published memoirs, storytelling, and collective memory have not always reflected this. Though this historical amnesia has diminished significantly in recent years, vigilance is still warranted. For example, the typical invisibility of women in many settlement projects, Mennonite and non-Mennonite alike, is evident in a "historic picture" of pioneers who attended the first Mennonite church service at Yarrow in April 1928. The photo—reproduced in several published histories—is of twenty men, though presumably women were also in attendance and also contributed to the start of formal religious life at Yarrow.[2]

This invisibility of women is also apparent in William Siddall's poem about the first Mennonite settlers in Yarrow: it mentions nary a woman, even though these "Twelve stalwart men from a Prairie Town" ate "Borscht, beans, bacon and corn" when they arrived home "all tired and forlorn." The poem also pays tribute to "Jacob Epp, that grand old man" who "loaned his house for church and song" when there was no church building.[3] We can only presume that Mrs. Jacob Epp (Elizabeth), a "yeowoman" of Yarrow, expended much energy preparing her house for those services. Women's work, especially work that is not given direct economic credit, is continually ongoing but publicly invisible, generally going unacknowledged in published community and church histories. In "Creating the Brotherhood," as Harvey Neufeldt has ironically titled an article,[4] the Mennonites of Yarrow created highly gendered structures of meaning and significance that fashioned the patriarchal history to follow.

This paper will describe the lives of yeowomen of Yarrow in two phases of settlement: first the initial settlement by the labouring pioneers who raised families and built the community, beginning in 1928 and continuing through the 1930s and into the war years, and second, the post-Second World War period, when many Mennonite refugees who were displaced by war and were fleeing Soviet oppression arrived in Yarrow.

In the pioneering period, the lives of these yeowomen consisted of a constant all-consuming cycle of labour—be it the physical labour required of subsistence living or the repeated labour of childbirth. Families arrived in the Fraser Valley with almost no financial or material resources. For the early settlers, the stark realities of life in the Valley during the difficult years of The Depression were also in sharp contrast to their remembered experience of comfort and culture in Russia. The years prior to the First World War, the Bolshevik revolution, and the ensuing famine were for many a period of economic prosperity in which education, leisure, and cultural activity were nourished in Mennonite households and communities. Aganetha Brucks, a Yarrow resident, was overwhelmed by her experience of economic reversal; in Russia her household had included domestic and farm servants. In contrast, one of her first homes in Canada was a rail car in Coaldale, Alberta, where she lived with her husband and nine children. When she moved to Yarrow, life became marginally easier.

Building homes and barns, tilling soil, harvesting crops, and tending livestock were the necessary initial steps in building the community, but routine daily life required many additional labour-intensive tasks—for example, sewing and mending, laundering clothes and bedding, preserving and preparing food, hauling and heating water for cooking and bathing. For women, keeping their families clean, warm, and fed, not necessarily in that order, filled the hours of most days. And these daily chores did not include the time they spent sharing in fieldwork and tending livestock. Household tasks were especially labour-intensive until basic utilities became available. For instance, electricity came to Yarrow in 1934, while a fresh water supply arrived only in 1946. Amenities like flush toilets and running water were not commonplace until well into the 1940s.[5]

In a journal entry, Gertrude Esau Martens recalls the challenges of the early years in Yarrow:

Life was not easy in those early years. The women worked hard in fields, milking cows, gardening, picking hops, haying. Often the women were left to do heavy jobs at home while the men tried to earn some cash to pay off the debt from their passage from Russia to Canada. After dark there was mending, sewing and baking to be done. But there was always time to go to Prayer Meeting on Saturday night, and always food prepared for Sunday's unexpected guests.[6]

Similarily, Edward Giesbrecht's memoir offers clues regarding the mammoth task of food preparation his mother faced as she baked weekly for 11 people: "On Saturday she bakes six pans of zwieback, 12 loaves of bread, butterhorns, cinnamon buns, and pies. Except for the bread, most of these are consumed by Sunday night. Often she bakes biscuits on Monday and pancakes on Tuesday to tide us over until Wednesday, when she bakes another eight loaves of bread. Her baking requires over 200 pounds of flour every month."[7]

In the early years, subsistence involved a degree of "making do" that demanded creativity, ingenuity, and economy. Preserving food was an all-consuming activity during the times of year when fruit and vegetables were in season. Sewing skills were taxed to their limit when the only fabrics available were unbleached flour sacks and worn-out clothing. Katherine Quiring Loewen, a noted Yarrow seamstress, was an expert at turning cuffs and collars inside out in order to give her husband's shirts a second life; later she turned those same shirts into blouses for her granddaughter. She was known to visit the local garbage dump to search for discarded clothing which she then cleaned and transformed into something new. When she turned her efforts to sewing for relief purposes, her first project—100 dresses all meticulously pieced together from scrap—was initially rejected at the Mennonite Central Committee office. Apparently the abundance of lace and trimming she had used to cover up the many puzzle-piece seams in the dresses was deemed "too fancy for starving children."[8]

Living on the edge of subsistence during the early years of settlement meant that families had to work together to build barns, harvest crops, and preserve food. Communal "work bees" became a common practice for everything from butchering pigs to sewing quilts. Thus, community building was a by-product of everyday activity, not something that happened only when people formally gathered together for church activities.

Community—albeit of a single gender—was also built amongst urban female workers. During the early years, while mothers laboured on the home front, in many families the daughters, some just teenagers, became the major breadwinners for their families. Beginning in the late 1920s and continuing well into the 1950s, many Fraser Valley Mennonites sent their daughters to work in domestic service in Vancouver, a sector of the economy in which jobs were plentiful, knowledge of English was not essential, and for which these newcomers had the needed skills. Mennonite families took advantage of the fact that domestic service was the dominant wage-labour option for women in Canada from the nineteenth century right up to the Second World War. Unlike women from some other immigrant groups, Mennonite women were not known for "defiance" or class-conscious resistance to exploitative treatment on the part of employers. Indeed, as Ruth Derksen Siemens has remarked, Mennonites were desirable as domestics because "they were white, submissive, quiet, hard-working and their lifestyles appeared as clean as their floors."[9]

When Mennonites settling in the Fraser Valley learned that such domestic work was plentiful in urban centres like Vancouver and Chilliwack, they readily put their daughters on the city-bound trains. In the summer of 1928, it was already reported that among the 40 families settled in the Sumas area, 35 daughters had gone to Vancouver and elsewhere for work. By spring of 1931, 50 young women from Yarrow were employed in Vancouver, averaging $25 a month in wages and sending most of that money home to help support their families.[10] Perhaps of even greater importance, the money they earned contributed directly to the payment of their families' travel debts: the total amount of travel debt owed by Mennonites in the Fraser Valley is estimated to have been $37 000.[11]

Fearful for the morality of these young women living amidst the perceived evils of the city, Mennonite church leaders established boarding houses —called girls' homes—in Vancouver. The homes functioned as employment bureaux and several later formed the nuclei of urban Mennonite church congregations. Once established, the girls' homes became immensely busy as the Mennonite reputation for reliable domestic service grew, and as rural parents, comforted by the knowledge that such supports existed, sent their daughters to the cities in greater numbers. At the Bethel Home in Vancouver, the number of women registered grew from 53 in 1934 to 81 in 1936 and, finally, to 350 in 1956.[12] Peter Thiessen reported that girls were being placed in the Vancouver homes "as rapidly as possible" after harvest.

The impact on these women of their urban working experiences was mixed. For some, their sojourn in the city was an adventure, an opportunity to sprout wings and explore sectors of society normally closed or forbidden to them. They undoubtedly brought back to their communities new skills, habits, and language that fused with their traditional Mennonite upbringing. However, for some young women, their time in the city was shaped by homesickness and ill-treatment by their employers. They were those who, as Anna Kornelsen wrote, went to Vancouver "with heavy hearts."[13]

The impact on Fraser Valley Mennonites of such a large number of women working in the city was not minor. For instance, in its first few years the Elim Bible School at Yarrow, established in 1929, had only male students, since most of the older girls and young women of the community were working as domestic help in Vancouver.[14] One might also wonder what impact this gender imbalance because of women working in Vancouver had on the marriageable population of Yarrow. Were men drawn to marry "English" women during these years when Mennonite women were absent? Were there eventually more unmarried Mennonite women in the Valley as a result? Fifteen years later, in 1944, this gender imbalance was reversed, when the 1944 Bible school class had 62 young women and 32 young men, of whom five were instructors. This gender reversal was likely due to the absence of young men involved in wartime military or alternative service and the return to Yarrow of young women who had previously been working in Vancouver.[15]

Work in the city was, of course, seasonally complemented by agricultural work. As the berry and hop industries in the Fraser Valley developed, both young boys and girls were employed as pickers, hoe-ers, and cannery workers. Teenage girls and women were the primary seasonal workers for night-time production lines at the canneries, where they would sort and pack berries for hourly wages. Some ambitious individuals would work the night shift, go home and sleep until noon, and then head for the berry fields to pick until their evening work in the cannery began once more.

Picking berries and also hops were central seasonal events for many families in Yarrow and elsewhere in the Valley. Anna Bartsch, whose early married life was spent developing a Christian mission station in remote regions of the former Belgian Congo, moved to Yarrow with her family in 1943. Her husband Heinrich was frequently away from home, engaged in missions promotion, so Anna with her four children kept their own small farm operating and also picked berries and hops in the summer. She recalled rousing her children at 5 a.m. in order to meet the truck that would carry them to the hop fields. After a long day in the fields, and after putting her exhausted children to bed, Anna would stay up until midnight canning her family's own fruits and vegetables. Like all the other hop pickers, the Bartsch family had specific financial goals; when a water system came to Yarrow in the mid 1940s, their goal was to earn enough money to install a bathroom in their house.[16] Thelma Reimer Kauffman also recalled the routine that ended a full day of hop-picking: "There was supper to be fixed, the garden to be tended, farm animals to be fed, sometimes milking to be done, and always clothes to be washed. First we'd set to scrubbing our hands to take off the tarry layer that had accumulated during the day. Often famished, we still had to pick the lettuce, make the Rollkuchen, or fry the chicken before we could sit down and eat."[17]

Women who laboured in the early years did not just chop wood and haul water for their own households, pick and pack berries for the co-op, or polish silver and sweep floors for urban households. In the midst of the dawn-till-dusk physical work demanded for building a community, women also laboured in childbirth and in child-rearing. So much of settlement history is about land-ownership, land-development, land-cultivation, and in the case of Yarrow, land-reclamation. We learn the names of male land-owners, male land-purchasers, and male heads of households on settlement and immigrant lists. The occasional widow or single woman on such lists is an aberration from the norm. Yet while land ownership and cultivation were an important part of establishing settlements, family re-generation was equally crucial. To the extent that women bore babies and raised families, their participation in the agenda of group settlement was just as important as that of the men, even if not measured in acreage, land deed, and crop yields.

Since most Mennonite families in Yarrow, as elsewhere, had many children—partly because of their church's condemnation of birth control—and since the settlement was quite distant from hospital facilities and trained physicians, up to the 1940s, most babies were born at home with the assistance of a midwife. The Mennonite pattern of creating social systems such as healthcare apart from the mainstream society was strongly manifest in Yarrow. This pattern was perhaps even more accentuated when the Mennonite settlers, in reaction to the disappointments of life on the Canadian prairies, attempted to create a community modeled in many ways on what they had known in Russia. As a result, Mennonite midwives played important roles in communities suspicious of outside intrusion into their public spaces, and even more so, into the private lives of individuals and families. For many early immigrant women, childbirth could be an extremely isolating and dangerous experience. Prior to the Second World War, maternal mortality rates in Canada were high and childbirth-related death was second only to tuberculosis as the cause of female deaths.[18] Repeatedly, in these life or death scenarios of giving birth, women relied on experienced midwives and the assistance of family members and neighbours, all the while hoping for uncomplicated births.

A number of Yarrow's yeowomen became experts in the art of "catching" babies. These included Elizabeth Harder Harms, who not only helped women deliver their babies but also provided a wide array of medical care when she moved to the immigrant community in the early 1930s. She mixed her own pharmaceutical compounds and created a successful remedy to treat an infection under the fingernails caused by strong cleaning solutions that plagued Mennonite women who worked as domestic help in Vancouver.[19] In 1928, Margaretha Klippenstein Enns moved with her family to Yarrow and was "well accepted" as a midwife, especially since she had birthed nine children of her own.[20] Margaretha eventually set up a birthing room in her own house, where post-partum women stayed for up to 10 days, sometimes to the chagrin of their husbands who declared that their wives were desperately needed at home.

Like the families of church ministers, the families of midwives coped with the ramifications of a parent's demanding career and with the frequent and sudden disruptions to family life that occurred whenever their mother was called away to "catch" a baby. The recollections of Margaretha Enns's family sound very much like stories told about male pastors:

> The family often felt that everything revolved around their mother's career; family birthdays and Christmas gatherings were frequently interrupted when she was called away. Relatives who attended these gatherings recall her being summoned while she was in the midst of distributing Christmas gifts and homemade fudge to the grandchildren. She would drop everything, pick up her brown bag, and leave on her mission.[21]

As the medical profession increasingly took over the birthing process, by the 1940s midwives in Yarrow, as elsewhere across the country, lost their pre-eminence in childbirth assistance. Mennonite women, like other Canadian women, were drawn to a more professionalized approach to giving birth in the security of a safe, antiseptic, and modern environment. While these changes were certainly beneficial, there were undoubtedly also losses, as midwives lost their prominent and crucial places in their communities.

The first group of yeowomen indeed performed great and laborious service as they assisted their menfolk and each other in creating homes and building communities in the land between the mountains. They had just paused to catch their breath when a postwar economic crisis and the catastrophic flood of 1948 hit the community of Yarrow. Even so, they were ready to welcome a second wave of yeowomen.

The second wave of settlers arrived in the Fraser Valley after the Second World War. These later immigrants were among the 8,000 Mennonite refugees accepted into Canada after having been displaced from their homes in the Soviet Union and Eastern Europe in the midst of the war. They were the "lucky" ones; thousands more who fled went missing on the warfront, were sent back into exile in the Soviet Union, or went to Paraguay where a much more difficult frontier experience awaited them. A large portion of these refugees were "women without men," female heads of fragmented families that had lost husbands, fathers and brothers in the tumultuous events affecting Mennonites living under the regimes of Stalin and Hitler. Women outnumbered men by nearly two to one, a ratio that increased in older age groups. Susan Braun Brandt of Yarrow recalled the many cousins that her family assisted: "Anny Klassen with her children ... Anny's sisters, Margaret, Mary, Katie, and Helen; Lydia Penner; and Helena and Renate Penner." All women and children.[22]

If the pre-war settlers arrived with a forward-looking sense of hope for the future, the post-war newcomers, though grateful for their own safety, were looking backwards in sorrow for the many loved ones they had left behind. Recalling her departure from a refugee camp in Germany en route to Canada, Anny Penner Klassen said:

> I thought about my dear Johann (her husband), my mother and my brothers Jakob and Hans. I found it very difficult to leave Germany, because it meant that I would be so much farther away from them. Would we ever meet again? ... It was a hard struggle for me. I would have liked to run off the ship![23]

Thus, Yarrow was a bittersweet destination for women like Anny—she was physically safe; she could attend church and be baptized; she was connected with relatives who shared her culture and language. But she lived daily with knowledge of and perhaps guilt over the suffering of family members left behind. She also had to live for years with uncertainty about her marital status, not knowing whether or not she was a widow. To these women who arrived in the aftermath of the 1948 flood and the collapse of the berry market, Yarrow did not seem like a land of promise at all: as Anny stated, "[they] immediately discovered that this was Canada, not Canaan!"[24]

As elsewhere in Canadian Mennonite circles, the arrival of Mennonite refugee families after the Second World War resulted in a bulge in membership in Fraser Valley Mennonite churches. British Columbia received about 3,000—over one-third—of the postwar refugees. Many churches also experienced a gender imbalance with this sudden increase in the numbers of both young and old women.

Many female-headed families were drawn to the Fraser Valley because of the abundance of seasonal agricultural labour that required only a limited education and no experience. Because of the constant demand for workers in urban domestic labour as well as in rural agriculture, immigrant women could easily obtain work as househelp in Vancouver or Chilliwack during much of the year, quit their jobs to pick hops and berries in summer, and then return to domestic jobs after the picking season. The need to maximize their earning power was crucial for these women, especially because many of their families had no male breadwinner. In the fall of 1948, two sisters, Maria and Katja, arrived in the Fraser Valley with their two young sons. The two women drew lots to decide which one would seek employment in Vancouver and who would stay at home with the children. Maria earned forty dollars per month working at a delicatessen in Vancouver, while Katja supplemented those wages through seasonal work on the berry fields. Before long, however, Katja was also offered household work in Vancouver and reluctantly left the two boys living with relatives until the end of the school year when they could join their mothers in the city.[25] Because of their industriousness, many of these families quickly repaid their transportation debt and the money they owed to sponsoring relatives; many even managed to purchase their own homes.

British Columbia was also attractive to these refugee women because of the B.C. Mennonite Relief Committee's special loan program for widows who wished to purchase houses. Concerned that there were so many women with small children who lacked male-breadwinners, and recognizing also that most banks would not issue loans to women, the Committee offered widows interest-free loans up to $500, re-payable over five years. Anny Penner Klassen, widowed with two children, borrowed $500 in 1950 and bought three-quarters of an acre of land in Yarrow onto which she moved a one-room house. She expressed her gratitude, stating, "We were thankful to have our own home, even though it was small."[26] By November 1950, the $12,000 in the fund was already exhausted, though repayments were starting to come in, and a significant number of women were still on the waiting list. Quite likely, the existence of this fund attracted female-headed families across Canada to British Columbia: one Committee member complained that the fund was stretched because women from other provinces were moving west to take advantage of the assistance available in BC.[27]

While the loan fund was a generous and welcome form of assistance for refugee widows and their families, in some cases it was granted only after applicants had undergone some informal moral screening on the part of fund administrators, who were also leaders in the Mennonite churches. In one case, the Committee withdrew approval of a woman's application when it was discovered she was living with her brother-in-law, both of them having spouses missing in the Soviet Union.[28] In the 1950s, the issue of common-law marriages that developed in Canada when newcomers from Russia were uncertain of the fate of a first spouse in the Soviet Union increasingly chal-

lenged Mennonite churches in Canada. And likely, in Yarrow, these common-law marriages were also one of those not-talked-about issues.

These kinds of incidents reveal the gap, manifest in both values and
behaviour, which two decades of dramatic history had created between the
two Mennonite immigrant groups. Strain was also manifest in church life.
The newcomers were happy to be worshiping freely once again, after years of
secretive religious expression. In this predominantly female immigrant group,
religious life had been nurtured mainly by mothers and grandmothers—
almost all the male religious leaders had been arrested and exiled—and so
the newcomers may well have been startled and disheartened by the official
silence of women in BC Mennonite churches. The presence of so many self-
supporting female-headed families in the Valley likely contributed to women
receiving the right to participate and vote in church meetings in the late
1950s.

The postwar newcomers were also by and large unfamiliar with the
moral and ethical legalisms that permeated Mennonite churches in Canada
in the 1950s, legalisms based on fundamentalist interpretations of Christian
belief but also derived from gender-based power structures. The patriarchal
social control inherent in the programs at the girls' homes for women workers and in the closely monitored loan program for widows is evidence of the
belief that a utopian existence in this land of promise could only be realized
through close regulation of the community's members. As other scholars
have already observed, with no official power base within the Mennonite
community, women were easily regulated.[29] Inner religious piety was seen as
reflected in a woman's outward physical presentation; thus for instance,
women were chastised for the use of cosmetics, for cut or curled hair, for
short sleeves, bare necks, or for wearing shorts or slacks.[30]

The church leaders of Yarrow were responding, like other conservative
evangelicals, to the new liberties that women were generally demanding and
receiving in society. One history of the Fraser Valley describes the trend
thus:

> The individual self-expression emanating from younger women [was]
> represented by such dangerous trends as smoking; bathing suits
> which exposed more than ankles; high heels and make-up; and the
> propensity of some young women to surrender to the lure of the
> dance floor saxophone on the arm of some whippersnapper.[31]

Young Mennonite women may not have been smoking or dancing like
"other girls," but they were not immune to fashion trends that saw dresses as
well as hair shortened and that spawned shoes with open toes allowing one to
reveal at least something. Ironically, of course, the tighter the control is, the

greater the temptation to rebel from such measures. The woman who wore a shawl over her head to hide the "cut and curl" that she received at Hank Giesbrecht's newly opened hair salon in the 1950s was expressing her rebellion, however timidly.[32] So was my own grandmother, who went against my grandfather—a powerful and conservative minister in British Columbia at the time—and allowed her daughter-in-law, my mother, to give "hair perms" to her own daughters.

In many ways, the development of the community of Yarrow represented a sincere effort to create a utopia—a place of escape, separation, prosperity, and idealism. Such attempted utopias are places that evoke strong and indeed mythical memories. Why else would a village such as Yarrow evoke so many vivid stories as are contained in the recent two-volume history? However, utopias may be experienced differently by the women who serve in them than by the men who imagine them. The women of Yarrow supported, assisted, and laboured to raise families and build community in a land of promise. As such, they were indeed yeowomen who are now finding their place in history.

Endnotes

[1] Leonard Neufeldt, Lora Jean Sawatsky, Robert Martens, eds., *Yarrow, British Columbia: Mennonite Promise*, vol. 2, *Village of Unsettled Yearnings* (Victoria, BC: Touch Wood Editions, 2002).

[2] Agatha Klassen, ed., *Yarrow: A Portrait in Mosaic* (Yarrow, BC: author, 1976), 27.

[3] Ibid., 40.

[4] Harvey Neufeldt, "Creating the Brotherhood: Status and Control in the Yarrow Mennonite Community, 1928-1960," *Canadian Papers in Rural History*, vol. 9, ed., Donald H. Akenson (Gananoque, ON: Langdale Press, 1994), 211-38.

[5] Ruth Derksen Siemens, "'Pick the Berries, Don't Paint Them': The Odyssey of Three Artists in a Mennonite Lotus Land," in *Village of Unsettled Yearnings*, 130-32.

[6] Gertrude Esau Martens, manuscript excerpt in Leonard Neufeldt, ed., *Yarrow, British Columbia: Mennonite Promise*, vol. 1, *Before We Were the Land's* (Victoria, BC: Touch Wood Editions, 2002), 176-77.

[7] Edward, R. Giesbrecht, "The Everydayness of a Dairy Farm," in *Village of Unsettled Yearnings*, 187.

[8] Gladys A. Loewen, "Grandmother's Nimble Fingers," in ibid., 124-26.

[9] Ruth Derksen Siemens, "Quilt as Text and Text as Quilt: The Influence of Genre in the Mennonite Girls' Home of Vancouver (1930-1960)." *Journal of Mennonite Studies* 17 (1999): 121. See also Varpu Lindström-Best, *Defiant Sisters: A Social History of Finnish Immigrant Women in Canada* (Toronto: Multicultural History Society of Ontario, 1988).

[10] Peter Penner, "Chauncey Eckert, the CCA, and Early Settlement," in Neufeldt ed., *Before We were the Land's*, 140.

[11] Ibid., 140.

[12] Derksen Siemens, "Quilt as Text," 121.

[13] Anna Goosen Kornelsen, "Diary Excerpts," in *Before We Were the Land's*, 247.

[14] Klassen, ed., *Yarrow: A Portrait in Mosaic*, 89.

[15] See class picture in ibid., 91.

[16] Anna Bartsch, *The Hidden Hand Story of My Life*, trans. Art Bartsch (Nelson, BC: Author, 1987), 195.

[17] Ibid., 180.

[18] Wendy Mitchinson, *Giving Birth in Canada, 1900-1950* (Toronto: University of Toronto Press, 2002), 262.

[19] Irma Epp, Lillian Harms and Lora Sawatsky. "Midwifery: A Ministry," in *Village of Unsettled Yearnings*, 20.

[20] Ibid, 20.

[21] Ibid., 27.

[22] Braun Brandt, *Village of Unsettled Yearnings*, 218.

[23] Anny Penner Klassen Goerzen, *Anny: Sheltered in the Arms of God: A True Story of Survival in Russia* (Fort St. James, BC: Author, 1988).

[24] Ibid., 219.

[25] Marlene Epp, *Women without Men: Mennonite Refugees of the Second World War* (Toronto: University of Toronto Press, 2000), 123.

[26] *Sheltered in the Arms of God*, 220.

[27] Epp, *Women*, 129.

[28] Ibid., 130.

[29] Harvey Neufeldt, "Creating the Brotherhood," 211-38.

[30] Ibid., 225.

[31] John Cherrington, *The Fraser Valley: A History (*Madeira Park, BC: Harbour Publishing, 1992), 259.

[32] Harvey Neufeldt, "M Hank," *Village of Unsettled Yearnings*, 302.

Bibliography

Bartsch, Anna. *The Hidden Hand Story of My Life*. Trans. Art Bartsch. Nelson, BC: Author, 1987.

Braun Brandt, Susan."Pioneers Johann and Susanna Braun." In *Yarrow, British Columbia: Mennonite Promise*. Vol. 2. *Village of Unsettled Yearnings*. Ed. Leonard Neufeldt. Victoria, BC: Touch Wood Editions, 2002.

Cherrington, John. *The Fraser Valley: A History*. Madeira Park, BC: Harbour Publishing, 1992.

Derksen Siemens, Ruth. "Quilt as Text and Text as Quilt: The Influence of Genre in the Mennonite Girls' Home of Vancouver (1930-1960)." *Journal of Mennonite Studies* 17 (1999): 118-29.

Derksen Siemens, Ruth. "'Pick the Berries, Don't Paint Them': The Odyssey of Three Artists in a Mennonite Lotus Land." In *Yarrow, British Columbia: Mennonite Promise*. Vol. 2. *Village of Unsettled Yearnings*. Ed. Leonard Neufeldt. Victoria, BC: Touch Wood Editions, 2002.

Epp, Irma, Lillian Harms and Lora Sawatsky. "Midwifery: A Ministry." In *Yarrow, British Columbia: Mennonite Promise*. Vol. 2. *Village of Unsettled Yearnings*. Ed. Leonard Neufeldt. Victoria, BC: Touch Wood Editions, 2002.

Epp, Marlene. *Women without Men: Mennonite Refugees of the Second World War*. Toronto: University of Toronto Press, 2000.

Esau Martens, Gertrude. Manuscript Excerpt. In *Yarrow, British Columbia: Mennonite Promise*. Vol. 2. *Village of Unsettled Yearnings*. Ed. Leonard Neufeldt. Victoria, BC: Touch Wood Editions, 2002.

Giesbrecht, Edward, R. "The Everydayness of a Dairy Farm." In *Yarrow, British Columbia: Mennonite Promise*. Vol. 2. *Village of Unsettled Yearnings*. Ed. Leonard Neufeldt. Victoria, BC: Touch Wood Editions, 2002.

Goosen Kornelsen, Anna. Diary Excerpts. In *Yarrow, British Columbia: Mennonite Promise*. Vol. 1. *Before We Were the Land's*. Ed. Leonard Neufeldt. Victoria, BC: Touch Wood Editions, 2002.

Klassen, Agatha, ed. *Yarrow: A Portrait in Mosaic*. Yarrow, BC: author, 1976.

Lindström-Best, Varpu. *Defiant Sisters: A Social History of Finnish Immigrant Women in Canada*. Toronto: Multicultural History Society of Ontario, 1988.

Loewen, Gladys A. "Grandmother's Nimble Fingers." *Village of Unsettled Yearnings; Yarrow, British Columbia: Mennonite Promise*. Ed. Neufeldt, Leonard. Victoria, BC, Touch Wood Editions, 2002.

Mitchinson, Wendy. *Giving Birth in Canada, 1900-1950*. Toronto: University of Toronto Press, 2002.

Neufeldt, Harvey. "Creating the Brotherhood: Status and Control in the Yarrow Mennonite Community, 1928-1960." In *Canadian Papers in Rural History*. Vol. 9. Ed. Donald H. Akenson. Gananoque, ON: Langdale Press, 1994.

———. "M Hank." In *Yarrow, British Columbia: Mennonite Promise*. Vol. 2. *Village of Unsettled Yearnings*. Ed. Leonard Neufeldt et al. Victoria, BC: Touch Wood Editions, 2002.

Neufeldt, Leonard, Lora Sawatsky and Robert Martens, eds. *Yarrow, British Columbia: Mennonite Promise*. Vol. 1. *Before We were the Land's*. Victoria, BC: Touch Wood Editions, 2002.

———, ed. *Yarrow, British Columbia: Mennonite Promise*. Vol. 2. *Village of Unsettled Yearnings;* Victoria, BC: Touch Wood Editions, 2002.

Penner Klassen Goerzen, Anny. *Anny: Sheltered in the Arms of God: A True Story of Survival in Russia*. Fort St. James, BC: Author, 1988.

Penner, Peter. "Chauncey Eckert, the CCA, and Early Settlement." In *Yarrow, British Columbia: Mennonite Promise*. Vol. 1. *Before We Were the Land's*. Ed. Leonard Neufeldt. Victoria, BC: Touch Wood Editions, 2002.

Reimer Kaufman, Thelma. "Hop Season." In *Yarrow, British Columbia: Mennonite Promise*. Vol. 2. *Village of Unsettled Yearnings*. Ed. Leonard Neufeldt et al. Victoria, BC: Touch Wood Editions, 2002.

Arriving, Working, Learning, and Leaving: The First Four Decades in an Immigrant Community

Ruth Derksen Siemens and Lora Sawatsky

In reflecting on the dynamics of displaced people, researchers have discovered that new immigrants tend to form relationships between a particular place, their memories of this place and their inevitable nostalgia. Leo Spitzer names this experience "rootless nostalgia."[1] Such nostalgia is not simply homesickness or the longing to return to a lost origin, but rather it is a desire to establish a bridge between a remembered past and a lived present. This kind of longing embodies a need to repair the ruptured fabric of a painfully discontinuous, fragmentary history, even as it simultaneously acknowledges the impossibility of such reparation.[2]

In the 1920s, a group of displaced ethnic people, looking for a place to live their lives in peace and freedom, arrived in Canada. These settlers had survived the horrors of the Bolshevik Revolution in Russia, the civil war, the resulting famine and disease and the beginning of Stalin's "Reign of Terror." As displaced Mennonites, they envisioned a community that would replicate the village culture they had known in Russia for almost 150 years. In February, 1928, a group of families moved with their belongings from their first places of settlement in the prairie provinces of Canada to Yarrow, British Columbia, an elysian site in the shadow of Vedder Mountain: this location became the locus of connection between an idyllic past and their present conditions. A utopian vision of a rural place with a mild climate, rivers, streams and fertile soil provided the impetus for this group of émigrés.[3]

Predictably, the pioneers patterned this new village in a way that replicated the settlements of their homeland. The church, school and commercial enterprises were located at the core of the village, with a central road supporting the long narrow building sites on each side. Just outside the perimeter, livestock could graze in a common pasture. Although these Russian Mennonite immigrants *transplanted* many of their notions of an ideal socio-cultural milieu, Harvey Neufeldt notes that they also *adapted* them in order to conform to their Canadian realities.[4] But overall, a utopian vision inspired and sustained many of these displaced people for four decades.

What drives this kind of mythic vision? What generates the energy and commitment required to make the colossal sacrifices needed to maintain such an "imagined community"?[5] How much will settlers endure, work, or strive to sustain the dream? How do religious, socio-economic, and educational processes evolve in such a place? Which factors contribute to, or detract from, the creation of this desired space? How do we measure these factors?

With these questions as our impetus, we have conducted a study that traces the patterns, habits, lifestyles, and choices of the inhabitants of early Yarrow. In the process, we have attempted to measure how these phenomena change over time. We have examined distinct local practices and have attempted to forge cohesive ties between the various factors that resulted in the formation and dissemination of the community called "Yarrow."

In particular, our research project was propelled by a central question: Why did the dispersion of Mennonite people from Yarrow begin so soon after settlement and in such great numbers? As the graph below reveals, the Mennonite population of Yarrow experienced both rapid growth and swift decline. This central query led to others: What factors contributed to the rapid decline in population? Which socio-cultural strata initiated the changes? Which stratified sampling most clearly delineates the nature of the decline and dispersion? How did these Mennonite *Russlaender* integrate into the surrounding Canadian society? Which generation was the first to become bi-cultural (both Canadian and Russian-Mennonite)?[6] To what extent did education and employment opportunities affect individuals' decisions to leave Yarrow? Did the early settlers' children choose the vocations of their parents? If not, how much digression is evident?

Our primary investigative tool for this research project has been a questionnaire. As a result, most of the data included in this study is quantitative and originates from those who responded to the questionnaire. However, we have been wary of the reductionist potential of quantitative research and the ways in which it can possibly misrepresent human subjects.[7] Consequently, we begin each section of this paper with an anecdote—a short retelling of an experiential incident by a resident of Yarrow. Thus, two sources inform our paper: the first is the quantitative questionnaire completed in 2001, while the second is a series of anecdotes from the recent publication *Before We Were the Land's; Yarrow, British Columbia: Mennonite Promise*.[8] We have included four narratives that reflect four aspects of the lives of Yarrow residents: arriving, working, learning and leaving.

In the process of conducting our survey, we have attempted to represent as wide a spectrum as possible of historical time-lines, age groups and genders. Specifically, this study is based on 149 responses to the questionnaire. Females represent 59% of the respondents and males constitute 41%. Although many of the earliest settlers have died, the historical timeline represents some of the respondents who moved to Yarrow in the late 1920s, as well as those who arrived or were born in Yarrow from 1930 to 1960.

Arriving

Mr. Martens traded his car in on a 1927 one ton flat deck, former coal truck. He built sides on the flat deck and stretched a tarpaulin over the top. Now with the truck ready, they put an armchair in the back of the truck and loaded on their meager belongings. . . . They seated grandfather on the armchair [and with] John, Jake, nine-year-old Aron, and sister Sarah sitting on little benches and father Martens and mother in the cab, they were off. They rocked and rolled on the rutted roads and eighty-one-year-old Grandfather's bones and muscles ached, but he did not complain. The lure of the west and the perceived call from the land of opportunity beckoned and drove them onward.

The decision was made to go through Kingsgate, B.C. to the United States, across Washington State and north through the Huntington-Sumas crossing.

The only road leading to Yarrow was the Old Yale Road running through Arnold and up over Majuba Hill. . . . When they reached Yarrow Station on the B.C. Electric railway, at the junction of the Old Yale and Wilson road, they stopped to dip water from a creek and washed their dusty, travel-weary hands and faces. Below them they could see "The Promised Land," Yarrow, British Columbia.[9]

The following Sunday ... the Martens family went to church. . . . Mrs. Martens was sitting on the women's side behind one of the earlier residents, and overheard a lady say, "Have you heard, there have been more arrivals from Manitoba. They will surely take our jobs away from us." Mrs. Martens tapped her on the shoulder and commented[,] ". . . we will not take any work away from you . . . we will even create jobs for you."[10]

137

The Funk and Friesen families arrive in Yarrow (1933) having moved from Coaldale, Alberta. Back (left to right): Henry Funk, Cornelius Funk Jr.,Cornelius Funk Sr., Susie Thiessen Funk, Liese Thiessen, Mary Friesen, Mrs. Agatha Friesen. Front (left to right): Susie Funk Jr., Annie Funk, Betty Funk, Anna Friesen, Katherine Friesen.

When did they arrive?

Although the arrival of the Russian Mennonites began in 1928, half of the respondents (50%) stated that they moved to Yarrow sometime during the 1930s. During the next decade, the 1940s, an influx of Mennonites from Europe arrived in Yarrow. Of the respondents, 32% stated that they moved to Yarrow in this decade. Following World War II and the resulting dispersion of Russians and Europeans, many residents of Yarrow were able to sponsor their extended family members and friends who had not been able to emigrate in the 1920s. The defeat of the German army by the Russians in WW II opened the possibility for many Mennonites to escape Stalin's regime by following the retreating German army into parts of Western Europe. Yarrow attracted many of these refugees because of familial connections, ethnic ties and employment opportunities.[11] Most of these immigrants arriving after WW II joined the United Mennonite Church congregation. As the graph below indicates, the largest influx into the United Mennonite Church began in 1949. Very few of these post-WW II immigrants affiliated themselves with the Mennonite Brethren Church in Yarrow. This phenomenon accounts for the disparity in statistical growth during the late 1940s between the two Mennonite churches of Yarrow.

Despite this influx of refugees, for the total number of respondents providing information on the year they moved to Yarrow, the two most common years to begin residency were 1936 (16 respondents) and 1937 (11). Ten of these respondents indicated that they arrived in Yarrow in 1928. The latest date at which a respondent reported beginning residence in Yarrow was 1966.

How long did they stay?

The average number of years respondents lived in Yarrow was 19.3 years. The largest number of respondents (10) stated that they lived in Yarrow for

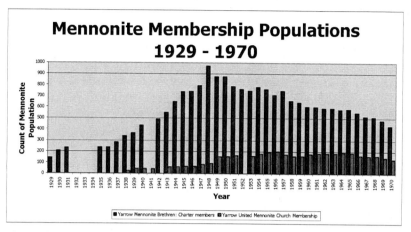

Mennonite Membership Populations 1929 - 1970

following number of years: 13, 14, 17, and 22. The first respondent to leave Yarrow left in 1932. Others reported that they continued to live in Yarrow and retired in the nearby community of Clearbrook at a much later time. Since many of the original settlers moved away from Yarrow, it is significant that several respondents who were among the early settlers to arrive in 1928 continue to live in Yarrow at the time of this study.

In light of the evidence that people from one particular ethno-religious group formed the core of immigration to Yarrow from 1928 onward, it is useful to measure the growth of the community by examining the rise and decline of the church populations. Specifically, the graph above indicates statistical growth of membership in the Yarrow Mennonite Brethren Church and the Yarrow United Mennonite Church.[12]

Where did they live?

Of the 140 respondents providing information about residence in Yarrow, the largest number reported *first* living on Central Road in Yarrow. The four streets, in order of settlement, were: Central Road (33 respondents); Stewart Road (20 respondents); Dyke Road (13 respondents); and Eckert Road (13 respondents). These four streets account for 56% of the responses (79 entries). Central Road was most comonly mentioned as the street in Yarrow to which the respondent's family relocated.

Where did they come from?

Almost one-third (27%) of respondents indicated that *they themselves* had emigrated from Russia.[13] However, most respondents reported that it was their parents, grandparents and relatives who had emigrated from Russia. A majority of respondents indicated that their fathers (96.6%) and mothers

(98%) had emigrated from Russia, making Yarrow truly a *Russlaender* community. In addition, 67.7% indicated that their grandfather had emigrated from Russia, while 70.4% reported that their grandmother had emigrated from Russia.

The most common geographical area of North or South America in which the respondents settled after leaving Russia but before coming to Yarrow was Saskatchewan. More specifically, for those who first settled in various regions of the Americas, the three most common provinces are Saskatchewan (17 respondents or 47.2%), Manitoba (12 respondents or 33.3%), and Alberta (3 respondents or 8.3%). Only four respondents indicated that they had settled in other parts of Europe after leaving Russia and before coming to North America. In addition, six respondents (5.7%) indicated that they emigrated from parts of Europe other than Russia.

When did they emigrate?

Respondents' grandparents were most likely to have emigrated from Russia to various parts of North and South America in the 1920s, most commonly around 1926. Although one respondent's grandparents had immigrated to North America in 1874, the earliest reported arrival date of respondents to North America was 1923 and the latest date was 1949. Of the 39 respondents providing years in which they settled in other parts of North and South America, 67% settled in the 1920s. Of the remaining, 21% settled in the 1930s and 10% in the 1940s.

Just under 30% (28.9% of the 97 respondents) indicated that they had settled in other parts of North or South America after leaving Russia and before coming to Yarrow. However, the majority of respondents settled only in North America after leaving Russia and before arriving in Yarrow. It is also significant that, after they had emigrated from Russia and settled in Yarrow, almost half of the respondents (46.8%) indicated that they sponsored refugees to Canada after World War II.

Working

When I was thirteen years old I was helping [my sister] Margaret at Ord's place when Mr. Ord [manager of the hop yard] asked me if I would like to work in the hop yard store. I was shocked because I felt I was far too young but I got the job and for five summers I had a steady job. I would go out and pick, then hurry and clean up by 10:00 a.m. I had to be at the store until 1:00 p.m. Then I went back to the field and then back to the store by 5:00 p.m. and worked until 10:00 p.m. The years when Dad and I worked at the store we could eat

Reverend Jacob Epp and son Peter picking hops in the Canadian Hop Company's hop yards.

corned beef, cheese, tomatoes, fresh bread, sardines and bananas because we did not take the time to cook. . . . We also had a team of horses and a wagon which was employed, hauling hop sacks from the fields to the kilns. Dave drove the team and looked after them in the evening. In the later years, when transportation was provided by trucks from Yarrow, mother and the small children lived at home. They cooked, baked, milked the cows and then caught the truck at 5:00 a.m. thus bringing us some fresh produce and baking daily.[14]

How long did they work for their families?

On average, respondents continued to work in the family home and on the family farm until they were 19.1 years of age. However, the oldest age that a female reported to be working on the family farm was 52 years of age and the youngest age that a male respondent reported beginning work on the family farm was five years of age. In respect to gender differences, of the 121 entries noted in this category, 70 were females and 51 male.

Although one female reported working in the home or on the family farm until 52 years of age and one male reported working in this capacity until 32 years of age, when the average age to which both females and males continued to work in the home or on the family farm is accounted for, gender disparity is almost non-existent. The average age for males is almost 19 years, while the average age for females is slightly over 19 years. Most entries for both females and males range between 15 and 21 years of age. Males provided 42 entries and females provided 65 entries for ages 15-21. These numbers appear to indicate that many respondents left Yarrow when they left the family home and/or farm. Perhaps the fact that there is little gender disparity is not surprising considering that many of the respondents were first-generation Canadians who left Yarrow as young people to find employment or continue their education.

A fairly large number (79.1%) of respondents reported that they were expected to find employment outside the home, while 20.9% indicated they were not expected to find such employment. The average age at which respondents first found part-time or full time employment outside of the family home was 15.7 years. The maximum age at which a respondent reported finding employment outside the family home was 23 years and the minimum age was 7 years. In respect to gender differences, of the 102 entries noted, 62 were provided by females and 40 by males. While the average age at which respondents found employment outside the family home was 15.7 years, the youngest age reported for females was seven years as opposed to ten years for males. The oldest age at which respondents reported finding employment outside the family home was 23 for females and 21 for males. If we eliminate those who reported picking hops and berries during their childhood as their *first* employment, both male and female respondents reported that they were expected to start employment outside the home as early as 12 and 13 years of age. The average for both males and females to begin employment outside the home is slightly over 16 years, with the female average being only slightly higher than that of males. There appears to be little or no gender disparity in terms of when dependent males and females were expected to find employment outside the home.

What kind of work did they do?

Approximately one-third (30.2%) of respondents indicated that cannery work was the kind of employment they found in the community of Yarrow, while an additional 23% indicated that they picked fruits, vegetables and hops outside the family farm or home. Even those who found work outside of Yarrow indicated that their first job involved some form of agricultural work. A large percentage (80.7% of respondents) indicated that their first job in the community was part-time, with a much smaller percentage (19.3%) indicating that their first job was full-time.

The following kinds of employment outside of the community were noted as a respondent's *first* job: agricultural work, factory employment, hairdressing, work in wood mills, truck driving, office work, retail employment, medical fields, educational fields, and the banking industry. Although in the later decades, cannery work was the primary source of employment for community residents, the memoirs of the early immigrants indicate that the hop industry was the major source of income for the first settlers; in fact, many of these families might not have been able to meet their minimal economic needs without this income.[15] Particularly in the first decades of village settlement, entire families of grandparents, parents and children picked hops. As the questionnaire reveals, over 75% of our respondents indicated that they worked in the hop yards during their childhood, adolescent and young adult years. As some early Yarrow residents recall, during the hop season, the streets and homes of Yarrow were empty from early morning until dinnertime.

How old were they when they worked outside the community?

The average age at which respondents first found employment outside of the community was 17.6 years. The maximum age at which a respondent found employment outside of the community was 25 years and the minimum age was 10 years. To provide further insight into these statistics, hop picking was considered by some respondents as work outside the community, hence the age of 10. However, if we eliminate hop picking, berry and bean picking as work found outside the community, the youngest age is 13 for females and 14 for males. The maximum age at which both males and females found work outside the community is 25 years. Further extrapolations for work outside the community are not useful since a number of respondents failed to answer this question and others omitted the age at which they started.

A majority (67%) reported that the income they earned helped support their families. It is significant that 61% of respondents indicated that all or most of their income helped to support their families. Most of these individuals (80 out of a total of 97) noted that their level of income support for their immediate families changed after they were married, although 17 indicated that they continued to support their parents despite their marital status. With respect to gender, of the respondents who indicated that their income helped to support their families, 59.3% were females and 40.7% were males. However, the average age to which female respondents continued to support their families was only marginally higher (21 years) than that of males (20.2 years).

143

What choice of career or profession did they make?

As is evident from the figures below, almost 30% of the 125 respondents eventually chose teaching as their career. The second highest choice of career was in the business sector, and the lowest number of respondents chose construction-related trades, such as plumbing or carpentry (along with engineering). Several female respondents commented that teaching and nursing were popular careers available to them at the time they made their choice. It is also clear that none of Yarrow's medical doctors responded to this section of the questionnaire. In particular, one male respondent who was born and raised in Yarrow and who is a retired medical doctor failed to answer this particular question or any of those relating to professional choices. Despite this omission, the chart below provides a fairly accurate portrayal of career choices among respondents.

Career Choice	Male	Female	Total	% of 149 respondents
1. Professor	2	0	2	1.3%
2. Teacher	22	22	44	29.5%
3. Engineer	1	0	1	0.7%
4. Nurse	0	7	7	4.7%
5. Farm/food production	4	1	5	3.4%
6. Bank teller	0	4	4	2.7%
7. Cashier/clerk	0	7	7	4.7%
8. Factory/lumber/ dockyard	5	1	6	4.0%
9. Sec/admin/bookkeeper	4	15	19	12.8%
10. Mechanic/driver	5	0	5	3.4%
11. Barber/hairdresser	1	1	2	1.3%
12. Self-employed	6	1	7	4.7%
13. Religious work	3	2	5	3.4%
14. Plumbing/carpentry	1	0	1	0.7%
15. Child/house/social work	1	8	9	6.0
Total	55	69	124	83.3%
% of 125	44%	56%	100%	

Where did their careers take them?

Of the 122 entries noted, 76.2% revealed that British Columbia was the area in which the respondents worked or conducted their careers. Specifically,

35.6% indicated Greater Vancouver and 8.1% stated that they continued to work in Yarrow.[16]

How old were they when they started their careers?

The average age at which respondents began their career was 23.7 years of age. Of the 107 entries noted for this question, the youngest was 17 years and the oldest was 51. Although one female eventually started her career as late as 51 years of age, it is clear that females tended to start their career/employment choices at an earlier age than their male counterparts. While 49 females began their careers between ages 17 and 24 years of age, 24 males started careers during this same age span. After age 24, only 10 females chose careers, whereas 25 males chose careers after age 24. Note that the few females who identified homemaker, mother or marriage as a career are not included in this count. It should also be noted that only four married females considered homemaking or raising children as careers. One female respondent entered "homemaker" as a career; another entered "marriage" as her career; and, a third commented that "I became a mother and that took up the bulk of my life." Eighteen married women chose not to answer the question as to choice of career or employment, whereas only five married men chose not to answer the same question. Our assumption is that the married women who chose not to answer this question did not consider homemaking and motherhood as a career/employment choice.

A rather impressive number of respondents made career/employment changes. One female respondent comments that as a college graduate, her choices were fairly limited to such career choices as teaching and nursing; however, she asserts that at midlife almost any choice was open to her if she wished to pursue it. A total of 18 females and 28 males chose a second career and one male chose a third. Males indicated that they made career changes between ages 21 and 55, while females did so between ages 20 and 50. Considering the fact that there are more female than male respondents to the questionnaire, career changes appear to have been more popular with males than females. However, there is relatively little disparity in the average age at which males and females made career changes. The average age at which males make career changes is slightly over 33 years, while the average age for females is between 31 and 32 years of age.

Who influenced their choice of career?

Regarding the freedom to choose a career, 38.9% of 82 respondents indicated that their parents did not choose their career, but left this choice to their discretion. Autonomy of career choice is also evident in the 24.8% of 74 respondents who indicated that their community did not influence their choice of careers.

Carl Wilson's first class in Yarrow, 1930. Wilson insisted that children wear shoes in the classroom.

Learning

It was in Yarrow where I started school. The cultural tensions in the elementary school years were minimal compared to those my genera-tion experienced within the high school system during the war years. In Yarrow the student population... was almost entirely of Mennonite descent with a common language which was either high or low Ger-man. For me to transfer to a high school in Chilliwack, BC occurred during the eighth grade. It was traumatic. Not only did we have to adapt to an entirely unfamiliar school culture with differing religious, moral and social values but our German speaking background made it almost impossible to become totally assimilated. My parents in-sisted that we speak German at home, yet in school we did not want to be identified with our Mennonite German background to the ex-tent that we attempted to deny this or at least to disguise it in every way possible.

One day my father... along with several church elders, appeared in the Chilliwack High School in order to petition the principal to ex-empt Mennonite female students from wearing slacks or shorts dur-ing PT (physical training) and to allow male students to wear slacks instead of shorts. When I noticed this delegation in the school hall-

way, I was most embarrassed and attempted to avoid them and certainly not to acknowledge that I knew any of these men.[17]

Where did they receive their education?

Fourteen respondents reported receiving village elementary education in Russia and two respondents noted that they had attended "other schools" in Russia. Six indicated that they received some education in Europe. However, it is evident from the questionnaire that the majority of individuals who attended school did so in Canada.

What kind of education did they receive?

The following figures reflect those who *attended* various educational institutions, but not necessarily those who completed or *graduated* from these institutions. In distinguishing between religious institutions, Bible schools were relatively small community schools associated with a local church that provided religious training for Sunday School teachers and church workers. On the other hand, Bible colleges, such as the Mennonite Brethren Bible College in Winnipeg, were degree-granting institutions. This Bible College provided religious education, music and theological training for Mennonite young people in many provinces.

Type of School in Canada	Male	Female	Total	% of 149 respondents
1. German	41	62	103	69.1%
2. Elementary	52	80	132	88.6%
3. Junior high school	50	76	126	84.6%
4. Senior high school	42	67	109	73.2%
5. Bible school	31	47	78	52.3%
6. Bible college	32	35	67	45%
7. University	15	14	29	19.5%
8. Music Lessons	5	27	32	21.5%
9. Community college	2	6	8	5.4%
10. Teacher training	18	24	42	28.2%
11. Nurse's training	1	8	9	6%
12. Other vocational	19	18	37	24.8%
13. Other job-related	9	11	20	13.4%
Total	320	483	803	
% of 803	40%	60%	100%	

The chart below reflects the respondents who *completed* specific educational institutions.

Kind of Education Completed in Canada	Male	Female	Total	% of 149 respondents
1. German school and Religious school	17	26	43	28.9%
2. Elementary school	34	64	98	65.8%
3. Junior high school	30	60	90	60.4%
4. Senior high school	32	57	89	59.7%
5. Bible school	20	29	49	32.9%
6. Bible college	15	14	29	19.5%
7. University	29	22	51	34.2%
8. Community college	1	2	3	2.0%
9. Music conservatory/ private	3	8	11	7.4%
10. Teacher training	19	21	40	26.8%
11. Nurse's training	1	7	8	5.4%
12. Other education/ training	11	12	23	15.4%
Total	212	322	534	
% of 534	39.7%	60.3%	100%	

It appears evident from these statistics that many women had the opportunity for education at almost all of the levels represented. Specifically, more women than men chose a music education. However, while more women than men enrolled in post-secondary studies, more men than women completed their degree programs. This finding might be explained in part by the varying effects of marriage on males as opposed to females, particularly in the sphere of career and education choices. However, it remains significant that such a large number of men and women furthered their education, though not all of them completed certification or degree programs in their chosen initiative.

Which educational goals would they have chosen had they had the opportunity? The 88 responses noted below have been coded into seven categories (two with sub-categories).

Several phenomena are evident in this chart that enumerate the ideal goals the respondents would have chosen had they had the opportunity. First of all, a greater variety of educational goals is evident. Secondly, the data in

Categories	Male	Female	Count	% of 150 respondents
1) Education				
a. graduate school	1	2	3	2.0%
b. university	2	6	8	5.4%
c. high school	3	1	4	2.7%
d. elementary	0	1	1	0.7%
2) Religious Education	0	1	1	0.7%
3) Professional Training:				
a. nursing	0	13	13	8.7%
b. teaching	0	12	12	8.1%
c. social work	0	1	1	0.7%
d. airline pilot	0	1	1	0.7%
e. engineer	2	0	2	1.3%
f. accountant	1	0	1	0.7%
4) Musical training	0	2	2	1.3%
5) No educational goals	2	8	10	6.7%
6) Own Choice	11	17	28	18.8%
7) Miscellaneous (prep for marriage)	0	1	1	0.7%
Total	22	66	88	100%
% of 88	25%	75%	100%	

the previous table demonstrates that a significant number of individuals did complete a religious education in either a Bible School or Bible College, yet this table indicates that very few respondents would have chosen this kind of education if they had been offered other opportunities. In particular, female respondents appear to have had a greater degree of unfulfilled career and educational aspirations. One explanation, although not the only one, is that the community of Yarrow functioned within a rubric of patriarchy and thus the impetus for women to find employment in their early years of marriage was to support their husbands' education and career aspirations. Anecdotal evidence suggests that some women continued their education when their children were old enough to attend school. Religious education was also perceived through a patriarchal lens; as a result women would have been unlikely to find paid employment within the Mennonite churches, regardless of their religious training.

Leaving

When the war ended and Frank came home to Yarrow . . . Mother Sawatsky was pleased to have him back; his life had been spared, and she was grateful. With Frank now being in the position to care for his mother, Abe and I knew the time had come to continue our education.

We applied to the Mennonite Brethren Bible College (MBBC) in Winnipeg in 1945, but had to wait until the January 1946 semester to begin studies. It was an exciting day when with our seven-month- old baby we left to prepare for whatever lay ahead.[18]

When did they leave Yarrow?

Respondents can be divided into at least three groups of people who left Yarrow at different times and for different reasons.

1. When the immigrants first arrived, many of the young women (some still adolescents) moved to Vancouver and Chilliwack in the 1930s to find employment as domestic workers. Some of these women returned to Yarrow only in the summer season to assist in harvesting agricultural crops. Others returned to Yarrow when they married, but many remained in the city to pursue various vocations, attain an education, and eventually raise their families. Having had to overlook (through economic necessity) the traditional Mennonite resistance to city living and finding it less evil than imagined, the parents and siblings of many of these young women eventually joined them in the urban centres, especially in Vancouver.

2. A noticeably large exodus of both young men and women from Yarrow occurred during the 1950s and 1960s. These young people left for various urban centres to both seek employment and further their education.

Mary Jane Epp, a graduate nurse at Vancouver General Hospital, circa. 1950.

150

3. A smaller group of respondents, more advanced in years, left Yarrow to seek further employment and enjoy the conveniences of urban living as they approached retirement.

More specifically, of the 140 respondents providing information on the year they left Yarrow, the first respondent left the community in 1932. The largest number of respondents (49.3%) left Yarrow in the 1950s. A smaller quantity (20%) left Yarrow in the 1940s (30 respondents), and a further 20% left in the 1960s. It is clear that the decade of the 1950s proved to be a watershed for Yarrow. It marked the end of many of the dreams that the early Mennonite settlers of Yarrow once had for the community.

The following table reveals the relatively large number of Yarrow residents who left the village when they left their parents' home.

Question	Male count	% of 53 respondents	Female count	% of 90 respondents
1) Did you leave Yarrow when you left your parents' home?	34	64.2%	64	71.1%
2) Did you leave Yarrow with your parents?	3	5.5%	11	12.2%
3) Did you leave Yarrow at a later time?	16	29.6%	15	16.7%
Total	53	100%	90	100%

How old were they when they left?

The majority (two-thirds of the respondents) indicated that they left Yarrow when they left their parental home. On average, they indicated that they left their parental home at 20.3 years of age. The most common reasons cited were to find employment or to pursue an education. The reasons for leaving home reveal only a small degree of variation between men and women, with slightly more men leaving to live independently and slightly more women leaving to pursue their education.

Of the 164 entries noted, the reasons for leaving home are delineated in the chart on the following page.[19]

Where did they go?

When respondents left Yarrow, nearly 70% of them left for urban locations. Specifically, 60.8% indicated that they left Yarrow to move to Vancouver, British Columbia and 8.8% stated that they moved to Winnipeg, Manitoba.

Why leave home	Male count	% of 53 respondents	Female count	% of 90 respondents
1) Find employment	22	31.4%	30	71.1%
2) Marry, start family	19	27.1%	25	12.2%
3) Live independently	6	8.6%	5	16.7%
4) Further education	23	32.9%	34	100%
Total	70	100%	94	100%

Of the respondents who went to Vancouver, 70% were women and 30% were men. Of the respondents who indicated that they moved to Winnipeg, Manitoba, 55% were women and 45% were men. Although gender differences appear to be remarkable, if we consider the fact that we have a higher percentage of female respondents, the ratio of females to males moving to Winnipeg is not that striking. However, the 70% to 30% ratio of women and men going to Vancouver needs to be considered.

In conducting the survey, we were interested in the respondent's first employment outside the home. However, as noted in a published study of Mennonite domestic workers in Vancouver, many young Mennonite women from several provinces of Canada left their family homes to work in Vancouver. Two Mennonite *Maedchenheime* (Girls' Homes) were established in Vancouver in the 1930s and remained active until the 1960s. One was the initiative of the Mennonite Conference Church and the other (although initially founded by women) became affiliated with the Mennonite Brethren Church. Many of the women working in the city returned to their parental homes in the countryside to work in seasonal agricultural occupations in the Fraser Valley. They then returned to their urban employment for the fall and winter.

Another plausible explanation for more women than men moving to the cities is that women moved to Vancouver to pursue careers in nursing or teaching. Although they were initially employed as domestics in Vancouver, this source of income was considered a transition to a career in nursing or teaching, or as a pathway to employment in the business sector. The main attraction in Winnipeg was the Mennonite Brethren Bible College, which was sanctioned by the church community and which attracted many young people, both male and female.

Why did they leave?

Some of the 143 respondents to this question provided more than one reason (many of them reflected in the previous discussion), resulting in 150 re-

Reason for leaving Yarrow	Male	Female	Count	% of 150 respondents
1) employment	31	34	65	43.3%
2) education	14	21	35	23.3%
3) religious education	1	6	7	4.7%
4) nurses training	0	3	3	2.0%
5) farming or farming related	3	5	8	5.3%
6) marriage reasons[20]	2	15	17	11.3%
7) miscellaneous reasons[21]	7	8	15	10%
Total	58	92	150	100%

sponses. The chart above provides an overview of the dominant reasons for leaving Yarrow.

Conclusion

While this is not a definitive study, a number of findings both predictable and unforeseen have become evident. For example, we were not surprised when the tabulated results demonstrated that the search for employment and educational pursuits strongly influenced individuals to leave Yarrow, especially in the 1950s, when the largest number of respondents (over 48%) left. The village of Yarrow was not a large settlement and could not have been expected to be self-sustaining in all aspects of education and employment unless many of the younger generation had remained on the family farms and followed the agricultural vocations of their parents. By the 1950s, it was becoming clear that the small farm supplemented with an income from the hop industry or raspberry fields was no longer a viable economic institution, let alone attractive to the second generation immigrants. It is also not surprising that the trend toward the urbanization of the Mennonites who left Yarrow was initiated by first-generation, Canadian-born citizens. The move to urban centres was significantly augmented by the many respondents who moved to Vancouver or Winnipeg to find work or to attend an educational institution. However, it is significant that within the group of approximately 59% of residents who left Yarrow to move to Vancouver, a large majority (70%) were women. This factor substantiates our belief that many of the young women, particularly from 1930-60, were able to find employment in the city (many as domestic workers in middle to upper class homes).

Another notable phenomenon is that the number of females attending and completing secondary school is higher than that of males attending and completing studies in these institutions. Admittedly, a somewhat higher percentage of female respondents completed the questionnaire, which accounts for some of the variance. Yet, considering that the early Yarrow Mennonite community was patriarchal in its expressions of public service, vocational pursuits and church leadership (in the Mennonite Brethren Church, women did not receive voting rights until 1959), we had expected that the number of females completing secondary school would be fewer than the number of males.

Also according to our findings, more women than men *attended* university. However, it is important to note that more men than women *completed* university degrees, although equal numbers of men and women report that they practiced their profession as teachers. Overall, the results of our research indicate that much less gender disparity than we had anticipated is evident in almost all fields queried.

It is also apparent from this study that the most popular career chosen by respondents (30%) appears to be teaching. The fact that 12 females, but no males, selected teacher training as their educational goal exposes a particular gender preference that is significant. Meanwhile, farming was one of the least chosen occupations by the children of the Mennonite settlers of early Yarrow. In regard to the choice of vocation, we were expecting to find that the respondents' parents and the greater community would have had a more significant role in influencing their choice of careers. It was therefore surprising that almost 40% of individuals reported that they were free to choose their vocations. Granted, we as authors of the questionnaire did not provide a definition of "choice", but assumed that the respondents would reply within the parameters of their social constructs.

Although we attempted to conduct a comprehensive survey, further questions have emerged that require additional scrutiny:

1. How does the rapid decline of the Mennonite population in Yarrow compare with the demographics of Mennonite villages in other parts of Canada at a similar historical time? How does this decline compare to conditions in non-Mennonite immigrant communities during the same era? How do the issues examined in this study compare to those of other contemporary ethnic immigrant groups?

2. In light of the evidence that the largest number of respondents left Yarrow in the 1950s, to what extent did the collapse of the berry market, the subsequent closure of the Yarrow Growers' Co-op, and the closure of the Mennonite private secondary school contribute to the exodus of residents from Yarrow?

3. Would integration have occurred at a slower pace had WW II not had an effect on the unassimilated Mennonite population of Yarrow?

4. Why did Abbotsford experience such a strong influx of Mennonites as the Mennonite population in Yarrow declined?

Overall, it is evident that the factors that facilitated the rapid urbanization and integration of the residents of Yarrow into the dominant Anglo society were complex. To some extent, one could measure the negative impact that WWII had on this German-speaking, immigrant minority who identified themselves as pacifists. The failure of the berry market following WWII and the subsequent closure of two institutions (the Yarrow Co-op and the private secondary school) certainly influenced young people to look beyond the village boundaries for their career and employment opportunities. Furthermore, the impact of Carl Wilson, a long-time teacher and principal of the Yarrow Elementary School must not be disregarded. To what extent did Wilson achieve his mandate to "use the schools to promote assimilation of the Mennonite identity into Canadian culture and society."[22] Despite the number and complexity of the reasons for the demise of the distinctly Mennonite village of Yarrow, it is evident that the first generation of Canadians born of Mennonite immigrants rapidly moved from their parents' vision of cultural separatism to a bicultural heritage: one that retained a connection to the past, yet formed a bridge to a lived present.

Endnotes

[1] Leo Spitzer, *Hotel Bolivia: The Culture of Memory in a Refuge from Nazism* (New York: Hill and Wang, 1998).

[2] Spitzer observes the experiences of displaced Jewish refugees in the mid 1930s until the end of the first year of World War II. These emigrants fled to Bolivia to escape potential imprisonment and death in Nazi-controlled Europe. Spitzer examines the refugees' recollections of their experiences in Austria and other European countries, as well as their memories of their "Bolivia experience" in the U.S. approximately fifty years later. He notes the interrelations of a sense of place, historic memory, and the ensuing predictable nostalgia. Further to this concept, Ian McKay asserts that rural living has the possibility of providing a "psychic space" that reminds its inhabitants of the "*Gemeinshaft* world" they have lost (Ian McKay, *The Quest of the Fold: Antimodernism and Cultural Selection in Twentieth Century Nova Scotia* [Kingston and Montreal: McGill-Queen's University Press, 1994], 13).

[3] Writers, artists, musicians, historians, and common folk have long expressed the desire for a place where all would be well. As early as 375 BCE, Plato described a utopian *Republic*. Ironically, the etymological definition of "utopia" translates as *no place;* perhaps this best reflects the unreality of actually achiev-

ing such a state. Or perhaps Sir Thomas More's *Utopia* (first published in 1516) provides the guide to establishing a place of idealized perfection. Or does Samuel Butler's more recent publication, *Erewhon* (1872), an approximation of *nowhere* backwards, more closely describe the location of an idyllic place?

[4] Harvey Neufeldt, "Creating the Brotherhood: Status and Control in the Yarrow Mennonite Community, 1928-1960," *Canadian Papers in Rural History* 9 ed. Donald H. Akenson (Gananoque, ON: Langdale Press, 1994).

[5] Benedict Anderson in *Imagined Communities* (London and New York: Verso, 1983) examines the creation and perpetuation of "imagined communities." He explores the relationships between religious faith, the decline of a monarchy, the practice of capitalism and language acquisition in light of communities imagining themselves as peculiar.

[6] We consciously use "integrate" rather than "assimilate" because in our view, the identity of Yarrow Mennonites did not get *absorbed* into the Anglo Canadian culture, but rather their identity was formed *alongside* the dominant group.

[7] Ethnographers have increasingly become aware of the potential misrepresentations inherent in quantitative data and, conversely, the value of qualitative research practices. Examples of ethnographic studies that resist reductionist processes and which exemplify a more wholistic practice are found in Laurie Finke's study of "Knowledge as Bait: Feminism, voice, and the pedagogical unconscious,"; John Hagedorn's examination of gang-related drug organizations, "Neighborhoods, markets and gang drug organizations"; and Sonia Livingstone's investigation of gender and conversation. See the bibiography for full publication details for these works.

[8] Leonard Neufeldt, ed., *Yarrow, British Columbia: Mennonite Promise*, 2 vols. (Victoria, BC: Touch Wood Editions, 2002).

[9] Jacob Abrahams, "Aron and Helena Martens Family," in *Yarrow, British Columbia: Mennonite Promise*, 1:118-119.

[10] Ibid., 195.

[11] Marlene Epp notes that these families were "women without men" who, with their children, had survived the Russian Revolution, civil war, and WWII. They were attracted to the Fraser Valley "because of the already significant Mennonite population" and because of the agricultural and domestic work available to them (Marlene Epp, *Women Without Men: Mennonite Refugees of the Second World War.* [Toronto: University of Toronto Press, 2000], 122).

[12] The source for statistics of the Mennonite Brethren Church membership is the *Membership Profile of the Yarrow Mennonite Brethren Church* compiled by Erma Wiebe (statistician for Yarrow MB Church, 1988-1996). She procured her statistics from the annual reports of the Yarrow MB Church.

The source of membership statistics for the Yarrow United Mennonite church is from the following:

- *Jahrbuch 1939 der Allgemeinen Konferenz der Mennoniten in Canada*, Mennonite Historical Society of British Columbia, Abbotsford, BC.
- *Jahrbuch der Konferenz der Mennoniten in Canada*, 1940-41; 1943-1950; 1953-1964, Mennonite Historical Society of BC, Abbotsford, BC;
- *Jubilaums Ausgabe Jahrbuch der Konferenz der Mennoniten in Canada*, 1902-1952, Mennonite Historical Society, Abbotsford, BC;

- *Yearbook of the Conference of Mennonites in Canada*, 1965-1970, Mennonite Historical Society of BC, Abbotsford, BC.
- H. H. Hildebrandt and H. J. Fast, *Des Bestehens Der Vereinigten Mennonitengemeinde Zu Yarrow, B.C., 1938- 1963.* (Yarrow, BC: Columbia Press, 1963).

[13] In light of the relatively recent formation of Ukraine as an independent nation in 1991, respondents who left their homeland in the 1920s consider their country of origin to be Russia. Currently, however, the geographic areas represented are in either the countries of Ukraine or Russia.

[14] Neufeldt, *Yarrow, British Columbia*, 1:161.

[15] For further information on the history and effect of hops as an agricultural crop in British Columbia, see Ron Denman's article in this volume. Also note Thelma Reimer Kaufman's article in Neufeldt, *Yarrow, British Columbia* 2: 175-83, in which she describes the rituals and culture of the hop industry in Yarrow

[16] The cities of Vancouver, Burnaby, New Westminster, Richmond and Surrey were included in the definition of "Greater Vancouver."

[17] Neufeldt, *Yarrow, British Columbia*, 1:184.

[18] Leona Warkentin Sawatsky, *Close to the Earth: A Memoir* (Van-couver: Benwell Atkins Ltd., 2000), 93.

[19] It should be noted that the 164 entries indicate that some of the 149 respondents listed more than one category.

[20] Find husband or husband's employment.

[21] Left with parents; left because of war-time conscientious objector status.

[22] For further illumination of Carl Wilson's perception of himself as an agent of assimilation for students into his Anglo-Canadian culture, see *Yarrow, British Columbia,* 2: 87-94.

Bibliography

Anderson, Benedict. *Imagined Communities.* London and New York: Verso, 1983.

Derksen Siemens, Ruth. "Quilt as Text and Text as Quilt: The Influence of Genre in the Mennonite Girls' Home of Vancouver (1930-1960). *Journal of Mennonite Studies* 17 (1999): 118-29.

Epp, Marlene. *Women Without Men: Mennonite Refugees of the Second World War.* Toronto: University of Toronto Press, 2000.

Finke, Laurie. "Knowledge as bait: Feminism, voice, and the pedagogical unconscious." *College English* 55 (1993): 7-27.

Hagedorn, John M. "Neighborhoods, markets and gang drug organizations." *Journal of Research in Crime and Delinquency* 31 (1994): 264-94.

Livingstone, Sonia. "Watching talk: Gender and engagement in the viewing of audience discussion programs." *Media, Culture and Society* 16 (1994): 429-47.

McKay, Ian. *The Quest of the Fold: Antimodernism and Cultural Selection in Twentieth Century Nova Scotia.* Kingston and Montreal: McGill-Queen's University Press, 1994.

Neufeldt, Harvey. "Creating the Brotherhood: Status and Control in the Yarrow Mennonite Community, 1928-1960." *Canadian Papers in Rural History.* 9 Ed. Donald H. Akenson. Gananoque, Ontario: Langdale Press, 1994.

Neufeldt, Leonard, Lora Sawatsky and Robert Martens, eds. *Yarrow, British Columbia: Mennonite Promise*. Vol. 1 *Before We Were the Land's*. Victoria, BC: TouchWood Editions, 2002.

—— . *Yarrow, British Columbia: Mennonite Promise*. Vol. 2. *Village of Unsettled Yearnings*. Victoria, BC: TouchWood Editions, 2002.

Sawatsky, Leona Warkentin. *Close to the Earth: A Memoir*. Vancouver: Benwell Atkins, 2000.

Spitzer, Leo. *Hotel Bolivia: The Culture of Memory in a Refuge from Nazism*. New York: Hill and Wang, 1998.

Presenting Promise:
The Mennonite Memoirs of Yarrow, BC

Royden Loewen

The so-called "linguistic turn" has shifted historians' interests from the contents of a particular set of documents to the process of their genesis. Those contents are no longer considered to be "facts" useful in writing "*Geschichte wie es eigentlich gewesen*," history as it actually was, the aim of the nineteenth-century German historian, Leopold von Ranke.[1] Rather they are seen as interpretations of the past that authors publicize for unspecified reasons. The preoccupations of the post-modern critics with "discourse" have their limitations.[2] Nevertheless, speculating on the reason authors publish may reveal as much about their communities, worldviews and life aims as focusing on the content of their writings. In this paper, I speculate about the reasons why Mennonite pioneers of the community of Yarrow, British Columbia, wrote their memoirs. I look specifically at excerpts from 28 memoirs (including two detailed diaries) edited by Leonard Neufeldt and published as Parts 2 and 4 of the 2002 local history, *Before We Were the Land's*.[3]

Certainly the memoirists had a general reason for writing. Unlike letters, sermons, account books and other personal writings, a memoir is usually written in the last decade or two of one's life, while a diary is written at the end of a specific day. Both are written to leave a personal record of one's life, usually for family members or one's community. Both are deliberate products of choice; some memories are recounted and publicized, others are deliberately ignored and kept personal. Walter Ong writes in his classic *Orality and Literacy* that "'backward scanning' makes it possible in writing to eliminate inconsistencies, to choose between words with reflective selectivity that invests thought and words with new discriminatory powers."[4] What was it that the authors of the Yarrow memoirs wished their audience to know?

First, the authors seem to want the reader to know that Yarrow was a specific place; it is in British Columbia, not in Russia or the Canadian prairies that the Yarrow residents had left behind. In Rohinton Mistry's *Family Matters*, the main character, Yezad, cries out in a particularly stressful moment that he should like to leave Bombay for Toronto to "breathe . . . the pure Rocky Mountain air." His wife, Roxanna, corrects him on Canada's geography, unless Ottawa "had quietly . . . shifted them one night," the mountains comprise a distinctive place in Canada.[5] The Yarrow memoirists announce boldly that they are pioneers, Mennonites who live in and have subdued a mountain valley. They are not prairie folks. Gerald Friesen's 1985 history of prairie Canada depicts a geographical frontier, a multi-cultural cacophony, a mono-crop economy, and a region of discontentment that is a victim of federal hegemony. Marking a distinctly different region, Ruth Sandwell's 1999 edited volume on rural British Columbia, *Beyond City Limits*, speaks of tight geographies, urban-rural continuity, upward mobility, flexible and variable household economies and rurality as an "'underground' . . . identity."[6] The meaning of rurality in BC was unique. The Yarrow Mennonites' encounters with aboriginal people, their relationships with the "large city," the processes of household formation, the agricultural economy, and their sense of ethnicity all differed from their experiences in their earlier places of residence. These are important differences for the writers of the Yarrow memoirs.

A second aim of the Yarrow memoirists seems to be to show their descendants that they have "made good" in a new land. Memoirs often follow a kind of Jungian trajectory, a battleground where personal struggle is enveloped in cosmic meaning.[7] One begins in a state of vulnerability—youthful, displaced, disadvantaged, ignorant, primitive, and poor—and moves through life, acquiring experiences that leave one wiser, settled, educated, respected, wealthier, integrated, and sophisticated. The missing portions of the memoirs published in *Before We Were the Land's*, that is, references to the decade of displacement in Russia, are crucial for the intended readership, for the tragedy of Russia seems to be the beginning point in the road to the redemption that Yarrow represents. American immigration historian Orm Overland has argued that immigrant memoirs deliberately highlight cultural traits meant to win respect in the new land.[8] Were the memoirs published in *Before We Were the Land's* meant to demonstrate good Canadian citizenship? Certainly immigrant accounts of survival and triumph following encounters with Soviet atrocities would have merited the respect of Cold War Canada. "Making good" in BC with their gifts and talents would further have secured the writers their rightful and respectable place within Canada's middle class. For most of the memoirists, it was important that Yarrow was Mennonite and Christian, with its cultural markers of hard work, honesty, thrift and sobriety and thereby a full citizen in the new land.[9]

The writers describe a specific place and time, anchored in specific networks and articulated in social boundaries. The Yarrow constructed from these conceptions seems to hold a profound meaning for the memoir writers.

Place

The writers of the memoirs leave no doubt that Yarrow represents a distinctive space; therefore the move to Yarrow is not a simple relocation. It is invariably depicted as a "promised land" at the end of a treacherous journey, the end of a life that begins in Russia and crosses the Canadian prairies. And once the move to BC begins, Russia falls out of view. The "special hour of prayer for ... the Mennonites in Russia['s] ... near annihilation" held by Dietrich Rempel is unique, as is the note by Anny Goerzen that in 1954 she finally "heard that my Mama had died in [a Soviet] prison in 1941 or 42."[10]

For the majority of the memoirists, the move to British Columbia leaves Russia far behind and the new space in BC is juxtaposed with their most recent home on the Canadian prairies. Landscape becomes the symbol of that separation. As Simon Shama notes in his *Landscape and Memory*, "landscape that we suppose to be most free of our culture may turn out, on closer inspection to be its product."[11] In the Yarrow memoirs, the prairie landscape, especially its semi-arid and frigid features, is universally denounced as harsh and unsuitable for human settlement: for example, John Bargen came to Yarrow in 1927 for the simple reason that "we found the Alberta weather too severe"; Aron Martens moved after deciding "to leave the harsh winter climate of Manitoba"; Dietrich Rempel was propelled by the "dry grain fields" of Saskatchewan where wheat ears are "no higher than an upright-sitting field mouse."[12] But landscape does not only push the migrants westward, it draws them. British Columbia's temperate climate appears frequently in the travelogues. Typical is Jacob Abrahams' recollection of the "many letters from our uncle and aunt" telling "of the balmy winters, the 'Mediterranean' type climate, the abundance of fruit ... away from the icy Saskatchewan blizzard" (121). These were the elements sought after and reported by the arriving immigrants: Nickolai Reimer, for example, remembers November's fragrant roses; Jacob Krause, February's "mild spring breeze" (151, 152).

Rarely did BC's physical features spell discontent.[13] Importantly, only the two diaries that recorded memories at the end of the day contain any significant scepticism: Dietrich Rempel's diary for 23 February 1937 ridicules his neighbour who descended on Yarrow in 1935 thinking that in "BC there is no winter" (126), while Anna Kornelsen's entry for 3 December 1948, the second day in their new abode, notes that her family rose "cheerfully" that day only to face "the tall mountains around us [that] gave a gloomy impression" (246). Where problematic physical features are described in the memoirs, they almost always lead to a sort of redemption. Mountain passes become the narrow road to "Canaan." The memoir of Aron and Helena Martens speaks of fear of "very treacherous" mountain roads where unreliable brakes could spell doom, but at journey's end, at the mountain junction of Yale and Wilson on "Old Yale Road," the Martens see "below them . . . the 'Promised Land,' Yarrow, British Columbia," bidding them to hurry down the valley; once they arrive in the valley their contacts, the Janzen family, "served up a cup of coffee and a bite to eat," and all this on a balmy May evening (119). Other memoirists utter similar sentiments: John V. Friesen notes the "especially rough . . . long and all gravel" road through the Fraser Canyon, but again the road is portrayed as a "narrow passage" leading to "rich soil . . . fresh water . . . [and] fruit trees . . . that . . . surpassed the orchards . . . in the old country."[14]

The new land also provided a different kind of redemption, that is, of economic success in a new physical environment. Before the settlers lay unprecedented obstacles, especially costly land, labour-intensive agriculture, and a moist climate. Consider the comparison of Yarrow to Russia or the Canadian prairies in Elizabeth Janzen Epp's note that the farm her family purchased in 1932 had a total of 6.63 acres, and that when further acquisitions of 12 and 26 acres were made, their raspberry farm suddenly produced enough yield to provide work for 20 seasonal harvesters. In Russia the typical farmstead was 65 desiatini, or 175 acres; on the prairies, 160 acres. The annual precipitation in Russia and the prairies was little more than 15-20 inches a year; in the region between BC's coast and interior it was 40-80 inches. The main crop in both Russia and the prairies had been wheat that, with the exception of harvest day, could be produced mostly with family labour. And the newcomers' corporate poverty, rooted first in the ravages of civil war a decade earlier and then later in a costly secondary migration from the prairies, increased the economic obstacles. Still, the new conditions were tackled head on. Henry Neufeldt writes of the acquisition of 10 acres and 4 cows in Yarrow in 1929 as constituting "our third pioneering" (177). And as the settlers courageously tackled the obstacles of the new land, the land in turn promised to share its innate abundance.

As the memoirs indicate, economic success was the result of hard work and unrelenting experimentation. It is commonplace for agricultural historians to link ethnicity to a particular culture of crop selection.[15] But this argument does not extend to Yarrow. These farmers left old practices and tried new crops, unabashedly obtaining advice from the ever-present and paternalistic Chauncey E. Eckert, land agent and developer of the Sumas Plain. Without reserve the settlers recorded failures with their experimentation, but usually their final triumphs as well. The testimonials are numerous. Nickolai Reimer tried field peas for three years before worm infestations sent him to Eckert, who advised him to grow rhubarb and pole beans. While the rhubarb thrived in cow-manure rich soil, the pole beans went mouldy, so Reimer raised chickens until liver disease struck. He grafted fruit trees—apple, pear, plum, peach and cherry—and rose bushes, then, despite early losses to frost, he could exclaim that "God placed me into this vocation" and utter the valley's typical understatement of upward mobility, "we . . . did well for the next several years."[16] Other farmers readily contested cultural restraints in their farm strategies: Peter Unger who arrived from Alberta in 1940 turned the traditionally female commodity of chickens into a capitalistic endeavour—he "maximized the free help of his sons" by having "a chicken barn built for about 1500 layers." Three years later he built one for 3000 layers and, finally, earned the nomenclature "Chicken Unger" when he achieved a farm of 10,000 birds. He entered "forbidden" domains with equal bravado, trying tobacco, only to retreat after "church leaders in Yarrow...asked that he discontinue" the "nicotine weed" or "forfeit his membership."[17]

By the mid 1930s, however, a fool-proof formula had been secured by most farmers. As Aron Martens notes, Yarrow farmers "found that they could grow raspberries and supplement their income by shipping milk" (196). By the time of the post-war migration to Yarrow, the brave-hearted went directly into raspberries. Cornelius Penner notes that on a scouting trip from Regina to Yarrow in 1946, he "bought a farm with a small new four-room house and three acres of raspberries for $5000, mostly borrowed money" (240). Kathryn Regehr Neufeld writes that, in 1945, when she and her husband arrived in Yarrow from Winnipeg with the intention of establishing a printery, they at once "bought two acres of raspberries to tide us over until the print shop would bring in enough for our livelihood"(239). Raspberries would betray the Yarrow writers after World War II, but even the frequency with which the great berry bust of 1948 is mentioned in the memoirs is evidence itself of the raspberry's dominance in the valley.

Time

The Yarrow memoirists also seem eager to indicate that the early years in Yarrow constituted a specific time in their life histories. The settlers' very first challenge as refugees farming in a high-cost region was to find a source of immediate income. Money was needed for food and shelter, but also for the down payment on farmland. The settlers, unlike farm settlers on other frontiers—Russia in the eighteenth century and Manitoba in the nineteenth—

sought wage labour without hesitation or consternation. Such work could be found at the Canada Hop Company Yards and, if necessary, in nearby to-bacco fields. In fact, so many people worked in the hopfields, writes Peter Giesbrecht, that "at harvest time, the town was empty since everyone, young and old, was out picking hops" (159). The work was tedious and back-break-ing. Jacob Krause summed up his life with the following description: "the days were long then, swinging hoes in the hop gardens for eight hours, fre-quently walking all the way home, quickly consuming a meal with the family and with renewed resolve devoting additional hours to work on the house and preparing our farm land" (158). Hop fieldwork was significant for the Yarrow settlers because it was never seen as simply work, but as a step to-wards the final goal of procuring an independent farm. Heinrich Harms hints that the hopyards represented a necessary evil: "slowly but surely our farming began.... For the dairy [of two cows] the bank gave us a short-term loan, but our request for a loan to build further on the house and barn was turned down: thus we were strongly advised to find employment [and]... virtually all of us were urged to work in the Canadian Hopyards... " (167).

The work in the hopfield is described as hard but rarely exploitative. Of the 32 memoirs, only two mention any sense of class-based conflict and neither reference relates to the hopfield work. In one instance Bible School teacher Peter Loewen asked the dairyman Mr. Wells for $1.00 a day instead of 80 cents a day for his fellow workers and himself; in another instance, young Jacob Derksen and a friend confronted the rancher Mr. Spencer about an attempted "strike with the seasonal workers." Perhaps the hopyard work-ers were quiescent because they knew that Wells and Spencer had the power to fire the offending Mennonite "agitators" without hesitation. More likely, the Mennonite workers were deferential because wage labour was a path to the promise of Yarrow, the achievement of an independent farm. Neither Loewen nor Derksen relied for long on wage labour: one became a chicken broiler king, the other a successful trucking firm owner (191,187).

If the time of "field labour" marks an early state in the Yarrow commu-nity, so too does life in crude, austere and earthy conditions. A powerful symbol of primitive beginnings is the frequent reference to an intimacy with animals. A recent history, *Awe for the Tiger, Love for the Lamb,* published by UBC Press, speaks of the emotional and evocative relationships possible between people and animals.[18] As farmers, Mennonites were especially close to animals. In the wider diasporic literature of the Dutch-Russian Mennonites, these creatures of God—spiders, mice, dogs, pigs, monkeys, cows, horses, bulls—bring shame to the greedy, humour to drudgery, companionship to the lonely, and salvation to the vulnerable. The animals in the Yarrow

Mennonite memoirs possess all of these qualities, and references to animals create an atmosphere of innocent, romantic, and earthy primitiveness. Often animals put farmers to shame: farmer Sawatsky wishing to drive away the cows that moo at his bedroom window "puts on his slippers . . . steps over the threshold right into the warm calling card of a cow," leaving him "not very friendly"; apiarist Reimer drives wild bees into the hive by felling their natural habitat of a willow tree, only to face attack from a bee "commando group" leaving him with a "thickly swollen head"; farmer Harms' cousin, emulating the greed of Lot, selects the largest birds from a flock of goslings, only to find half a year later that his geese fight one another and lay no eggs. But the animals are also partners and even co-habitants in pioneer Yarrow: the horse that Jacob Krause and D. Rempel share in their travel to the Hopyards — "one of us [would] ride a stretch and then tie the horse to a tree and proceed on foot" — expedites travel and fosters a close friendship; the 10 chickens at the Peter Giesbrecht farm are welcomed inside the first residence, one designed by father and daughter Elizabeth in 1928 as a chicken barn (146, 145, 167, 232, 154, 167, 159).

According to the memoir writers the ultimate reward of this harmony with nature, of the hard work in the fields, and of the adaptation to a new climate is prosperity; early primitiveness grows into later sophistication. Innovations leading to ease are celebrated: "as soon as electricity came to the farms," writes farmer Peter Loewen, "I built our first modern chicken barn," and then he successively marks his embrace of scientific feed formulas, state-supported "supply management," and barn automation, all leading to a life that "was not difficult" (194). Diligence leading from rags to riches is given a "Horatio Alger" welcome: Cornelius Penner records the rise of the Yarrow Growers' Cooperative Union and its four nearby satellites and then, following the raspberry bust of 1948, the rise of the Mennonite-owned Sun-Ripe Fruit Packers to become the sole supplier of raspberries and strawberries for the Birds Eye and Dominion Store chains in Canada (243). Cornelius Funk juxtaposes a time when "we were poor, but we had food, shelter and clothing . . . health and happiness " with one in which he rose against odds and Eckert's advice to become a respected Yarrow miller and retailer who also owned a subsidiary in Clearbrook and planned for another in Abbotsford.[19] Often setbacks are turned into steps of advancement to prosperity: when Nickolai Reimer saw the flood of 1948 "cover . . . our nursery stock to a depth of several feet . . . we enlarged our stock," and when the frost of November 1955 killed the roses on his farm and in the entire valley, he raised his plantings by "40,000 rooted rose cuttings" (182, 152, 212). Even personal histories of individuals who never acquired the coveted independent farm could be triumphant: Henry Janzen who worked in the hopfields for eight seasons, firing one of the three hop kilns, and then sold his dairy cows and most of his land, took pride in finding "hard work" at "higher wages at the Elk Creek Waterworks" and then "profitable employment" at Pacific Coast Packers (212).

Success was seen as the well-deserved fruit of one's labour. Thus the depiction of an early, primitive life was the necessary base from which to recount upward mobility and full participation in the Fraser Valley's middle class.

Networks

The story of the community transplanted is yet another theme interwoven through the Yarrow memoirs. Yarrow is portrayed as a replicated Russian Mennonite village where church, family and street culture offer a close-knit place, set off from the wider British Columbia society.

Family and kinship lie at the heart of the so-called "group migration" that took the Mennonites to Yarrow. Sometimes the migration separated family members. When Annie Penner Klassen left for Canada in 1948, for example, she thought about "dear Johann, my mother and my brothers, Jacob and Hans" and wondered "would we ever meet again?" (127) For most of the migrants, however, the migration was a familial effort, often consisting of the entire extended family: Aron and Helen Martens arrived on a "1927 one-ton flat-deck . . . coal truck" holding an extended family; "Grandfather [was seated] on the armchair" on the deck of the truck, with "John, Jake, nine-year-old Aron and sister Sarah sitting on little benches and Father Martens and Mother in the cab."[20] And upon arriving, the whole family—father, mother and children—put their shoulders to the hoe. At the Peter and Margaretha Unger farm, "the oldest brothers had to help feed and milk the cows" and prepare the "milk for shipping," all before the "school bus arrived at 7:45 a.m.," and then "after school and in the summer all the children had jobs to do," including "working the land, planting, pruning, hoeing, picking . . . much of it . . . heavy manual work, especially for those of us who were not yet in our teens."[21] Traditional gender relations, no doubt, were tested by the unprecedented requirement for a breadwinner to leave home for the day. As the diary of Anna Goossen Kornelsen notes, shortly upon arrival in Yarrow, "the time for the men to find jobs had come" (246). For the majority of settlers, however, the daily scattering of family members was a necessary sacrifice for the familial aim of establishing an independent farm household.

In many memoirs, the transplanted family is linked closely to the replicated Mennonite community. John Bargen's January 1928 prayer, "Our Father in Heaven, give your power and blessing to make this a Mennonite settlement," does not express an isolated sentiment: Heinrich Harms recollects that everyone was "totally devoted...at the outset on establishing a closed Mennonite community"; Anne Funk Bartsch is pleased that Yarrow consists "of about 2000 persons, almost all of which were Mennonites" (170, 231). Certainly, early settlers were eager to establish networks among fellow Mennonites. Sometimes the networking began even before migration: John Bargen and Aron Martens, like many of their fellow congregants, were introduced to Yarrow through an informal letter published in the *Mennonitische Rundschau*. Subsequent conversations among its readers created a pre-Yarrow network (112). Others settlers met Mennonites en route to Yarrow. Peter D. Loewen encountered two young BC-bound Mennonite women on the train; at Abbotsford they in turn introduced him to a man who just happened to be "brother Johann Derksen," bound for Yarrow.

According to the memoirists, the new arrivals who contacted Eckert for housing often find themselves placed in communal residence: Nickolai Reimer, his wife and two children share a small cottage with a total of 15 persons, all Mennonites (145). Soon the newcomers integrate into a close-knit Mennonite community. Neighbourhoods are created and after settlement, more neighbours are added by squeezing farms in between existing ones: Rudolph Boshman's parents are able to obtain a four-acre raspberry and dairy farm in fully-settled Yarrow in 1932 because "Mr. Henry Enns was willing to sell two acres on the north side of his farm and Mr. John Dyck... two acres on the south side of his farm" (212). Occasionally it seems neighbours live too closely together and tensions arise: when Dietrich Rempel's chickens stray into the garden of J. Dyck in 1932, the Dycks have at least one for dinner and chase the others home with a note addressed to "Neighbour Rempel "that asserts "if you don't want all of your chickens ... slaughtered ... keep your feathered animals at home" (199).

Social life also develops on the streets. In the morning the hopfield workers group together to make their way to the distant fields, or as one memoirist puts it, the workers "rode their bicycles in a huge swarm, so to speak" as "those farthest away would start earliest [while] others would join them along the way to ride together" (213). In the evening, neighbours meet to discuss issues and enquire about one another's well being: when Heinrich Harms returns by BC Electric from the Chilliwack Hospital where his wife and first child first child have survived a difficult birth, upon disembarking he is accosted on the street by three to four enquiring women (168).

Close-knit community relations also led to instances of inter-Mennonite benevolence. For many settlers, it was important that mutual aid was offered at the moment of arrival. Gertrude Esau Martens writes that when her family came to Yarrow in 1928 "the railway station was too full with other families, so the John Bargens opened their house to the Esau family." Cornelius Funk, arriving in a mature community in 1933, noted that "during the first days in Yarrow we experienced the help and warmth of many friends," for "Petrus Martens . . . brought us some bread and the C. Isaak family . . . brought us a stove." Anna Goossen Kornelsen records that when she disembarked in Yarrow in December 1948, "two men, N. Reimer and J. Martens, approached," and after greeting her, "J. Martens pressed 50 dollars into my hand . . . then we went in" and life in Yarrow began. A general culture of benevolence directed all settlers. No sooner had Cornelius Funk settled in Yarrow than he returned the favours he had received as a newcomer. He cut fire wood for minister John Harder, the infirm "Mr. Boschman," and "a widow, Mrs. Wall." Peter Unger recalls that "whenever father and mother heard about a family in need, they sent us over with eggs, chickens and vegetables" (176, 217, 245, 218, 230).

At the centre of the community, of course, was the church. With remarkable consistency, however, the memoirists describe the life of the congregation not with reference to the sermons, but to the enthusiastic, corporate singing. "When all these people began to sing," writes Paul Unger, whose family had not previously attended church regularly, "I thought my ear drums would burst. I just looked around in amazement" (226). Singing was central to the religious life in Yarrow: significantly, Peter P. Giesbrecht's narrative on church life in Yarrow concludes with the words, "we had a nice choir and were happy and contented" (159). Few Yarrow residents were as revered as George Reimer, conductor of the Yarrow Mennonite Brethren Church choir. Leona Warkentin, who married in 1944, notes that "attending" Reimer's choir "became our main social outlet as a young couple." Henry Neufeldt seems to have been so energized as George Reimer's assistant that he left a successful transfer company, borrowed money and headed to Winnipeg's Mennonite Brethren Bible College to make a career of church music.[22] The culture of singing shaped the villagers' worlds at home and in public. Dietrich Rempel loved to "sing and play the piano to my heart's content" in private; after the funeral of his friend Nickolai Reimer, "when everyone was gone," he even sat down to sing "a few songs for Onkel Reimer"(198). Rudolph Boschman brought his singing to the wider world by helping to create the "Gospel Messengers Quartet" and by singing on Chilliwack Radio's Wayside Chapel, which was sponsored by the local Yarrow Freight and Fuels company and received frequent invitations to "valley churches and to weddings."[23]

The church's importance is also revealed by descriptions of church leadership, especially its power and presence in everyday culture. Some settlers celebrate the presence of Mennonite leaders. For example, when Peter Giesbrecht notes that "we had two preachers—Mr. Jacob Epp from the MB Church and Mr Bahnman from the United Mennonite Church," he also seems to announce the beginning of a legitimate community. Church leaders shape the community's very culture. They enforce strict lifestyles, descending into the tobacco field to stop the growing of the nicotine crop and entering the public school to insist that Mennonite girls wear skirts and not slacks or shorts during "PT" classes. They are the guardians of sexual purity, admonishing "church teen-agers" not to visit the Cultus Lake swimming area and counselling youth to avoid long courtships, which they see as "a poor testimony" and unnecessary in a community where "everybody knew everybody." The ministers enforce church teachings such as millennialist eschatology by excommunicating the sceptics, and they censure their critics by deliberately overlooking them in the annual New Years' ministerial housecalls. They guard the social boundaries, labelling English-language singing groups as "'tinged' with youthful rebellion" and criticize church workers who seek instruction from the outside: for example, admonishing choir conductors who travel to Vancouver to take voice lessons from "a teacher who is not a Christian" (159, 184, 173, 203, 207, 214, 182).

Boundaries

This concern for social boundaries was a crucial component of the Yarrow community. Some memoirists highlight the institutions that kept Mennonites isolated from the dynamic central Fraser Valley society. This separation took both secular and sacred forms. Henry Neufeldt describes Yarrow's local municipal council, formed because the community was "somewhat isolated from the Chilliwack Municipality," but secured by the council's willingness to organize work projects and to circumvent the Chilliwack authority if necessary by appealing directly to provincial powers in Victoria (154,180). John Harder describes the Yarrow Bible School as attracting a small, earnest group of students wishing to maintain the cultural boundaries around Yarrow. At age fourteen he was enrolled at the Bible School "against my wishes" in order that he might be provided "with a grounding in the scriptures and an understanding of our Mennonite heritage." He returned to school again at age seventeen when World War II broke out because his parents again "feared for my spiritual welfare."[24]

The frequent expressions of boundary maintenance reflect a binary opposition between the inside and the outside worlds. Because the Mennonite newcomers arrived in a densely populated part of a province in which they themselves did not have a critical mass, themes of inter-ethnicity take on particular meaning. The personal writings of Ontario and prairie Mennonites note many instances of inter-ethnic friendships, marriages, and business arrangements, as well as encounters with government agencies, both helpful agricultural representatives and threatening school inspectors. But the nature of inter-ethnic relations in BC was unique, shaped by the province's history. The rural districts of British Columbia, for example, were much less ethnic than those of the three prairie provinces. In British Columbia, only 25% of the population in 1931 was ethnic, non-British, non-French and non-Aboriginal, compared to 44% in Manitoba, 45% in Alberta and 52% in Saskatchewan. This meant that an Anglo-Canadian culture dominated on the coast in a way it did not on the prairies, home to large numbers of Germans, Ukrainians and Scandinavians.[25]

Several memoirists note that BC residents of British descent were not especially friendly towards the Mennonites. Jacob Krause recalls that Mennonite newcomers were confused with the radical anarchist Doukhobors, frightened by a so-called "local friend" who "reminded us that high water would soon drive us out" and disparaged by predictions that Mennonites "would undoubtedly become a burden to the taxpayer." John Harder recalls that discrimination at the Chilliwack school because of "our German speaking background" made us "not want to be identified with our Mennonite German background." Susie Alice Giesbrecht Derksen recalls that "the people of the valley were not too happy with the immigration," that in school Anglo-Canadian children forced Mennonite braids into ink wells, that attendance at Normal or Nursing School was discouraged because "Mennonites were discriminated against," and that when Mr. Rowlands, the storekeeper, hired her, "a Mennonite girl," clients threatened that they would "never come into his store again.[26]

Most often, however, it was Mennonites who constructed the social boundaries. In fact, they referred to the wider society that lay outside of Yarrow as "Jantzied," meaning "the other side."[27] Although references to other groups are rarely openly hostile, tell-tale signs of insecurity, fear, and condescension interlace the memoirs. With the exception of British-Canadians to whom the Mennonites defer, or Dutch or German-speaking associates with whom they work, members of other ethnic groups remain unmentioned by name. Inevitably they are kept at a distance, notwithstanding an oftentimes implicitly warm regard for them. Susie Alice Giesbrecht Derksen recalls with gratitude that her family was directed to Nelson, BC, by Doukhobors familiar with that community, and she seems to respect the aboriginal field workers at the hopfields, recalling visiting them "from cabin to cabin" to sell them "our produce" and observing them "several times a week as they had powwows." But with neither the Doukhobors nor the aboriginal neighbours are there signs of more than a passing secondary relationship.[28] In fact, usually outsiders are cast sceptically. They include the Vancouver merchant who convinced the Mennonite farmers to entrust him with their pea harvest, just before both "the man and the peas disappeared" and the Lindberg-baby-kidnapper copycats who attempted to extort money from Mennonite families in which there were baby daughters (196,185). Oftentimes, members of specific groups are disparaged: Chinese gardeners are admired from a distance, but close up their thrift and haggling brings mistrust (200,232). Members of some racial minorities go unseen: the only mention of Japanese neighbours is by farmer Abram Esau, who refers to them quite indirectly: Esau writes that because "hundreds of Japanese families were moved to various places in Alberta," Esau's neighbours, the Balzers, were able to "move onto a Japanese berry farm," a move that in turn allowed the Balzers to "make their house available to us," the Esaus.[29] Ironically, even the Mennonite Conscientious Objectors [CO] who encountered members of other racial groups created personal boundaries; in fact some of the memoirists imply that working alongside members of racial minorities somehow spells humiliation: when one Yarrow CO encounters Chinese Canadians, it is in the context of being sent to the "very 'bottom' of the ladder," sledging lime rock alongside "a few Chinese"; when another CO encounters "natives" on a ranch, it is in a context of intolerable "conditions"(174, 185).

However, the social boundaries created by the Mennonites enabled secondary relationships with British-Canadian business associates and neighbours and German-speaking labourers and travellers. When Susie Alice Giesbrecht, the woman who encountered Doukhobors and Aboriginal people, prepared to marry Jake Derksen, she went out of her way to invite "our English speaking friends" (164). Peter and Margaretha Unger also cultivated warm relations with "first a Dutch family and then a German family" who ran their dairy, and similar ties linked Heinrich Harms to a "woman, already a grandmother, who had emigrated from Europe some years ago," who loyally supervised a work gang to harvest his raspberries (229, 171). Deference characterizes business relationships with Anglo-Canadian or Anglo-American businessmen. In these memoirs, Chauncey Eckert sells land parcels to the Mennonites on credit, advises them in settlement strategies, sells commodities on their behalf, lends rooms in his houses, and at all times is "a very patient man while waiting for payments... not hard on anyone who could not pay" (159, 146, 145, 201, 217, 218). Other Canadian businessmen are venerated. No one, however, is iconized as much as lumberman Orion Bowman, who agreed to exchange lumber to build the new Mennonite Brethren church building for labour at his sawmill, plus the perk of being allowed to "play his violin for the congregation during an evening service."[30]

In summary, these memoirs reveal that the Yarrow Mennonites constructed imagined boundaries around their community. On a primary level they fully trusted only members of their own religious and ethnic community; on a secondary level they respected English and German economic associates. Members of racial minorities were usually faceless folks, given to strange customs and a "trickster" trading culture, people definitely on the "other side" of the social boundary that demarcated Yarrow.

Meaning

What did Yarrow mean for the writers of the memoirs? The documents certainly possess enough religious content to suggest that memoir writing itself was a religious act, an opportunity to witness to one's faith. Leona Warkentin Sawatsky relates how she poured out "her heart to God" on behalf of her children, scattered between Saskatchewan, war-time France, and the Soviet Gulag (225). Henry Janzen who arrived in Yarrow in 1932 at a time when even "established old farmers could hardly manage to stay afloat" credits "the good Lord's help...that we made it." Abram Esau recalls his day off from the Sardis dairy farm, "walking by myself and talking with the Lord about what He might have for me" (225, 211, 172, 168). But just as indicative of Yarrow's deeply religious culture are the descriptions of religious conflict that pit elders against youth, lay people against preachers, and pious mothers against careless fathers. Religion was important enough to generate deeply felt emotions. Cornelius David Toews's father chastises the conscientious objectors who have "no personal convictions about pacifism," seeking only "to avoid joining the armed forces"; Dietrich Rempel cites church ministers for "glib, habitual expressions" and for ignoring "the suffering that exists in such abundance"; John Harder writes that his baptism occurred to "allay my fears and in response to my parents' wishes as well as to peer influences" (235, 208, 186, 184). Religious practice in Yarrow was encased in emotion and highly intentional.

The memoirs themselves, however, clearly indicate that other motivations besides religious duty shaped the course of life for the Yarrow Mennonites. The Yarrow Mennonites, like all immigrants, came with multiple aims. They came with religious purpose, desiring to turn their daily struggle into a cosmic battle, one in which God guided, led, chastised, rewarded, and then blessed with close communion during the singing of German hymns of heartfelt thanksgiving and spiritual submission. But the Yarrow settlers also wished to build a familiar community, one which facilitated a dynamic interface between earthy Low German and pietistic High German. Here they could take steps to embrace what bits and pieces of isolation were given them. And here they embellished the geographic lines around Yarrow by envisioning non-Mennonites as outsiders, by being sceptical of the racial minorities below them on Canada's "vertical mosaic" but deferential to the cultural groups above them. The Mennonites also clearly wished to survive and thrive financially; they seemed to welcome wealth and ease when they presented themselves, not for their own sake, but as cultural markers of well-being and worthiness. In these memoirs the bar of respectability is reached when both financial resources and evangelical faith are secure. The Yarrow memoirs are the record of a people in an envisioned "promised land." Presumably, the villagers who did not make good in the "promised land" did not write their memoirs. But then we may never know.

Endnotes

[1] Leopold Von Ranke, "The Ideal of Universal History," in *The Varieties of History: From Voltaire to the Present*, ed. Fritz Stern (London: McMillan, 1970), 54-62.

[2] Paul A. Bové, "Discourse," in *Critical Terms for Literary Study,* ed. Frank Lentricchia and Thomas McLaughlin (Chicago: University of Chicago Press, 1995), 50-65.

[3] See: Leonard Neufeldt, Lora Sawatsky and Robert Martens, eds., *Yarrow, British Columbia: Mennonite Promise*, vol. 1, *Before We Were the Land's* (Victoria, BC: Touch Wood Editions, 2002).For a fuller account of the community, see also the companion volume, Neufeldt, *Village of Unsettled Yearnings.* To have so many primary sources—collected, translated, edited, introduced—at the ready, in front of the historian, is itself like walking into a "promised land." Several notes of caution are necessary before proceeding to use these memoirs as primary sources. These works are abridged versions of the original memoirs and thus have undergone two "selection" processes, first, by the original author and second, by the editor, who has shortened the documents to enable their publication. Then, too, there is no guarantee that these literary pieces were representative of the community: about 21 of the writers were men and 11, women; 26 were Russlaender Mennonites who left the Soviet Union in the 1920s and of these 23 were secondary migrants from the prairie provinces (4 from Alberta, 9 from Manitoba, 10 from Saskatchewan); 4 were secondary migrants from Mexico; of the migrants, 11 arrived in BC in the late 1920s, in 1927 or 1928, 12 came in the Depression years, 5 during the war years, and 3 were Displaced Persons who arrived in 1948. Of the memoirists, 20 were adults upon arriving in Yarrow, 9 were children, 3 were not yet born when their parents moved to Yarrow. Only a full demographic analysis of Yarrow could judge the representativeness of these memoirists. In the end, however, the facts that the editor's self- described task was to shorten the memoirs without losing the integrity of the authors' voices and that certain themes reoccur in these personal writings suggest that mean-

ingful observations of the world view of the Yarrow memoirists and diarists can be made.

[4] Walter J. Ong, *Orality and Language: The Technologizing of the Word* (New York: Methuen, 1982), 104.

[5] Rohinton Mistry, *Family Matters* (Toronto: McClelland and Stewart, 2002), 263.

[6] Gerald Friesen, *The Canadian Prairies: A History* (Toronto: University of Toronto, 1985). Ruth Sandwell, ed. *Beyond the City Limits: Rural History of British Columbia* (Vancouver: UBC Press, 1999), 5, 11.

[7] Carl G.Jung, "Approaching the Unconscious," in *Man and His Symbols*, ed. C. C. Jung (New York: Doubleday, 1964), 3-94.

[8] Overland Orm, *Immigrant Minds, American Identities: Making the United States Home, 1870-1930* (Urbana, Illinios: University of Illinois Press, 2000).

[9] Adamoski, Chunn and Menzies, *Contesting Canadian Citizenship* (Peterborough, ON: Broadview, 2002).

[10] Neufeldt, *Yarrow, British Columbia: Mennonite Promise*, 119, 124. Subsequent citations from this volume will be indicated in the text

[11] Simon Scahma, *Landscape and Memory* (New York: Knopf, 1995), 9.

[12] Neufeldt, 112, 118, 120, 116. See other examples in the memoirs of Jacob V. Friesen and Dietrich Rempel, ibid, 115 and 201.

[13] See also the memoirs of Nickolai Reimer, who blames "rain . . . every day and a heavy cloud cover" in February 1928 for not being able to establish cardinal points, Annie Goerzen, who complains of "high mountains silhouetted against the sky" standing between her and Yarrow, Dietrich Rempel, who describes the flooding Sumas River in 1935 [as] "water . . . claiming its [historic] rights" and the October 1936 frost that killed "carrots, beets and apples." Significantly, each of these descriptions is followed by very positive notes about BC's weather. See Adamoski, 146, 127, 205, 206.

[14] Ibid., 116. For other examples see the memoir of Jacob Abrams, who describes the very narrow "Canada . . . Number One," ibid., 121.

[15] For a discussion of this phenomenon see Loewen, "Ethnic Farm Culture in Western Canada," *Canada Ethnic Group Series* 29 (Ottawa: Canadian Historical Association, 2002).

[16] Neufeldt, *Before we were the Land's*, 151. See also the memoir of Jacob Krause and Heinrich Harms, both of whom experimented with a variety of crops. Ibid, 156 and 171.

[17] Ibid., 227, 230. Eventually the Ungers also constructed a large 25-30 cow dairy, cultivated a 10-12 acre berry farm, built a 150 foot-long hog barn, experimented with "pole beans" and turkeys, and undertook custom work.

[18] Preece, *Awe for the Tiger, Love for the Lamb* (New York: Routledge, 2003). Animals, insects and birds, too, are intertwined with the divine in the thoughts of these agrarian people. See the following examples: of a mouse in Regehr, *Mennonites in Canada*, xv; of a spider in Wiebe, *Causes and History of the Emigration of the Mennonites From Russia to America*; of a herd of pigs in Loewen, *Family, Church and Market*, 189; of a dog in Abram Friesen, *The Von Riesen-Friesen Genealogy [Sic]*, 1756-1961, 31, 206. The story of a monkey sending a message from God to a kidnapped Mennonite was told to me by Klaas L. Friesen, while the account of a bull rescuing a driver stuck in mud near Rosenort, Manitoba, was told to me by H.K. Friesen.

[19] He concludes with a note of humility and thanksgiving: "who could ask for more than to be able to carry on a vocation that is thoroughly enjoyable and satisfying."Neufeldt, 217.

[20] Ibid., 118. When newcomers arrived, the kin that had preceded them often became a central resource: Abram Esau recalls that he and his family arrived late in 1928 to settle on a 10 acre parcel "reserved for us by our uncle," presumably Nickolai Reimer. Ibid, 171.

[21] Ibid., 227. When parents became incapacitated, children in school who were aiming for the professions had no choice but to support their family, as young Aron Martens experienced upon his father's death in 1938: "Aron had to get a job to support mother, grandfather Martens, grandmother Abrahams and brother Victor." Ibid, 197.

[22] Ibid., 225, 182. Another example of the value Yarrow residents placed on sacred music occurred when Aron Martens dropped out of school after his father died in 1938 to assist his younger brother Victor to study in Winnipeg and then in Detmold, Germany, for the simple reason that he "wanted to be a musician" and that "he was a talented young man" (Ibid., 197).

[23] Ibid., 215, 198, 208. When Dietrich Rempel was forced to sell the piano for financial reasons his only consolation was that "now the angels sing for me" (Ibid, 198).

[24] Ibid., 185. A measure of the limited success of the strategy of building a Bible School was John's decision to leave his position as conscientious objector on a BC interior ranch, hitchhike to Vancouver and join the Canadian Army as a medic, returning to Yarrow "dressed in full uniform" and then make the RCAF his career home after the war, where he worked, but only as an educator and social worker and not in a combat position. Ibid., 187.

[25] Roy, "British Columbia's Fear of Asians," 162-72. For related studies that link racism and rurality in BC see: Koppel, *Kanaka*; Adachi, *The Enemy that Never Was*; and Stadfield, 33-45.

[26] Neufeldt, *Before We Were the Land's*, 157, 184, 160, 163. It seems that at least some of these remarks came from members of a host society in a restrictive economic environment; in fact, one of the Mennonite writers recalled that upon arrival from Manitoba in 1930 he heard utterances in church that the newcomers "will surely take our jobs away." Ibid., 195.

[27] Conversation with David Giesbrecht, Abbotsford, BC, 2 June 2003. Ironically, the word "Jantzied" was used by Mennonites in Manitoba to denote the Mennonite community on the "otherside" of the Red River, thus giving it an inherently friendly meaning in Manitoba.

[28] In fact her family's stay at Nelson BC was short-lived because, as she put it, "there were no young people there except Doukhobors." Ibid.,114, 161.

[29] Ibid., 174. Despite charges of anti-Semitism that have been levelled against Soviet Mennonites, only one set of comments in these abridged memoirs counter the evangelical dispensationalist teaching of Jews being a privileged people; the only one that specifically mentions Jews, the memoir of Anny Goerzen, recalls "our Jewish friends, Mary and Joseph" who "were eager to help" them as they left the Soviet Union and "treasured the spiritual fellowship" and "asked that we pray . . . that God would have mercy upon them." Ibid, 125.

[30] Ibid., 196. E.D. Smith of Winona is praised by Cornelius Penner as the one who bought an initial "small carload of frozen raspberries" from Penner

and then allowed his firm to become Smith's "sole supplier for many years...."
Ibid, 242.

Bibliography

Adachi, Ken. *The Enemy That Never Was: A History of the Japanese Canadians.* Toronto: McCLelland and Stewart, 1976.

Adamoski, Robert, Dorothy E. Chunn and Robert Menzies. *Contesting Canadian Citizenship: Historical Readings.* Peterborough, ON: Broadview, 2002.

Bové, Paul, A. "Discourse." *Critical Terms for Literary Study*, Ed. Frank Lentricchia and Thomas McLaughlin. Chicago: University of Chicago Press, 1995.

Friesen, Abram P, et al, ed. The VonRiesen-Friesen Genealogy [Sic], 1756-1966. Steinbach, MB: Author, 1967.

Friesen, Gerald. *The Canadian Prairies: A History.* Toronto: University of Toronto, 1985.

Jung, Carl G., "Approaching the Unconscious," *Man and His Symbols.* Ed. C. C. Jung. New York: Doubleday, 1964.

——— , ed. *Man and His Symbols.* New York, Doubleday, 1964.

Koppel, Tom. *Kanaka: The Untold Story of Hawaiian Pioneers in the Pacific Northwest.* Vancouver: Whitecap, 1995.

Loewen, Royden. "Ethnic Farm Culture in Western Canada. *Canada Ethnic Group Series*, Booklet # 29. Ottawa: Canadian Historical Association, 2002.

——— . *Family, Church and Market: A Community in the Old and New Worlds.* Urbana, IL: University of Illinois Press, 1993.

Mistry, Rohinton. *Family Matters.* Toronto: McClelland and Stewart, 2002.

Neufeldt, Leonard, Lora Sawatsky and Robert Martens, eds. *Yarrow, British Columbia: Mennonite Promise.* Vol. 1. *Before We Were the Land's,* Victoria, BC: Touch Wood Editions, 2002.

——— . *Yarrow British Columbia: Mennonite Promise.* Vol. 2. *Village of Unsettled Yearnings.* Victoria, BC: Touch Wood Editions, 2002.

Orm, Overland. *Immigrant Minds, American Identities: Making the United States Home, 1870-1930.* Urbana, Illinios: University of Illinois Press, 2000.

Ong, Walter J. *Orality and Language: The Technologizing of the Word.* New York: Methuen, 1982.

Preece, Rod. *Awe for the Tiger, Love for the Lamb: A Chronicle of Sensibility to Animals.* Vancouver: UBC Press, 2002.

Regehr, T.E. *Mennonites in Canada: A People Transformed.* Toronto: University of Toronto Press, 1996.

Roy, Patricia. "British Columbia's Fears of Asians." *Histoire Sociale/Social History*, 25 (1980).

Sandwell, Ruth, ed. *Beyond the City Limits: Rural History of British Columbia.* Vancouver: UBC Press, 1999.

Scahma, Simon. *Landscape and Memory.* New York: Knopf, 1995.

Stadfield, Bruce. "Manifestations of Power: Native Resistance to the Resettlement of British Columbia." *Beyond the City Limits: Rural History of British Columbia.* Ed. Ruth Sandwell. Vancouver: UBC Press, 1999, 33-45.

Von Ranke, Leopold. "The Ideal of Universal History," *The Varieties of History: From Voltaire to the Present.* Ed. Fritz Stern. London: McMillan, 1970. 54-62.

Wiebe, Gerhard. *Causes and History of the Emigration of the Mennonites from Russia to America*, 1898. Trans. Helen Jantzen. Winnipeg: Manitoba Historical Society, 1981.

Personal Communication

Friesen, H.K., Steinbach, Manitoba, June 2002.
Friesen, Klaas, L. Spanish Lookout, Belize, December, 1992.
David Giesbrecht, Abbotsford, British Columbia, 2 June 2003.

PART IV

Educational Institutions
and the Arts

"Where berries grow and rivers run to sea": Memory and Metaphor in Leonard Neufeldt's *Raspberrying*

Maryann Tjart Jantzen

Literary writing by Mennonite Canadians has flourished during the past two decades, with authors like Rudy Wiebe, Sarah Klassen, and Di Brandt receiving national acclaim. In their fiction and poetry, these writers have communicated important insights into the larger Mennonite story and how it has shaped contemporary Mennonite life narratives, capturing complex emotional and thematic nuances often not communicated by historical details. These authors have helped Canadian Mennonites move from being the "quiet in the land" to becoming more actively engaged with Canadian culture. But thus far, few Mennonite authors writing out of a British Columbia context have been acknowledged in critical discussion. Leonard Neufeldt, who grew up in Yarrow and served as editor for the recently published two volume history of Yarrow, has also published the poetry collections, *Raspberrying* (1991) and *Yarrow* (1993), which significantly contribute to understandings of the cultural dynamics of mid-century Mennonite life in the central Fraser Valley.

Through literary analysis of a representative selection of poems from Neufeldt's *Raspberrying* volume, I want to imaginatively revisit the rich cultural past constructed in his poetry. I work from the assumption that mid-twentieth-century raspberry culture contributed significantly to both Mennonite economic survival and cultural continuity while also facilitating assimilation into the larger economic and social framework of the central Fraser Valley. Through examining Neufeldt's literary landscape and by utilizing the symbiotic relationship between poetry and memory, I will access a unique and transient historical moment (the 1930s-60s) in a particular place (the central Fraser Valley village of Yarrow). Poetry and memory have obvious affinities; both often function as embodied history, not history of facts and figures but of emotional and sensory remembering, mediated through an impressionistic tactile recreation of the sights, smells, and emotional ambiences of a specific place and time.

I) Memory and Metaphor

The poem "Raspberries Are Not Easily Gotten Rid of," which playfully articulates the memory motif that informs the entire volume, metaphorically explores the power of the past to imaginatively inform the present. Emphasizing the tenacity and unpredictability of raspberry plants, Neufeldt writes,

> Raspberries have ways of coming back
> years later in fields turned out to pasture
> or littered with food wrappers, posts without wires
> rotting full-length in wet grass[1]

Here Neufeldt uses raspberry plants as a metaphor for the pervasiveness of the past. Like raspberry shoots which sprout up where they are least expected, memories emerge out of nowhere, reminding us of the past from which we come. The poem suggests that we are irrevocably shaped by past environments and experiences, carrying traces of them wherever we go. Just as in the poem we can see traces of the past (the pasture field, the rotting posts) on present landscape (in this poem "the builder's stakes and gravel for the new road"), we bring with us into the present unavoidable and unpredictable traces of the past.

In stanza two, Neufeldt humorously suggests that in unlikely places (Texas, Indiana, Princeton, Lake Champlain) far from home, places perhaps not hospitable to either raspberry culture or inherited cultural traditions, remnants of the past will emerge when least expected, like "vines" which in "ones and twos will cross the hot pavement" and "root where rattlers wait for the sun to set." I'm sure all of us have experienced, in unexpected moments, the way that a memory remnant—a recalled image, word or deed, smell or taste—can impact us, despite our present geographical and psychological locations. Recently while I was pruning an ornamental hop vine for the winter, the acrid smell of the crushed hop flowers, an odour I had not encountered since early childhood, instantly transported me back almost fifty years to the sights and smells of the hop fields in Sardis, where I had picked alongside my mother and grandmother. Thus, sudden memories, like raspberries, reach "out beyond the row" and "catch each part of [us] unawares," sometimes in very uncomfortable and prickly ways. It's as if memories are the visible evidence of a past that still unconsciously inhabits and informs our present sense of self.[2]

The poem uses the lines "more than once raspberries have crossed oceans/ as lost luggage" to further develop this idea. The playful assertion that, "When that happens Newbergs come as Washingtons, / and Washingtons as Willamettes, / and Willamettes as all-season/ all-weather blight resistant stock" emphasizes the way in which memory is simultaneously persistent and subjective, but not necessarily always factually reliable. It's the imaginative essence of a thing, its emotional power, which both poetry and memory bring back to us, not linear time lines or exact recreations of behaviour or belief. Thus, individuals who have shared similar experiences can have very different impressions, something I discovered again when, in preparation for writing this paper, I gathered some friends for a lunch spent discussing raspberry memories. I remember being anxious at age eleven to starting picking raspberries at a neighbouring farm, eager to encounter "the blond new berry stand with its dusty feet, / and bushes triumphant with red/ of ripened berries" (15). I viewed picking as a privilege, as an initiation into a larger world, a social extension of my limited horizons. In contrast, one of my friends remembers it as childhood slave labour, claiming she was dragged kicking and screaming at age nine to berry patch drudgery. Likewise, even now each summer I can hardly wait for the taste burst of the first berry of the season, while my sister has vowed to never again eat a raspberry, so sated did she become after numerous summers spent picking and processing berries.

II) Beginnings

The two recently published Yarrow history volumes, especially Volume 2, *Village of Unsettled Yearnings*, provide ample documentation of the importance of raspberry growing in central Fraser Valley Mennonite communities during the 1930s and 1940s, as Mennonite refugees arrived, lured by newly available rich agricultural land created by the diking and draining of Sumas Lake. Growing raspberries, along with other labour intensive cash crops, provided welcome economic opportunities, while also facilitating familial and cultural continuity as the tasks of planting, pruning, weeding, picking and processing provided local employment for family members of various ages, from mothers with young children and adolescents in the berry patch to young adults and primary wage earners working in the canneries which sprang up to process the crops.[3]

The poem entitled "Message by the Rev. Peter Neufeldt" speaks of the desire and longing of displaced Mennonite refugees arriving in Yarrow for a new homeland into which to sink their roots. Focusing on the immigrants' discovery of a new world while they are still lamenting the old, the poem communicates a strong longing for cultural continuity, articulating the communal intent and desire to transplant important long-held values, beliefs and cultural practices into a new context. The speaker of the poem tells us, "we travelled lightly when we left the Old World" (38), reminding us that these refugees could bring very little of economic value with them, but suggesting also that they travelled not so lightly in emotional and cultural baggage. The travelers are "ready to protect whatever came with us: for example, the solitude of growing seasons." Here the speaker seems to be alluding to the traditional Mennonite quiet-in-the-land lifestyle of cultural and geographical separation from the larger world. A subsequent line, "Exile, obedience, freedom, departure, song" merges the sorrow of exile and departure from the old homeland with the new hope of freedom to live according to inherited values and cultural prac-

Man and woman with raspberry stand

tices in a new promised land. As historical scholars have observed, spatially the village of Yarrow was modelled on the layout of Russian Mennonite villages, an orientation that visibly reminds us of the Mennonite settlers' desire to retain their traditional cultural values.

In this poem, Neufeldt's use of a song motif alerts us to how cultural values are passed on through music and also points to the process of merging the departed past and the insecure present into a hopeful future. Words from a well-known German hymn—*"Ich kenn einen Strom dessen herrliche Flut/ fliesst wunderbars stille durch's Land"* (38) [4]—transform the majestic view of the Fraser River greeting the weary travelers into a metaphor for God's grace. Significant lines in the poem create an image of a fluid harmonious river of song that merges the identities of the past with the emerging present to create a longed for future:

> starting what we know, what our children will complete,
> that part of ourselves that sings when the next page
> is missing, when we're unsure
> and watch each other for half-formed words.

The travellers are singing their way into the new land of "Yarrow," where

> the river would turn from the rock-blue wall
> to find a valley and the deep centre of the Canal
> running to the Fraser behind Sumas Mountain (39).

Further, the image of the travellers pausing earlier at the "the Great Divide/ . . . There, the cordillera of a new continent" separating a "future from the past," also emphasizes the enormity of the new beginning, the finality of the past and the hope of a healing future.[5]

III) For Better or Worse

Stanza 3 of "Dyke Berry Farm" celebrates the economic prosperity of the early 1940s, when berries hung "like jewels on overladen bushes." Yarrow bustled with "crops palpable as geese/returning by thousands" (11), carried on their way to market in the United States by "fresh-painted Co-op trucks " leaking "raspberries/ down Highway 11 past the U.S. Customs officers . . . ." Each spring saw optimistically planted new fields of raspberry canes. But as anyone who has grown raspberries knows, raspberries are fragile and, like roses, have thorns. Twentieth-century raspberry horticulture in the Fraser Valley was characterized by boom and bust cycles. Although small-scale raspberry production remained a vital part of Mennonite rural life until the 1970s, the growing prosperity of the early and mid 1940s gave way to the disappointment and economic hardships of the post-WW II period as the British market for raspberries dried up and many central Fraser Valley raspberry fields were destroyed by the 1948 flood.

Two poems, "The '48 Flood," and "Mother," focus on the thorny side of raspberry growing while also alerting us to cultural and social nuances of the period. The first one, "The '48 Flood," depicts the power of the surging Vedder River to sweep away all in its path. Its rapidly swelling waters are pictured as threatening to wash away the restraining dykes, imagery which also metaphorically points to the "softening" of the dykes of cultural isolation and the coming flood of cultural assimilation through its depiction of young men, who like the river feel the urge to "break out/ the other side" (41). The Vedder "uproots berry fields, two-room shacks/ and corkscrew willows in the flood plain," softening "the heart of the dyke," and "seeping from field to berry field/ finding basements from below, filling them/ with shimmering night, drowning/ salamanders, spiders, stray cats." Like the flood-force of the rising river, with its power to breach the dykes, a current of desire swells in restless young men who "feel the desire to rush overtop/ this one time, to break out/ the other side," while "Mothers past childbearing chide daughters/ and pray indulgently for sons in the fields."[6] As is typical in first-generation immigrant communities, the adolescents and young adults seek to breach the boundaries between themselves and their larger cultural context, while the older adults resist the onslaught of assimilation, attempting to retain cultural continuity.

While the second poem depicting this period is simply called "Mother," its first section narrates the speaker's memories of Charlie Fong, the anomalous Chinese man who lived his solitary life "on land leased from Mrs. Riesen" (24), raising "the largest potatoes I had ever seen," while speaking to his Mennonite neighbours of his "children north of Canton, / where they had moved because of the war" (25). Section ii focuses on the speaker's mother conversing with Charlie Fong, both "speaking too fast for me to understand, / diaspora of sentences, dialect of the displaced." English, a second language for both, is their common mode of communication. As the speaker listens, he shivers "among potato sacks/ that turned to stone soldiers," an evocation of steely coldness that ironically reminds the reader of the violent history of these displaced persons who meet in this land of peace.

The poem ends with a litany of economic hardships as the speaker relives his mother's evening prayers, "her fingers berry-stained," praying to a God "immune to Co-op statistics and red potatoes" (27), who could "shape a new world out of/ falling prices, raspberry fields,/ Clay harder than jute sacks of new potatoes,/ and all the dispossessed from Adam/ to Yarrow, British Columbia, and you, Charlie Funk,/ and her children, children's children/ walking up Sabbath-ripe rows, raspberrying." Here, the young speaker's humorous ethnocentric linguistic transposition of Funk for Fong suggests the process, typical of displaced individuals, of trying to understand difference by viewing it through a familiar filter. Also significant is the way Neufeldt again picks up the promised land motif through use of Sabbath and edenic new world imagery; however, here this biblical allusion is ironically juxtaposed with the harsh reality of Charlie Fong, perpetually displaced, unable to bring his family to Canada because of the exclusion laws. The poet reminds us that not all hopeful travellers to British Columbia found the promised land of their dreams. And yet the poem also reminds us of how personal experiences of hardship are often crucial in motivating us to offer hospitality to strangers. The common experience of cultural and economic displacement creates an unlikely bond between the Mennonite mother and the Chinese father: significantly, the mother's hope for the future includes not only her children, but also Charlie Fong's children, all "raspberrying" together.[7]

IV) Growing Up Raspberrying

The poem "Handbook for Berrypickers" provoked in me powerful personal memories rich with sensory impressions: the majestic visual canvas of mountains and sky, changing light playing against grey-green sun-dappled bushes, the red jewel tones and sharp taste tingle of sun-warmed raspberries, the scratchy prickle of tiny thorns, and the sun-baked smell of dusty earth.[8] In stanza one, the speaker of the poem recreates for the novice picker the sensory sights, sounds and smells of a Fraser Valley raspberry field at dawn —

the sky will awaken with purple, the
mountains south and north, then the sun.
Blue insouciance will walk through mists
on the valley floor for another hour (14).

— and later, the speaker cites the sight and sound of "two dive-bombing killdeer protecting nests unseen" and a "spider's thread of light, transparent." Then, as the picking begins, we hear the "power of voices in dying shadows" and "laughter of pure colour" juxtaposed with the "endposts bold with jackets and yellow straw hats."

In my adolescent experience, the raspberry patch was an intensely social place, even though pickers, with their "lightly stained fingers," were separated by rows often higher than they were. While mothers might forego conversation, too busy with supervising young children and checking rows to make sure that older children had picked all the ripe raspberries, restless adolescents found creative ways to interact across the rows, "baring shoulders one at a time, slowly as a confession." Singing "unguarded songs" was a popular way to pass the time, throwing the occasional berry or dirt clod at one's picking neighbour was an exciting misdemeanour, and when transistor radios became common in the early '60s, worldly rock 'n roll music often censored at home would float across the rows, energizing lagging pickers and speaking seductively of another more exotic world. Adolescent romantic ardour also occasionally blossomed, often communicated in socially inept ways, as is humorously depicted in Neufeldt's "Garter Snakes" poem, where the adolescent speaker and his complicit peers, their entranced eyes caught by "Betty Wedel," who walks "the shimmering rows/ upright as a hallelujah" (17), show their interest in her by sending "our best berries from hiding, aim surer than the messages/ we wanted to be found out/. But only half understood" and by dropping "A frantic garter snake/ into the wind-filled back of her blouse."[9]

Of course, lunch time also provided opportunities for social interaction, as sandwiches tinted red by raspberry-stained hands were devoured in the cooling shade of berry bushes. Experienced raspberry pickers will also remember the "numbness" of standing "against the rain . . . / breast to breast with mostly unpicked berry bushes" (15). At the end of the day, chilled pickers would be thankful for the appreciated luxury of a hot cleansing bath and a rejuvenating hearty Mennonite meal prepared from the first harvests of the summer, perhaps Cabbage *Borscht* or *Bohnensuppe* (bean soup) or, on a sunnier day, *Erbose* (watermelon) and *Rollkuchen* (fritters), or fresh cucumbers in *diche milch* (clabbered sour milk). Poignantly, however, the poem also emphasizes the power of a particular place to leave its traces on our personal identity, no matter how far we travel from our origins. Neufeldt suggests that this youthful raspberry patch experience will indelibly shape the picker's sense of self, no matter how far he or she will wander in the future:

> The day will bring your life
> this far, will lose it nearer the light,
> will attach what remains of you
> to the hard earth underfoot ... (15).

V) Passing away: Assimilation and Autonomy

From the berry-picking endeavours of early adolescence, many young people in Fraser Valley Mennonite communities moved on to working in local canneries, where they could earn, in the early '60s, the princely starting wage of approximately 70 cents an hour. By the early '70s this had increased to about $1.25 an hour. The poem "The Cannery Manager, Mr. Penner" poignantly captures not only the routine busyness of "another week of picking, processing, shipping" (36) during a rainy summer, but also the cultural and generational tension between the manager and the young men he has fired for their "folly of writing the Labor Board" about the perceived deficiencies of their working conditions. Mr. Penner strains to grasp the growing gap in understanding between those who have experienced "the harvest requisitions,/ [the] "drought and hunger" of life lived at the beck and call of the Soviet communist regime, and the brash young who attempt to "steal morale in this summer of rain," accepting individual rights and economic advancement as their birthright. He puzzles over the growing generational divide as "children born of blandishment / have come like exiles among us."

This generational tension also emerges in the poem, "The Young Women of Yarrow," where in church the young women defer to the "bosswoman" (29)—the stern and authoritative "woman's usher" who keeps them in their place, both physically as she seats them in the prescribed pews and culturally in her role as communicator of the cultural conduct code. However, in the berry patch they reveal their growing independence in the way they "[talk] and [pick] faster/ in the fields than young men," pushing up their sleeves and looking to a future when they will "stop breaking their backs" and burst out of the bounds of their insular community. The poem suggests they dream of a time when their lives will no longer be only about picking and washing, ironing and starching men's shirts, but about new vistas equally shared with the men in their lives. This desire for new horizons is acknowledged and

Young woman picking raspberries

poetically realized at the end of the poem when they climb together with their men to the top of Mt. Cheam, "to see the Pacific / separate itself left and right, / slowly, from the slate-green sky / a hundred miles away"(30).

VI) Lament for a Lost Past

In a poem significantly entitled "Anataeus," Neufeldt uses playful but sad language to lament the passing of a transient but significant time period during which, through the growing of raspberries and other cash crops, many residents of Yarrow lived in close connection with the rich earth that gave the community its beginning. In Greek mythology, Anataeus is a powerful giant who was invincible as long as he remained in contact with his mother the earth, for she supplied him with his strength. He was eventually defeated by Hercules, who, discovering his secret, separated Anataeus from the life-sustaining ground and overcame him by strangling him. "How can Yarrow feel her juice?" (44), laments the poet, when "derelict kids burn vacant picker's cabins" and there are "PICK-YOUR-OWN / signs everywhere" and the only sights to see are the "Winnebagos" that "snubnose into town" on their way to the lake. In this lament for the past, violent imagery is used to demonstrate that something essential is dying, as "Raspberries are ripped from the earth, / "soil clinging" to their roots "like something you see/ in the heart before it gets out / and dies."

But this rich volume of poetry is not only a nostalgic lament for a faded past. Even after the reader may have forgotten some of the sensory evocations and powerful images of the poems, the recurring thematic reminder that "raspberries are not easily gotten rid of" lingers. As a whole, these poems powerfully remind us that present realities and future potentials are powerfully shaped by the lessons of the past. Since we live in such a transient and tentative present, we need to find creative ways of productively negotiating our connections to the past in order to utilize its rich legacy.

I would like to conclude with an anecdote shared with me by Ruth Derksen Siemens while I was working on my paper. The context of the story is the demands of the raspberry harvest, during which a young mother and her three children who are picking at her parents' farm hear the constant refrain, "The berries are falling." However, "Yarrow was astir" because "the Queen and Prince Phillip were coming to Chilliwack." Knowing the desire of her children to witness this important Canadian cultural event, the mother pleads with her father-in-law to take her children to see the queen. When he refuses, reminding her that "the berries are falling," she takes matters into her own hands. Prepared with "blanket, food, drink, toys and plans," she and the children pick "furiously, motivated and driven."

As Derksen Siemens tells it:

> They were going to see the Queen! Near noon, they packed their food and blanket and began to walk across farmer's fields. They walked almost three miles north [to the highway]. Across freshly ploughed dirt, mud, pastures, seeded ground, they marched ceremoniously. The side of the highway was level enough for their blanket and lunch. Predictably, the entourage appeared: motor cycles, police escort, and an open convertible with a chauffeur, Prince Phillip, and Queen Elizabeth. The parade moved closer. It stopped! Breathless, we must have watched in horrified wonder that they might actually approach us. But it was only a driving exchange. The Prince changed places with the chauffeur, likely a last opportunity for him to take the wheel before the formalities of Chilliwack. But we saw them. All of them at close range, and they saw us. Waves and beaming grins followed them until they disappeared. We must have floated back across those fields.

> Despite grandfather's repeated refrain, 'The berries need picking. They're falling off the branches', the children are filled with glee, shouting, 'We saw the Queen! We saw the Queen!'[10]

As I interpret it, this poignant anecdote illustrates well a Mennonite mother's creative negotiation between the obligations of the past (the need to respect the values of the past, represented by the authority of her father), the demands of the present (the urgency of the berry harvest) and her hopes for the future (she is careful to acknowledge and accommodate her children's desire for an expanded cultural horizon). Her creative ability to achieve new horizons (not realized, however, without much personal effort!) while still being faithful to the legacy of the past models the kind of strategies we need to successfully negotiate the conflicting demands of our present reality and the legacy of the past.

Endnotes

[1] Leonard Neufeldt, *Raspberrying* (Windsor: Black Moss Press, 1991), 54. Subsequent citations will appear in the text.

[2] Neufeldt also develops his theme of the past in the present in the title poem "Yarrow" from the volume of the same name where he writes, "you pass through me; scattering wind inside trees, / softest shudder in the spine/ not letting go . . . *A psalm wanting to speak its love/ to those who learned it by heart/ but forgot the words, too much expected"* (54).

[3] While the arrival of the Mennonite immigrants coincided with an economic raspberry "boom", they were not the first to attempt to grow berry crops in the Fraser Valley for commercial production. Early settlers had grown raspberries for sale as early as 1908, when the Chilliwack Canning and Preserving Company was established and during the harvest season handled five tons of soft fruit daily, mostly raspberries, strawberries, and blackberries. The cannery closed by 1912 because of declining production. See "Early Fruit Farming in Chilliwack," in *Down Country Roads: Chilliwack's Agricultural History*, ed. Pat Jepson and Ron Denman (n. p.: 1991), 10-12.

[4] These lines can be translated literally into English as, "I know of a heavenly stream that flows wonderfully peacefully through the land," or as more commonly known, "O have you not heard of that beautiful stream/ that flows through the promised land."

[5] And, indeed, for some refugees, raspberry growing facilitated emotional and economic renewal. See Helen Rose Pauls, "One Who Survived" *Transitions. Sophia.* 8:3 (Fall 1998): 10-11, for an article in which a war weary refugee woman speaks of the renewed hope she found in the raspberry fields of her central Fraser Valley farm.

[6] It's interesting to note the subtle hint of a gender double standard here: within the context of the breaching of the dykes of cultural conformity daughters are chided while sons are indulgently prayed for.

[7] See Leonard Neufeldt, ed., *Yarrow, British Columbia: Mennonite Promise,* vol. 2, *Village of Unsettled Yearnings* (Victoria, BC: Touch Wood Editions, 2002), 305-313, for Robert Martens' chapter on Yee Fong, who lived a solitary life, separated from his family because of Canadian immigration laws. Fong farmed in Yarrow from the mid 1930s until his death in 1968.

[8] See "Our Raspberry World" by Thelma Reimer Kauffman in *Village of Unsettled Yearnings,* 165-174 for more raspberry memories.

[9] A friend recounted a similar example of bean patch tomfoolery, in which beans were thrust down the front of her blouse, an event that did nothing to facilitate her romantic interest in the perpetrator!

[10] Derksen Siemens, Ruth. E-Mail communication to Maryann Jantzen, April 2003.

Bibliography

Derksen Siemens, Ruth. E-Mail communication to Maryann Jantzen, April 2003.
Jepson, Pat and Ron Denman, eds. "Early Fruit Farming in Chilliwack." In *Down Country Roads: Chilliwack's Agricultural History.* N. p.: 1991.

Neufeldt, Leonard. *Raspberrying*. Black Moss Press: Windsor, 1991.

——. *Yarrow.* Black Moss Press: Windsor, 1993.

——, Lora Sawatsky and Robert Martens, eds. *Yarrow, British Columbia: Mennonite Promise.* Vol. 2. *Village of Unsettled Yearnings.* Victoria, BC: Touch Wood Editions, 2002.

Pauls, Helen Rose. "One Who Survived." *Transitions. Sophia.* 8:3 *(*Fall 1998): 10-11.

Planting the Cross in the Wilderness: Saint Mary's Indian Residential School in the Fraser Valley

Rev. Mark Dumont, OSB

As I prepare this paper I am looking east out my monastery window over the majestic Fraser River, towards Chilliwack Mountain, the Cheam Range and Mount Baker. I see three eagles soaring overhead, just as the natives saw eagles several thousand years ago when the *Stó:lõ* peoples first settled in the Fraser Valley.[1]

In this paper, I will examine Saint Mary's Indian Residential School which existed from 1863 to 1984 in the Mission area of the Fraser Valley. I define the Fraser Valley as the area from Agassiz to the mouth of the Fraser River, which is about 120 kilometres as the eagle flies. Today, from Agassiz to Ladner, there are 18 Catholic parishes, all within 13 kilometres of the Fraser River. It is impossible, within the scope of this paper, to write a complete history of each parish, let alone one parish, so my efforts will focus on Saint Mary's.

Oblates of Mary Immaculate

The first permanent Catholic missionaries to the BC mainland were the Oblates of Mary Immaculate (OMIs), a congregation founded in France in 1826 by Eugène de Mazenod (1782-1861), the future Bishop of Marseilles. He was canonised, or declared a saint, in 1995 by Pope John Paul II. The first five Oblates to the Pacific Northwest were sent by Mazenod in 1847.[2]

Unfortunately, these French missionaries did not get along with the French-Canadian Bishops installed in Oregon and Washington territories. They came therefore to Esquimalt in 1858 at the request of Bishop Modeste Demers, who was desperate for priests; he assigned them to the mainland under their Vicar, Louis D'Herbomez (1822-1890). The latter, who had come in 1850 from France to Olympia, Washington Territory, became the second superior to the local OMIs in 1856, and moved the majority of his men first to the Victoria area and later to the mainland. In 1864, he was made the first Vicar Apostolic of the BC mainland and ordained a Bishop. According to Gresko, D'Herbomez' long-range plans for his missions to the natives was to establish agricultural villages modelled on the reductions established by the Jesuits for the Indians in Paraguay in the seventeenth century. In these church-centred villages, separate from the debauched gold-rush towns, the Indians could live a temperate life, learn Christianity and agricultural methods, celebrate Catholic feasts instead of traditional Indian ones, and have their children educated in an industrial school.[3]

There were two types of native schools: the boarding school and the industrial school. Industrial schools were simply a chain of better-funded residential schools, established by the government of Canada after 1883, but administered, like the boarding schools, by the churches.[4] In the United States, industrial education was viewed as especially relevant first for natives and later for ex-slaves and poor whites. Critics have argued that this perspective represented a race and class bias (see Anderson). Since Canada modelled its residential school system after the American example, accusations of class and race bias have also been levelled against its residential schools.[5] One should be careful, however, in making historical judgements based on current values. It is likely that since the land base needed for a traditional lifestyle was rapidly disappearing, European Canadians considered farming to be the only possible alternative to widespread starvation among the First Nations. In retrospect, it is obvious that due to a lack of demand some of the "industrial" courses such as shoemaking were unsuitable for natives from remote rural reserves. However, there is no doubt that this approach followed the conventional wisdom of the day.

In 1860, the Oblates first established a centre in New Westminster—St. Peter's Parish for whites and St. Charles' Mission for the natives—then in 1861 a centre in what is now Mission. In July of 1861, D'Herbomez sent Father Leon Fouquet (1831-1912) some 56 kilometres upstream from New Westminster to locate a site for the future St. Mary's Mission. The location, with its cedar and fir forests, was ideal, with a magnificent view of Mount Baker to the southeast. It was centrally located and within easy paddling distance of the estimated 5000 Stó:lō people who lived along the Fraser River, their main transportation route both east and west. The most important food-gathering expeditions of the natives were the salmon harvests in the summer and fall. These expeditions also drew some natives from Cowichan and Nanimo on Vancouver Island. A boys' school for the Stó:lō children was begun in 1863 under Father Florimond Gendre, the first principal. It was named St. Mary's and began with 42 boys (Cronin, 89). The work the pioneering Oblates performed was prodigious. By 1890, the 24 OMI priests and brothers had erected 70 churches, schools and houses on the BC mainland; these missionaries ministered to some 25,000 natives. The OMIs brought in religious orders of Sisters, including the Sisters of St. Ann, to staff schools and hospitals.

The Sisters of Saint Ann

In 1848, the Sisters of St. Ann were founded in Lachine, near Montreal, by Sister Esther Blondin, Sister Marie-Anne in religion. At the request of Bishop Demers, four sisters came west in 1858 to begin St. Ann's Academy in Victoria. From there the Sisters moved on to found St. Ann's Academy in New Westminster in 1865. From New Westminster, the Sisters continued to extend their work of teaching throughout British Columbia. By 1868, Bishop D'Herbomez asked them to begin management of a residential school for native girls at St. Mary's Mission. In response to this invitation, on November 5, 1868, a small party embarked from New Westminster on the river steamer. Included in the party were Bishop D'Herbomez, two Oblate Fathers, Sister Mary Providence McTucker, Sister Mary Praxedes Marceau, Sister Mary Lumena Brasseau, and Sister Mary Bonsecours Graff. The last two sisters were stationed at the new mission. Also arriving with the party were seven native girls, who became the first resident pupils of this new school.[6]

The first white-washed, rough lumber convent was a building 6 by 16 metres near the river bank. For 16 years it served as the general workroom and living room for thirty to thirty-six girls ranging in years from early childhood to marriageable age. In this room, too, they had school, learned sewing, played, and had mass receptions and festivities. Upstairs was the dormitory. A lean-to served as a dining room and kitchen.

Difficulties

To be effective, the first thing a missionary must do is learn the language of the people he or she is evangelizing. One difficulty at the residential schools was the missionaries' lack of knowledge both of English and of the native languages. The Oblates from France and the Sisters of St. Ann from Quebec naturally spoke only French and had to learn English as a second language. Besides English, the Fathers had to learn Chinook and several other native languages in order to preach and to hear the confessions of their charges on the reserves. The priests would have studied theology mainly in Latin or French, and conducted their liturgies, including the liturgical hymns at Mass and Benediction, in Latin. The native children naturally spoke only their own tribal Halkomelem dialect. The colonial policy, and later the provincial and federal policy, was to teach in English. Consequently, missionaries not fully fluent in English were teaching natives from as many as eighteen different language groups and dialects! Eventually D'Herbomez requested and

St. Mary's Indian Residential School from 1884 to 1961, located a kilometre east of Mission, BC. Credit: Mission Museum and Archive.

received some fluent anglophones from the Irish Oblate Province and from the Sisters of St. Ann to teach in the schools. The boys' and girls' classes were segregated until the 1950s, when their classes became co-educational.

Keeping the native children healthy was another major problem. Diseases such as smallpox, measles, pneumonia, Spanish influenza, scrofula and tuberculosis all took their toll. Tuberculosis, especially, was a scourge in the school—and also in society at large—for many years, especially in the '30s and '40s. Joe Aleck, for example, contracted tuberculosis after three years at St. Mary's and spent three years in the Coqualeetza Indian Hospital in Sardis before returning to St. Mary's in 1948.[7] Many of his predecessors and contemporaries in residential schools across the country were not so fortunate.

Buildings

In 1883-84, when the Canadian Pacific Railway (CPR) came through the valley and needed its right-of-way, new buildings for the school had to be constructed uphill on the plateau to the north. This second location is the present site of the Fraser River Heritage Park. The school sat on a property of about 144 hectares, which was owned in the name of Louis D'Herbomez by the Oblates under the pre-emption laws of the colony. The OMIs also bought some property across the Fraser River in Matsqui, to serve as a hayfield for the school's animals. The boys' and girls' school buildings, each three stories in height, measured 11 by 19 metres. There were various outbuildings for workers as well as a laundry, sawmill, flourmill, dairy barn and church. The church burned down in 1929 and was never replaced. From then on, liturgies were held in the boys' or girls' chapels. Both schools had septic tanks. The buildings were lit by electricity generated at the school's own plant and heated by a central coal-fired steam generator. Water was piped one kilometre from St. Mary's Creek, since renamed D'Herbomez Creek.

The new St. Mary's School and Residence from 1961 to 1984. Credit: Fraser Valley Record.

The Oblates tried to make St. Mary's as self-sufficient as possible. During the two World Wars and the Depression years they had to "economize to the bone in every department."[8]

Two new classrooms were built in 1928 and some further construction was done in 1933. In 1960-61 a brand new fireproof school for 300 students, costing over $1 million, was erected by the federal government on an adjacent site about a kilometre to the east. The old buildings, including the Grotto, were razed in 1965 while Fr. Herbert Dunlop was administrator. The Grotto was rebuilt in 1996 and continues to be a pilgrimage destination each summer. Natives continue to play a prominent role in these pilgrimages.

Enrolment

St. Mary's started with 42 boys when it opened in 1863. By 1874, there were only 18 boys and 24 girls attending. The dramatic drop in the boys' enrolment was probably due to health problems. Subsequent figures for select years were 26 pupils in 1884 and 66 in 1894. By 1925, there were 108 pupils; this number increased to 212 by 1947 and 270 in 1958.[9] Students came from as far away as Mount Currie, Seton Portage, Lillooet, Darcy, Skookumchuck (north of Harrison Lake), and even Vancouver Island. Children of former traditional tribal enemies intermingled in the same dormitories, dining rooms, classrooms and playing fields. They learned to tolerate and even become friendly with their former ancestral enemies. Naturally, the students prefered watching the CPR steam locomotives or catching rabbits and salmon to memorizing multiplication tables or learning long division.

The daily program at the school was composed of work, prayer, study and play. The studies, conducted in the mornings, consisted of "the four R's" (the fourth R being religion). Afternoons were devoted to learning domestic skills, including housekeeping, gardening and sewing for girls and farming, milking the cows and learning trades such as baking and milling for the boys. Later, boys were taught trades such as shoemaking, blacksmithing and woodworking.[10] Sports were regularly scheduled. The boys excelled in soccer, boxing and gymnastics. Also among school activities was the practice of musical instruments. Soon the school boasted a brass band which travelled to various parts of the province for concerts and parades.[11] In 1976, the band was photographed with Premier Bill Bennett.

Finances

Financing the institution was an ongoing problem, since money was always a scarce commodity. The motto of the Oblates is "To preach the gospel to the poor he has sent me." Thus, they took on even the poorest missions. The Oblates were almost entirely dependent on the charitable donations of local miners, farmers and loggers, although they did get some help from European missionary societies. The Oblates' own lay brothers had to do the brunt of clearing the land, farming and carpentry work. Brothers like Gaspar Janin (1798-1880) and Felix Guillet (1838-1903) built the original St. Mary's buildings near the riverbank.

After Confederation in 1867, the federal government promoted the establishment of the residential schools and funded their operation. The social engineering policy of John A. Macdonald and early Canadian politicians was to assimilate the natives into mainstream white culture and customs (Milloy, 20-21). Money, however, remained a scarce commodity, since the government was almost always parsimonious in funding the residential schools. Fr. Leon Fouquet obtained a small grant of $250 (50 pounds) for St. Mary's from the colonial government in 1866, but no federal money was granted until 1874, seven years after Confederation. During the war and depression years, the federal government even cut back on funds. From 1892 until 1957, this financial assistance was in the form of per-capita grants—funding was given yearly to the school based on the number of students enrolled. Limits were set on the maximum number of grants available per school, the religious community being responsible for supplementing costs for students above the quota, as well as for expenses surpassing the remuneration received from these grants. Apparently, the government would not pay for Métis children, so the school had to absorb their costs if the parents could not pay. In general, government funding remained inadequate, and the resulting hardship was borne by the OMIs, the SSAs and the lay staff who ran St. Mary's (Lascelles, *Schools*, 57-60). This lack of financial resources was another reason for agricultural training—the schools needed the food or the natives would have starved. As late as 1940, the government was paying only 44 cents a day to feed, clothe, house, and educate each native child at St. Mary's. By 1956, this amount was increased to $1.16 per day for each of the 245 pupils (Lascelles, *Schools*, 69).

Problem of Non-Matriculation

Although not limited to residential schools, an ongoing problem in native education was the limited advancement of students beyond the primary grades. In 1920, over 80 percent of Canada's native children enrolled in schools were in grades one to three, and the remaining 20 percent, in grades four to six. Not until 1950 do we find even 2 percent of native children in grades ten to thirteen. But even then about 65 percent were in grades one to three, 25 percent in grades four to six, and only 7 percent in grades seven to nine (Lascelles, 10).

At least part of the problem of non-matriculation can be attributed to the fact that prior to 1948, residential schools had no permission from the government to offer a high school curriculum. The reason for this regulation, in my opinion, was wholly financial. It costs much more to educate secondary students than primary ones. When permission was finally granted that year, it was only after persistence by the Oblates, and only two schools— Kamloops and St. Mary's Mission—received it. Yet even this concession facilitated great advances for many native students. Until the 1960s, most native children left St. Mary's school before completing secondary education. The first high school students graduated in 1952, encouraged to complete their education by the principal, Father John Hennessy, OMI.[12]

A Change of Attitude

St. Mary's remained under OMI direction and control until 1973, when control was given over to the Department of Indian Affairs. The last OMI administrator was Brother Terry McNamara. St. Mary's then served as a residence for students under Joe Aleck, a native administrator, for eleven

Students lead procession before the start of the final Mass closing St. Mary's, the last native residence to close in B.C. Credit: Fraser Valley Record.

years. Beginning around 1963, the students, at least at the secondary level, attended integrated classes at local Mission schools.

In the 1950s and '60s, the federal government's attitudes towards native education were beginning to change. The twin goals of "Christianising and civilising" Canada's native peoples gradually gave way to the new goal of "integration." No longer was the concept of a separate school system for native children appealing. Since this system had not been successful in integrating or assimilating the natives into white society, the government decided that a new model was needed—one where native and non-native children would learn to live and cooperate with one another. There were also other motivating factors, such as a broader concept of a multicultural society. The shift from "civilising" to "integrating," although originally resisted by the Oblates and the Catholic residential schooling system, eventually received the OMIs' endorsement. After 1963, the majority of newcomers sent to residential schools came from dysfunctional families or from very remote areas. In the 1950s and '60s, because of various federal-provincial agreements, more and more native pupils were sent to public day schools. Between 1969 and 1976, nine of the Catholic residential schools in BC closed. The last of them, St. Mary's, would follow suit in 1984.

Observations

The Indian residential schools of BC have disappeared as institutions of formal education. In recent years, they have become an issue of much controversy. Generally, this controversy is based upon the accusation that the schools were culturally oppressive in nature. The natives contend that through the schools, members of the dominant white society set out to impose their customs, language, culture, attitudes and religion onto BC's native people; as a result, native languages were prohibited, and physical punishment, often unheard of in the children's homes, was commonplace in the schools. In addition, the curriculum was European-oriented, with little consideration of the natives' heritage and history; the focus on agriculture, husbandry and trades was at the expense of the native way of life. Students were indoctrinated with the Christian religion through required participation in prayer and church services. These criticisms have merit, even though residential school policies seemed reasonable in their day.

However, while it is important to acknowledge the limitations and shortcomings of past perspectives, we cannot judge the standards of the past by today's standards. In the nineteenth century, as Thomas Hobbes once said, life was "nasty, brutish, and short," not only for the First Nations but also for many newcomers to British Columbia. In earlier times, murderers were hanged by order of Judge Matthew Baillie Begbie and also well into the 1960s by orders of later judges; the paddle was used on penitentiary offenders, and the strap was used in both public and private schools into the 1960s. The missionaries were also influenced by the major social ideas and customs of discipline current at the time.

While it is clear that neither the schools nor those responsible for their operation were without weaknesses and prejudices, it is also obvious that they made a valuable contribution to the lives of many children who attended them. As one former graduate of the residential system remarked, "I know for so many years we as natives got further education only because the Oblates built residential schools to help educate us" (Lascelles, *Schools*, 34). Another student, Mary Charles wrote, "I suppose all of us experience things in our own way. There are some who never liked boarding school life. For myself, I can only say that St. Mary's was good to me. It was strict but so was everything else in those days. We had only a half day class but outside class I learned to knit, to sew, to cook, to dressmake and to needlework, to look after vegetables and of course to scrub and wash."[13]

When St. Mary's closed in 1984, the *Fraser Valley Record* interviewed former students and teachers, all of whom had good words to say about the school. "It'll be like leaving home," said Joe Aleck, a former student, later a teacher of woodworking and drafting, and finally the first and only native administrator of the school. Joe was associated with the school for over 40 years. "The residence has been good to me," he reminisced. "If it wasn't for St Mary's, a lot of people from the more remote bands wouldn't have got an education" (15 July 1984).

Attitudes were to change, however, over the years. Joe Aleck's assessment of the residential school system is more nuanced in a recent (2001) interview with Terry Glavin:

> The residential school situation affected all our people. It's why I lost my language, my home. My parents were no longer my parents. They weren't able to bring me up because I wasn't home and it seems like I lost my ties for a while. I think the emotional and mental impact was the greatest on all our people and it's going to take a long time to bring people back to normal. Our grandparents were in the residential school and the impact is affecting my children .... The federal government needs to realise what was done. If it was the proper thing it sure wasn't done in the right way (Glavin, 89).

The Fraser River Heritage Park

The municipality of Mission, out of respect for the OMI pioneers, in 1986 established a heritage park at the former site of St. Mary's Mission and the Indian Residential School. Altogether some 550 Oblates have ministered in British Columbia over the past 150 years. About 100 of these OMIs worked at St. Mary's at some time in its 120-year history.[14] The OMI cemetery lies next to the twenty-hectare Fraser River Heritage Park. The Oblates sold most of their land to the government in 1973 except for one hectare for their cemetery. Here lie over 130 Oblates, including Bishops D'Herbomez, Durieu and O'Grady.[15]

The Catholic community and indeed the whole province of British Columbia owe a great debt of gratitude to these pioneers for, in the words of Scripture, "bringing the good news to the poor." The very name of the City of Mission perpetuates the memory of the Oblates' work at St. Mary's, and Mission has features named after some of them, including Durieu Street, and Durieu hamlet, north of Hatzic Lake; D'Herbomez Drive and Creek, Tavernier Terrace, and Peytavin Place. The Oblates planted the cross firmly in the Fraser Valley.

Conclusions

Regardless of the success or failure we attribute to the Indian residential school system in general, we cannot but note the great cooperative effort which sustained it, as well as the sacrifices missionaries made, at times bordering on heroism. Persons of varying cultures, languages, and religious persuasions all made their contributions. Church, state, and native people collaborated with one another to make schools like St. Mary's possible and real—bishops, chiefs, politicians, priests, religious sisters, Indian agents and employees, lay people, both native and white, parents and children. Certainly, St. Mary's will long remain fresh in the memory of those who have played a part in it. The Oblates of Mary Immaculate and the Sisters of St. Ann gave some of their best men and women to St. Mary's. They sacrificed both physically and economically for the good of their native charges.

We cannot change history. Indian residential schools were the conventional wisdom of an earlier era, not only for the Catholic Church, but also for the Anglican, Methodist, Presbyterian and United Churches. These schools were established not only in Canada, but also in the United States and in Australia, for aboriginal students. As far as their success in Christianising the natives, the 1991 Census of Canada (Catalogue 93-319) shows that fully 85 percent, or 401,000 of Canada's 471,000 aboriginal people, considered themselves Christian.

Perhaps a century from now, historians, political scientists, sociologists and anthropologists will look back upon the residential schools and call them "a noble experiment," as President Hoover called Prohibition in the United States. In my science classes, my experiments sometimes turn out poorly. I do not call them failed experiments but "limited successes." So too the residential school system might be called a "limited success." In the light of eternity, if the residential schools helped prepare four or five generations of natives for eternal life, imbued spiritual values of humility, discipline and industry at work, respect and love for neighbours and even enemies, then the residential schools were successes, albeit limited. As scripture states, "By their fruits you shall know them." The Mary Charleses, the Mary Englunds, the Joe Alecks, the Peter Jameses, the Philomena Frasers: all have made their mark in Native and B.C. annals.

* * *

As I came to the end of preparing this paper, I drove down to the site of the Fraser River Heritage Park and walked past the foundations of the old St. Mary's buildings. I thought of the hundreds of students educated here for 80 years and more. It was a glorious sunny afternoon, after a week's heavy rain. I walked past the venerable chestnut trees that were planted some 80 years ago, as depicted in historical photographs. Mount Baker was splendid to the southeast. There were at least two black rabbits hopping on the property. I walked to the OMI cemetery and mused over the graves of pioneers such as Fouquet, D'Herbomez, Durieu, Chirouse, Peytavin, Tavernier and the two

Collinses. I thought, "Your work here among the natives was not in vain." And then I looked up to the sky and saw an eagle flying in the heavens. "No, your work has not been in vain. Yours was a labour of love. You planted the cross steadfastly in the wilderness."

Endnotes

[1] The word *Stó:lō*, variously spelled *Stalo, Stallo, Stahlo,* or *Sta'lu,* means simply "river." See Wilson Duff, *The Upper Stalo Indians of the Fraser Valley, British Columbia* (Victoria, BC: British Columbia Provincial Museum, 1952), 11. The *Stó:lō* peoples spoke Halkomelem dialects.

[2] Kay Cronin, *Cross in the Wilderness* (Toronto: Mission Press, 1976), 4. Subsequent citiations will appear in the text.

[3] Jacqueline Gresko, "Herbomez," in *Dictionary of Canadian Biography*, vol. 9, *1881-90* (Toronto: University of Toronto Press, 1966), 402.

[4] Robert Choquette, *The Oblate Assault on Canada's Northwest* (Ottawa: University of Ottawa Press, 1995), 219.

[5] John S. Milloy, *A National Crime: the Canadian Government and the Residential School System, 1879-1986* (Winnipeg, MB: University of Manitoba Press, 1999), 7.

[6] Sister Edith Down, SSA, *A Century of Service*. 2nd Printing (Victoria, BC: The Sisters of Saint Ann, 1999), 62-64.

[7] Terry Glavin and Former Students of St. Mary's, *Amongst God's Own: The Enduring Legacy of St Mary's Mission*. (Mission, BC: Longhouse Publishing, 2002), 88. Subsequent citations will appear in the text.

[8] Milloy, *A National Crime*, 120. Fr. Victor Rassier, O.S.B., of the Christie School, Kakawis, used the expression in a letter to the Secretary of the Department of Indian Affairs, 15 April 1934.

[9] Thomas A. Lascelles, *Roman Catholic Indian Residential Schools in British Columbia* (Vancouver: Order of the OMI in BC, 1990), 69. Subsequent citations will appear in the text. It is estimated that over the 110 years the Oblates and SSAs directed the school, about 2,500 natives received some education at St. Mary's.

[10] Gresko, "Some Research Notes: Roman Catholic Indian Brass Bands, 1865-1915," in *British Columbia Historical News* 2 (Winter 1983): 95 and n47.

[11] Ibid., 12-15.

[12] Glavin, 43. Father John Hennessy (1910 - 2003), and his predecessor, Father Fergus O'Grady, were outstanding principals at St. Mary's in the '40s and '50s. Both promoted the introduction of high school studies in 1948 at their respective residential schools, St. Mary's and Kamloops.

[13] Jody R. Woods, "St. Mary's Roman Catholic School: A Spatial Analysis" in *A Sto:lo-Coast Salish Historical Atlas*, ed. Carlson, Keith Thor (Vancouver: Douglas & McIntyre, Ltd., 2002), 68.

[14] Thomas A. Lascelles, O.M.I. "Father Leon Fouquet, Missionary among the Kooteneys," in *Western Oblate Studies*, 1, Proceedings of the First Symposium of the Oblates (Edmonton: Western Canadian Publishers, 1990), 71.

[15] John Fergus O'Grady (1908-1998) was Principal of St. Mary's from about 1936 to 1942, later Principal of the Kamloops Residential School, then Provin-

cial leader of the OMIs, and finally Bishop of the Prince George Diocese (1956-1986). He was awarded an Honourary Doctor of Law degree in 1986 by the University of British Columbia for his lifelong commitment to the welfare of Natives and non-Natives in B.C.

Bibliography

Anderson, James. *The Education of Blacks in the South, 1860-1935*. Chapel Hill: University of North Carolina Press, 1988.

Carlson, Keith Thor, ed. *A Sto:lo-Coast Salish Historical Atlas*. Vancouver: Douglas & McIntyre Ltd, 2001.

Cassidy, Thomas, OMI. *Roots and Branches: A Diary of St Peter's Province*. Ottawa: English Oblates of Eastern Canada, 1988.

Choquette, Robert. *The Oblate Assault on Canada's Northwest*. Ottawa: University of Ottawa Press, 1995.

Cronin, Kay. *Cross in the Wilderness*. Toronto: Mission Press, 1976.

Down, Sister Edith, SSA. *A Century of Service*. 2nd Printing. Victoria, BC: The Sisters of Saint Ann, 1999.

Duff, Wilson. *The Upper Stalo Indians of the Fraser Valley, British Columbia*. Victoria: British Columbia Provincial Museum, 1952.

Glavin, Terry, and Former Students of St. Mary's. *Amongst God's Own: The Enduring Legacy of St Mary's Mission*. Mission, BC: Longhouse Publishing, 2002.

Gresko, Jacqueline. "Creating Little Dominions Within the Dominion: Early Catholic Indian Schools in Saskatchewan and British Columbia." *Indian Education in Canada*. Vol. 1. *The Legacy*. Ed. J. Barman, et al. Vancouver: University of British Columbia Press, 1986.

Gresko, Jacqueline "Herbomez." *Dictionary of Canadian Biography*. Vol 9. *1881-90*. Toronto: University of Toronto Press, 1966: 402.

——. "Some Research Notes: Roman Catholic Indian Brass Bands, 1865-1915." *British Columbia Historical News*, Number 2 (Winter 1983): 12-15.

Haig-Brown, Cecilia. *Resistance and Renewal: Surviving the Indian Residential School*. Vancouver: Tillicum Library, 1988.

Lascelles, Thomas A., OMI "Father Leon Fouquet, Missionary among the Kooteneys." In *Western Oblate Studies* 1. Proceedings of the First Symposium of the Oblates. Edmonton: Western Canadian Publishers, 1990.

——. *Roman Catholic Indian Residential Schools in British Columbia*. Vancouver: Order of the OMI in B.C., 1990.

Miller, James R. *Shingwauk's Vision: A History of Native Residential Schools*. Toronto: University of Toronto Press, 1996.

Milloy, John S. *A National Crime: the Canadian Government and the Residential School System 1879-1986*. Winnipeg, MB: University of Manitoba Press, 1999.

Whitehead, Margaret. *Now You Are My Brother*. Victoria, BC: Provincial Archives of British Columbia, 1981.

——. *They Call Me Father: Memoirs of Father Nicholas Coccola*. Vancouver: UBC Press, 1988.

Woods, Jody R. "St. Mary's Roman Catholic School: A Spatial Analysis." *A Sto:lo-Coast Salish Historical Atlas*. Ed. Keith Thor Carlson. Vancouver: Douglas & McIntyre, Ltd., 2002.

"I Want to Become a More Efficient Worker for the Lord": Mennonite Bible Schools in the Fraser Valley, 1930-1960

Bruce L. Guenther

"I want to study God's word and to become a more efficient worker for the Lord," explained one prospective student in his application for admission to Yarrow Bible School. While his actual motives for attending Bible school were likely more varied, his explanation was typical of the approximately 6,000 young people who attended a Bible school in the Fraser Valley during the first half of the twentieth century.[1] This article explores the contribution of Bible schools in the development of the central Fraser Valley during the first half of the twentieth century.

The sixteen Bible schools started in British Columbia prior to 1960 were part of a much larger phenomenon among evangelical Protestants in Canada. Since the establishment of the first Bible school in Canada in 1885, evangelical Protestants have initiated approximately 300 such institutions throughout the country.[2] By training church workers, pastors and missionaries who have gone to virtually every corner of Canada and the world, by organizing innumerable Bible and mission conferences, and through the use of radio broadcasts and literature, these schools have influenced the lives of hundreds of thousands of people. Because of their contribution to the growth of evangelical Protestantism in Canada, Bible schools have arguably been among the most influential evangelical institutions of the twentieth century.

A vastly disproportionate number of Canadian Bible schools were located in the four western provinces. During the first half of the twentieth century less than 20% of the Canadian population lived in the region, yet it contained more than 70% of the Bible schools started in Canada prior to 1960. With more than 110 schools initiated between 1909 and 1960, this area contained the largest concentration of Bible schools anywhere in the world.

This Bible school phenomenon has been virtually ignored by historians researching higher education in Canada, and, until recently, only rarely acknowledged even by historians of religion. Many historical studies of higher education in Canada during the twentieth century exclude church colleges on the assumption that they "indoctrinate" and therefore do not "educate."[3] One, and perhaps the only, exception is Robin S. Harris's comprehensive history of higher education in Canada.[4] In addition, Virginia Brereton's recent work on Bible schools in the United States identifies the emergence of these schools as one part of a turn-of-the-century trend in educational reform that sought a closer tie between learning and practical experience. She demonstrates that these schools were not some kind of bizarre educational oddity: uninhibited by older educational conventions, early Bible school founders offered a flexible and inexpensive program of training for laypeople, including a large number of women who had not enjoyed access to theological education before. Without minimizing the way in which different denominational or theological traditions utilized and adapted the new educational genre of Bible schools for their own purposes, Brereton's observation describes accurately many of the Bible schools in western Canada.[5]

Whether Bible schools should be considered an educational alternative approximately equivalent to secondary schools or whether they should be categorized as a post-secondary options is an open question. However, the sheer number of individuals who spent time in such schools makes ongoing scholarly neglect indefensible. For example, a comparison of enrolment statistics between the fledgling universities and the Bible schools in western Canada reveals that for every 3.5 university students enrolled in 1940, at least one person was enrolled in a Bible school, or put differently, in 1940 proportionally 29% of the total university enrolment was studying at a Bible school. The percentage was considerably higher in Alberta and Saskatchewan (62% and 34% respectively) and considerably lower in British Columbia (11%). By 1950, this proportionate comparison within western Canada had declined, but still remained at an impressive five to one ratio (or 20%).[6]

Bible Schools in British Columbia

Sixteen of the 110 schools started prior to 1960 in the four western provinces were located in British Columbia. These sixteen schools were located in the southern part of the province, a geographical region containing more than one-half of the province's population, with all but two situated in the Fraser Valley. All but five schools were started in the 1930s and 1940s, during two of the most economically difficult decades in Canadian history. Nine schools managed to remain in operation for at least a decade or longer, with only one school started during this period still in operation. The first school in British Columbia (and one of the first in western Canada) was Vancouver Bible Institute, which was started in 1918 by the scholarly and ecumenically-minded Walter Ellis. It was unique for its denominational breadth, its tolerance for diversity in the areas of eschatology and ecclesiology, and its vigorous promotion of an experiential Keswick Holiness teaching that included an emphasis on consecration, personal holiness, daily communion with God, and active service, especially in evangelism and foreign missions.[7] The school served as a centre of influence for a network of conservatives within mainline Protestant denominations. Notably, it also had the highest cumulative student enrolment of any Bible school within British Columbia during the first half of the twentieth century period.

The Vancouver area became the centre for several discernible strands of conservative Protestantism, a number of which were involved in starting Bible schools. Together with Toronto and Winnipeg, Vancouver became a centre for Pentecostal activity during the 1920s. This aggressive new religious movement, which rapidly splintered into a variety of denominations, birthed at least four Bible training schools in the province. The two most notable were Life Bible College of Canada, which was opened in 1928 by the Kingsway Foursquare Church, and British Columbia Bible Institute (later renamed Western Pentecostal Bible College and now known as Summit Pacific College), which was initiated in 1941 by the Pentecostal Assemblies of Canada (this school continues to operate in Abbotsford to where it relocated in 1974 from North Vancouver). In addition to the Pentecostals, several Baptist groups started schools. In 1929, the Convention of Regular Baptist Churches of British Columbia (now known as the Fellowship of Evangelical Baptist Churches) initiated the Regular Baptist Bible Institute in Mount Pleasant Baptist Church in Vancouver; it, however, lasted only a year. In 1945, another effort was made to start a school in the area. After the denomination purchased the facilities of an Apostolic Church of Pentecost Bible school located in Port Coquitlam (a school that had operated for a decade), Northwest Baptist Bible College was started to train personnel for home and foreign pastoral and missionary service.[8] This school eventually relocated to the campus of Trinity Western University in Langley, where it continued to operate until 2000. The influence of these Pentecostal and Baptist schools was felt mostly within the immediate Vancouver area and within the particular churches and denominations they were intended to serve.

Unlike the denominational diversity of the Bible schools in and around the urban centre of Vancouver,[9] the situation in the central Fraser Valley was quite different. Here the most significant initiators were congregations from

Table 1: Bible Schools in British Columbia Started Prior to 1960

Name	Location	Denomination	Origin	Closure
Vancouver Bible Institute	Vancouver	Transdenominational	1918	1955
Faith Bible School	Victoria	Pentecostal Assemblies of Canada	1924	1925
Life Bible College of Canada**	Vancouver, Surrey	Foursquare Gospel Church of Canada	1928	1997
Regular Baptist Bible Institute	Port Coquitlam	Fellowship of Evangelical Baptist Churches	1929	1930
Elim Bible School	Yarrow	Mennonite Brethren	1930	1955
Fundamental Bible College	Port Coquitlam	Apostolic Church of Pentecost	1935	1945
Mennonite Brethren Bible Institute*	Clearbrook	Mennonite Brethren	1936	1970
Greendale Bible School	Sardis	Mennonite Brethren	1938	1945
Religionsschule	Itinerant	Mennonite Church Canada	1939	1944
Bethel Bible Institute*	Clearbrook	Mennonite Church Canada	1939	1970
Pacific Summit College (formerly Western Pentecostal Bible College)	Victoria, North Vancouver, Abbotsford	Pentecostal Assemblies of Canada	1941	
Black Creek Bible School	Black Creek	Mennonite Brethren	1942	1945
Western Bible Institute	Vancouver	Evangelical Church in Canada	1944	1953
Northwest Baptist Theological College	Port Coquitlam, Vancouver, Langley	Fellowship of Evangelical Baptist Churches	1945	2000
East Chilliwack Bible School	Chilliwack	Mennonite Brethren	1947	1959
Vancouver Bible College	Vancouver, Surrey	Baptist General Conference	1957	1978

Notes: * Merged in 1970 to become Columbia Bible Institute in Clearbrook (now known as Abbotsford).
** Merged in 1997 with Pacific Life College to become Pacific Life Bible College in Surrey.

two Mennonite denominations that were involved in starting a variety of educational institutions, including six Bible schools. The Bible schools embodied the priorities of the early settlers in the central Fraser Valley and served as one part of an educational strategy for the spiritual formation and denominational integration of their young people (along with Saturday language schools and Sunday schools). My purpose here is not to provide a detailed descriptive institutional biography of each of these six Mennonite schools, but rather to offer a skeleton outline of their historical development along with some interpretative reflections about their significance within the context of the larger Bible school movement in Canada and their specific denominations.

Elim Bible School

Attracted by the prospect of fertile land, a mild climate and natural beauty, in 1928, Mennonites began arriving in Yarrow, British Columbia, a whistle stop on the BC Electric Railway. Following the arrival of the first six families, this settlement became the fastest growing Mennonite community in the province.[10] These Mennonites were part of a wave of more than 20,000 German-speaking *Russlaender* Mennonites arriving in Canada during the 1920s and several subsequent decades. They had fled the Bolshevik revolution and its aftermath and had settled briefly in various places on the Canadian prairies before moving west. Indicative of their keen interest in rebuilding the community-based way of life recently left behind in Russia was the speed with which they established familiar institutions.[11] Despite their difficult financial circumstances, within two years Mennonite Brethren leaders were holding discussions about starting a local Bible school.

Instrumental in making the idea of a local Bible school become reality was Gerhard J. Derksen, whose interest in Bible schools had been kindled at Winkler Bible Institute.[12] He was living in Winkler when the sudden arrival of Abraham H. Unruh, a Russian-certified teacher, German specialist, and a former teacher at a Mennonite Brethren Bible school in Tschongrav, Crimea[13] became a propitious moment for the inauguration of a local Bible school. Unruh quickly recruited two of his former colleagues, Johann G. Wiens and Gerhard Reimer, to assist him, thereby virtually transplanting the Tschongrav school to Canadian soil. The school in Winkler proved to be an influential centre that had an ongoing influence on the Bible schools in British Columbia.[14] By the time the Yarrow Bible school began, the Mennonite Brethren were already involved in four Bible schools in western Canada in addition to the school at Winkler. In reflecting upon the energetic efforts of the early Mennonite pioneers to establish economically viable farming operations, Derksen concluded that "if these well-meaning people should be brought to think along the same lines, and if they were to be kept from becoming to [sic] materialistic, a Bible school had to be started in the near future" (Bargen).

Records of the Yarrow Mennonite Brethren Church, the first Mennonite Brethren church to be organized in British Columbia, note that during the summer of 1930 "several brethren expressed the thought, which soon grew into a conviction, that we are actually responsible to provide some form of religious education for our young people . . . we ought to provide an opportunity for our young people to use their free time in profitable study."[15] As a result, the church organized a Bible School Society in 1930, which hired Peter D. Loewen as the first instructor of Yarrow Bible School for $20/ month (Loewen had been a student at both Herbert Bible School and Winkler Bible Institute).[16] Loewen hurriedly organized a part-time twelve-week curriculum with four subjects: Doctrine, Bible, Bible History and German Language. During the first year, only young men were allowed to attend (most of the young Mennonite women were employed as maids in Chilliwack or Vancouver). But requests from some of the young women prompted a change in time for the second year: men attended on several evenings each week so that they could continue daytime employment, and young women who were not employed as domestic servants elsewhere attended during the day.[17] Although suggestions had been made at the outset to offer instruction in both German and English, the sole language of instruction was German. The school soon became a day school, and Johann A. Harder, pastor of the Yarrow Mennonite Brethren Church was added to the teaching staff. The school was sometimes referred to as "Elim Bible School," a name derived from a Hebrew word in the Old Testament meaning "springs of living water." Despite a brief closure during several economically difficult years in the mid 1930s, enrolment remained between 25-30 students until 1939 when a period of rapid growth began. The formal education level of incoming students was generally between Grade Seven and Nine, with some students having even less. The education levels of incoming students began to increase during the late 1940s as more young people, both women and men, completed high school.[18]

After the debut of a Bible school in Yarrow, a number of other British Columbia Mennonite Brethren churches, including South Abbotsford, Sardis and Black Creek made attempts at establishing Bible schools. The prominence and centrality of Yarrow as a community and the size of the Yarrow Mennonite Brethren church in comparison to other Mennonite Brethren churches in the vicinity meant that Elim Bible School remained the premiere Bible school in British Columbia during the 1930s and most of the

1940s. In fact, by the end of the 1930s, it was not only the largest Bible school in British Columbia, but for several years during the early 1940s it was also the largest Mennonite Brethren school in Canada, exceeding even the well-established school in Winkler. With enrolments in excess of 150 during the early 1940s and with great optimism for the future, the school increased the faculty to six and moved from a two-year program towards implementing a four- and then a five-year curriculum similar to that offered by Winkler Bible School. It also began plans for the construction of a six-classroom facility.[19]

Most young people in Yarrow attended the school for a year or more. Similar to the practice at Bethany Bible School in Hepburn, Saskatchewan, and Winkler Bible School, dozens of students were sent to scattered communities in southern British Columbia during the 1940s and 1950s to teach Vacation Bible School under the auspices of the newly founded West Coast Children's Mission. As Peter Penner notes, this practice helped widen the focus of the school beyond the local church and even other Mennonite Brethren churches in the region.[20] By the end of the decade, instruction was almost exclusively in English, a change justified in part by the need to communicate the gospel message more effectively to Canadian neighbours. Other incentives for young people to learn English included avoiding the stigma attached to German-speaking groups during the war years, and accessing educational and economic opportunities in this new land.

Misfortune struck the school during the mid 1940s, precipitating a decline that resulted in its eventual closure. The absence of many young men because of World War II hurt enrolment numbers. In 1945, fire destroyed the Bible school building. Although the church replaced the building with an enlarged structure, during the post-war years, the community was facing a severe economic decline as a result of a collapsing raspberry industry. In 1944, the addition of a secondary school in Yarrow created competition for both students and money.[21] Enrolment dropped dramatically to fewer than thirty students by 1948, the same year, ironically, that membership within the Yarrow Mennonite Brethren Church peaked at 971, making it one of the largest Mennonite Brethren churches in the country.[22] Nevertheless, the school continued to struggle until its eventual closure in 1955.[23]

Mennonite Brethren Bible Institute

As the Bible school in Yarrow declined, another school, South Abbotsford Mennonite Brethren Bible School (renamed Bethel Bible School in 1943 and Mennonite Brethren Bible Institute [MBBI] in 1955) gradually became both the more central and popular Bible school option for Mennonite Brethren students in the region.[24] The phenomenon of shifting geographical centres of Mennonite Brethren population and influence within British Columbia mirrored similar patterns experienced by the denomination across the country. New waves of immigrants, inter-provincial migrations due to economic conditions, and the transition towards urban centres redistributed Mennonite Brethren members each decade, thereby preventing any one Mennonite Brethren congregation or region from ever becoming *the* centre of influence within the denomination.

Like its sister school in Yarrow, MBBI was started by one congregation (the South Abbotsford Mennonite Brethren Church). It began as an evening school in 1936, but became a regular day school in 1943. This move prompted the support of the Clearbrook and Matsqui Mennonite Brethren congregations. There was a general consensus that "our churches cannot long continue in their God-ordained purpose unless its principles and policies are engraved in the hearts and minds of the young people."[25] Under the leadership of J.F. Redekop, MBBI gradually gained the support of three more local churches (Abbotsford, East Aldergrove and Arnold).[26] The two-year program expanded to three in 1945 and to four in 1947; a post-graduate year was added in 1951. Many MBBI students, like those at Elim in Yarrow, volunteered for service with the West Coast Children's Mission. During the 1950s, the school inaugurated a weekly radio broadcast and relocated its facility to the growing town of Clearbrook. By 1959, it was the sole surviving Mennonite Brethren Bible school in the province. The formal transfer of ownership from the six churches to the BC Mennonite Brethren Conference in 1960 helped formalize the school's new identity as the denomination's designated provincial school. Although the school's enrolment never exceeded the highest enrolment experienced by Elim Bible School in Yarrow, by 1960 the number of students enrolled was almost one hundred, making it the second-largest Mennonite Brethren Bible school in western Canada (second only to Bethany Bible Institute in Hepburn).

Concerned about academic recognition for Bible school work, the directors began promoting the school during the mid 1950s as a post-secondary college with a Bible-centred curriculum.[27] For many years Bible school had been seen as a substitute for high school, but as the proportion of young people completing high school increased, the remaining Bible schools tried to reshape their identity as a post-secondary option. In addition, they were now competing with universities and the two new Mennonite Bible colleges in Winnipeg. For MBBI, part of this process included the construction of its first dormitory and, during the early 1960s, the completion of a self-study review to receive accreditation as a degree-granting college by the Accrediting Association of Bible Institutes and Bible Colleges. Plans to pursue accreditation were, however, brought to an abrupt halt by opposition from the Canadian Board of Christian Education, which argued that a second accredited college within the denomination would result in harmful competition with the newly-formed Mennonite Brethren Bible College in Winnipeg.[28] The degree to which this decision was driven by denominational interests or regional interests is a question that remains unanswered.

In 1970, the school was involved in a unique inter-Mennonite merger with Bethel Bible Institute, a school belonging to the Conference of Mennonites in British Columbia. The two schools had jointly organized evening classes as early as 1963, which helped pave the way towards a larger and more permanent collaborative venture. Because Bethel Bible Institute desperately needed to escape from inadequate facilities and because MBBI was looking for a way to broaden its support base, the two schools joined together to form Columbia Bible Institute (now known as Columbia Bible College).

Greendale Bible School and East Chilliwack Mennonite Brethren Bible Institute

In addition to Yarrow and South Abbotsford, several other Mennonite Brethren congregations in the Fraser Valley initiated Bible schools. To avoid transporting their young people to Yarrow and to facilitate local Bible instruction, the Greendale Mennonite Brethren Church appointed a committee in 1938 to organize a local Bible school.[29] H.G. Dueck became the first instructor. Although enrolments grew to over forty during the early 1940s, the congregation did not have the resources to sustain the cost of this venture for long. The school closed in 1943, and prospective students were encouraged to attend other Mennonite Brethren schools.

A more substantial initiative during the late 1940s, known as East Chilliwack Mennonite Brethren Bible School, was organized by the East Chilliwack Mennonite Brethren Church (now Chilliwack Central) and Chilliwack Mennonite Brethren Church (now Broadway). Only three months after the inception of the East Chilliwack MB Church, a committee was formed to explore the possibilities of starting a Bible school (Giesbrecht, "Schools," 5-7). Within two years property had been purchased, and in October 1947 classes began with Gerhard Thielmann as principal. In keeping with trends elsewhere, the school offered a more rigorous two-year post-high school experience with a bilingual curriculum. When enrolments exceeded fifty during the first two years, leaders were optimistic about the future. Although the school served mostly the Menonnite Brethren young people from the two sponsoring churches, it did attract students from a number of other Mennonite Brethren churches and also from a local General Conference of Mennonites congregation. The emergence of this school during the late 1940s, as well as the growth experienced during this same time period by MBBI, occurred immediately after the demise of Elim Bible School in Yarrow and reflected the redistribution of the Mennonite Brethren population in the Fraser Valley. This initiative, however, proved to be unsustainable. Enrolments quickly settled in at around twenty-five during the 1950s as increased mobility made a greater range of options accessible to young people.[30] The school closed in 1959.

Bethel Bible Institute

The second Mennonite denomination involved with Bible schools in the central Fraser Valley was the General Conference of Mennonites (following a major reorganization in 1959, the name was changed to Conference of Mennonites in Canada, and following a recent merger, it is now known as Mennonite Church Canada). It was second only to the Mennonite Brethren as the denomination with the greatest number of Bible schools in Canada, starting more than a dozen schools across western Canada prior to 1960. However, significantly lower membership numbers in British Columbia made it difficult to compete with the vigorous efforts of the Mennonite Brethren. The churches of the General Conference of Mennonites nevertheless shared the same priorities and interests as their Mennonite Brethren counterparts for the religious education of their children, but in the absence of other local options, many of their young people attended Mennonite Brethren schools.

In British Columbia, the General Conference of Mennonites first discussed the possibility of a Bible training centre in 1937 at a conference of ministers. These leaders were torn between pressure to start a Bible program of their own and the economic constraints placed upon them by the Depression. This led to the organization of local *Religionsschulen*, or Bible classes, in four locations: Sardis, Yarrow, Coghlan and Abbotsford. The presence of Nicolai Bahnmann, a gifted teacher from Russia, helped the Bible class program at Coghlan (now part of Abbotsford) to expand into a day program in 1939.[31] Teachers volunteered their time, and students were not charged tuition.

Leaders in the denomination encouraged those interested in a Bible school to plan for a single, more integrated venture. Led by J. D. Jantzen, the program in Coghlan came under the supervision of a Bible school society that helped raise finances for the enterprise. This step towards a more formal organizational structure laid the foundation for the General Conference of Mennonites in British Columbia to assume full responsibility for the school.

Following the purchase of a tract of land adjacent to the West Abbotsford Mennonite Church and the renovation and construction of buildings including dormitories for students, the school became known as Bethel Bible Institute, the only General Conference of Mennonites in Canada school in British Columbia that survived any length of time. The school was well received, and by the 1950s its influence had touched virtually every General Conference of Mennonite congregation in the province.[32] Conflict emerged, however, during the early 1950s, when the West Abbotsford church withdrew from the Conference. thereby effectively reducing student enrolment by half, from over fifty to twenty-five. Other constituents began to raise questions about the fundamentalist and dispensationalist views promoted by faculty within the school.[33] As a result, student enrolment during the 1950s seldom managed to exceed thirty. In 1970, to the surprise and consternation of some, the school merged with Mennonite Brethren Bible Institute to become Columbia Bible Institute.[34]

Denominational Orientation of the Bible School Movement

The story of Mennonite Bible schools in the central Fraser Valley illustrates well some of the patterns within the larger Bible school movement. Contrary to the impression created by the prominent profile of large transdenominational Bible schools such as Prairie Bible Institute and Briercrest Bible Institute, during the first half of the twentieth century the Bible school movement was overwhelmingly denominational in its orientation, reflecting the religious free-for-all that was a part of the establishment of western Canada. The twelve transdenominational schools that existed in western Canada prior to 1960 were vastly outnumbered by a plethora of over ninety-five smaller schools operated by more than thirty different denominations. The cumulative enrolment in these denominational schools was more than double that of the cumulative enrolment in transdenominational schools.[35]

Although each school has its unique story, the dozens of individual institutional histories nevertheless share some significant commonalities in the way they are connected to the historical development of western Canada. A significant number of denominational Bible schools throughout western Canada had their roots within an ethnic immigrant community; many were at the outset extensions of much larger, more established denominational bodies located in the United States, many of which were already operating seminaries and liberal arts colleges. Despite the connection of many of the new Protestant denominations in western Canada to denominational groups south of the border, the competition between existing schools meant that

Bible schools were usually the most affordable and accessible religious training institutions possible for the pioneering communities in western Canada. The Bible schools in western Canada performed an integral part both in developing leaders for and nurturing a sense of Canadian identity within these small and often isolated denominations. Leaders within denominational Bible schools in western Canada struggled with the problems of economic hardship, geographic isolation, and their minority status compared to their larger denominational counterparts in the United States. Thus, they attempted to find local strategies that would both nurture an interest in Christian faith and guide the process of cultural assimilation within subsequent generations. The Bible schools were often the first denominational institutions to promote the use of English as the primary language and, as a result, they played an important role in helping the young people from various immigrant communities adjust to life in western Canada. Furthermore, many of the denominational schools served as a crucible for the convergence of European and North American theological influences.

The Mennonite Bible schools in the central Fraser Valley reflected many of these larger patterns. The Bible school was a practical educational genre adapted by Mennonite immigrants (and by other ethnic religious communities) as a supplement to public education. Even the *Russlaender* Mennonites, who readily endorsed education as valuable and had accepted the reality of public schools in Russia, were disappointed upon their arrival in Canada with the lack of opportunity for religious instruction within the public schools in western Canada. In Russia, the Mennonites had been able to devote one-third of their school term to the study of German and religion. These subjects were never given comparable space within the curriculum of the public schools in Canada.[36] Despite other differences that divided Mennonites, most agreed that the "national, god-less" public schools did not fully meet their needs. The Mennonites considered the responsibility to educate their children as part of a sacred trust from God. Moreover, all believed that "their identity as a people depended in large part on how successfully they would transmit their religious and cultural heritage to their children."[37] The perception of public schools as unfriendly and as potentially dangerous influences was exacerbated by the experience of Mennonite children who felt the stigma of being identified as "German" during the war years (Dahl, 27). Against this historical backdrop, the Mennonite Bible schools can be seen as one of several educational genres adapted by Mennonites in western Canada as part of a multi-faceted strategy for ethnic and religious self-preservation—Saturday German schools and Sunday schools being other strategies.

The Mennonite Brethren contribution to the Bible school movement, not only in British Columbia but also to the larger movement in Canada, cannot be overstated. They were among the first to start Bible schools in western Canada, and were by far the most aggressive, organizing more schools (over twenty) than any other denomination.[38] Despite their relatively small membership, their cumulative student enrolment significantly outnumbered that of any other denomination. In addition to being leaders in establishing Bible schools, individuals within the denomination were at the forefront of the movement to chart a path towards academic recognition and accreditation during the late 1950s.[39]

The Impact of Bible Schools

A substantial proportion of Mennonite young people in western Canada attended Bible school for at least a short period of time between 1930 and 1950. Estimates from the Greendale Mennonite Brethren Church indicate that approximately 75% of the young people baptized since the early 1940s had attended Bible school (Harder, 163). As a result, the most immediate impact of the Bible schools was experienced within the congregational life of churches. For almost two decades, beginning in the 1930s, the annual enrolment in Mennonite Bible schools was approximately 5% of the total membership within the Mennonite churches.[40] Over time, these schools created a common religious experience and a reasonable level of biblical literacy. They also generated an enthusiasm and predisposition for participation in the life of the church that was an ongoing source of vitality and energy for local congregations and that, over time, shaped the ethos of the entire denomination. A statistical study compiled in 1963 by A. J. Klassen highlighted the percentage of Bible school alumni involved in various areas of Mennonite Brethren life. He estimated that by 1963, 90% of missionaries working abroad, 86% of missionaries working in North America, 59% of Mennonite Brethren ministers, 67% of Sunday school workers, 100% of the Mennonite Brethren Committee on Evangelism, 90% of the Committee of Reference and Counsel, 87% of the Board of Education, and 88% of the Sunday School Committee had some Bible school training.[41]

The Bible schools left a distinct mark on the pastoral ministry of Mennonite congregations. For almost a century, leaders and pastors had been selected from within the ranks of the "brethren" after giving evidence of interest, good character, and ability. However, by the beginning of the 1930s, many of the new candidates for ministry within congregations had received prior training in Bible schools, since the practical courses and ministry work assignments offered by the Bible schools provided an ideal environment for identifying prospective candidates for ministry. Although the Bible schools did not set out to precipitate a movement towards a more professionalized ministry, they contributed, albeit unwittingly, towards the process. Ted Regehr concurs that the Bible schools "were the major training ground for an entire generation of Mennonite church leaders, preachers and lay workers who developed and maintained for many years close and intimate contacts with one another"(236). The Bible schools, particularly those partnered with larger congregations and those that survived to become conference schools, served as significant centres of influence for their denominations during a formative time in their development in Canada.

Cultural Change Agents

The Bible schools played a unique role in responding to some of the many influences that precipitated change among Mennonites in the Fraser Valley during the early-twentieth century. These schools were, at the outset, intended to serve as agents of cultural retention by grounding successive generations in the Mennonite faith, language and way of life.[42] They played a unique role as crucibles that forged new approaches towards the matters of language, acculturation, education and missions, eventually reshaping congregational and denominational practices. By helping to facilitate both the linguistic transition towards English—Bible schools were among the first Mennonite institutions to make the transition from German to English— along with a broader view of mission, the Bible schools undermined the cultural and religious separatism of the denomination and accelerated their integration into Canadian society.[43] The transfer of energy and resources into private secondary schools and a new Bible college coincided with the broader societal trend towards higher education, helping to facilitate the rapid transition among the Mennonites in the Fraser Valley from being a predominantly rural, agrarian community to a more urban, professional constituency. However, while Bible schools continued to be valued for their ability to influence the spiritual life of students, during the 1950s an increasing number of Mennonite young people did not see Bible schools as a necessary step on the path towards progress and opportunity.

Conduit for Evangelical Influence

The natural compatibility between the religious priorities of the Mennonites and evangelical Protestant groups in North America was quickly recognized by many Mennonite leaders. The Bible schools solidified Mennonite connections with North American evangelicals in a variety of ways. Some of the Bible school teachers trained at fundamentalist institutions such as Moody

219

Bible Institute, Northwestern Bible and Missionary Training Institute, and the Bible Institute of Los Angeles. The involvement of some schools such as Elim and MBBI, with the Evangelical Teacher Training Association brought not only a prescribed curriculum in the area of Christian education, but also a more familial affiliation with other evangelical schools and educators. As the need for English-language textbooks, library resources and Sunday school materials grew, Bible school teachers looked again towards the evangelical schools in the United States with which they were familiar. The use of textbooks written and published by American evangelicals was extensive throughout Mennonite Bible schools. Because the Mennonite Brethren community was in the midst of a language transition during the 1940s and 1950s, the denomination did not have writers who were capable of producing English language materials for use in the Bible schools. These schools, therefore, functioned as conduits for North American evangelical influences that then permeated the entire denomination. Although Mennonite denominations were removed by both distance and ethnicity from the divisive North American fundamentalist debates of the 1920s, the influence of fundamentalism nevertheless created internal tensions within these denominations that have lasted to the present day.

Criticism of Bible Schools

Despite their significant role within the denomination, not everyone is uncritical of the impact of the Bible schools. One common cluster of complaints centers on the low academic standards exacerbated by inadequate library resources and poorly-educated teachers, by simplistic, dogmatic answers to complex theological questions, and by a general environment which, if not openly anti-intellectual, prioritized personal piety and proper deportment above critical thinking. Despite the legitimacy of such complaints, the Bible schools nevertheless did prepare many individuals for advanced study when few other educational options were available.

A second cluster of complaints focuses on evangelical theological influences within the Bible schools that minimized the study of Anabaptist and Mennonite historical and theological distinctives. The early, and ongoing, influence of pietism, especially among the Mennonite Brethren in Russia, who stressed a personal salvation experience, thorough biblicism and missions, created a natural compatibility with the priorities of evangelical Protestants in North America. Despite linguistic and cultural differences between these groups, it did not take long before their affinities resulted in Mennonite Brethren contact with evangelical Protestant groups and an appreciative borrowing of resources. From this point onwards, the denomination readily identified itself as part of the larger evangelical Protestant community in North America, although internal conflict emerged concerning an appropriate response and relationship to transdenominational evangelical organizations and institutions. The General Conference of Mennonites was similarly affected: although somewhat slower in starting Bible schools, it borrowed heavily from the practices of the Mennonite Brethren and used many of the same resources, thereby importing the same influences.

Conclusion

More than forty of the approximately 110 Bible schools initiated in western Canada before 1960 were started by Mennonites. Moreover, the cumulative enrolment within Mennonite Bible schools during this period made up more than one third of the total student enrolment of all Bible schools in the region. (These figures do not take into account the fact that, particularly after World War II, a significant proportion of students attending trans-denominational schools came from Mennonite churches.) However, by 1960 more than 75% of these Mennonite educational endeavours had ended.

In the British Columbia Bible School legacy, only Columbia Bible College managed, late in 1983, to accomplish the goal initially set out by the leaders of MBBI of becoming an accredited and degree-granting institution.[44] John Redekop (one of the organizers of a February 2003 reunion of early alumni from the Mennonite Bible schools in British Columbia) notes, "While one can lament the closing of the other Bible schools, it is noteworthy that at present about twice as many students (over 500) receive accredited post-secondary Biblical and theological training at Columbia Bible College as received mostly high-school level education when the combined enrolment of the individual Bible schools was at its greatest."[45] This numerical calculation is accurate; however, without minimizing the work of the college, if enrolment at the college were to equal the same proportion of church membership as it was during the 1940s, its student population would exceed 2,500 students. Although all but one of the Mennonite Bible schools have disappeared, the recent alumni gathering demonstrated that for many Mennonites in the Fraser Valley the memories of these institutions still remain as "monuments of God's faithfulness" (Klassen 15-16).

Endnotes

[1] John Bargen, File 990.1.4.1, Yarrow Bible School, 1930-'1955, Box 990.1, Mennonite Historical Society. Subsequent citations will appear in the text.

[2] Bible schools typically offered a Bible-centred, intensely practical, lay-oriented program of post-secondary theological training. As educational insti-

tutions, they operated in a zone between the upper years of secondary education and the undergraduate years of post-secondary education. They need to be differentiated from Bible colleges, which are accredited and confer degrees, and whose curricula include significantly more liberal arts or general education courses alongside course offerings in religious studies (for an extensive overview of Bible schools in western Canada see Guenther, "Training for Service."

[3] For a thorough discussion of this issue, see Elmer J. Thiessen, *Teaching for Commitment: Liberal Education, Indoctrination and Christian Nurture* (Montreal: McGill-Queen's Press, 1993).

[4] Robin S. Harris, A History of Higher Education in Canada, 1663-1960 (Toronto: University of Toronto Press, 1976). Harris's work is commendable for the way in which it places theological colleges within the framework of professional education.

[5] Virginia Brereton, *Training God's Army: The American Bible School, 1880-1940* (Indianapolis: Indiana University Press, 1990), 115. Subsequent citations will appear in the text.

[6] University enrolments were obtained from Statistics Canada, *Historical Compendium of Education*; Bible school statistics are based upon compilations from my own research.

[7] Ellis was profoundly influenced at Wycliffe College by W.H. Griffith Thomas, one of the foremost proponents of Keswick Holiness teaching in North America. SeeRobert K. Burkinshaw, *Pilgrims in Lotus Land* (Montreal and Kingston: McGill-Queens University Press, 1995), 66.

[8] See *BC Baptist* 4.7 (1929): 5; John B. Richards, *Baptists in British Columbia: A Struggle to Maintain "Sectarianism"* (Vancouver: Northwest Baptist Theological College and Seminary, 1977), 102-33; and John H. Pickford, *What God Hath Wrought: Sixty Years of God's Goodness in the Fellowship of Regular Baptist Churches of British Columbia* (Vancouver: Baptist Foundation of British Columbia, 1987), 122-23.

[9] It is worth noting that the Bible school movement was not exclusively or even primarily a rural phenomenon, as is often assumed.

[10] In Yarrow, the Mennonites settled in what Alfred H. Siemens called, "a nucleated agricultural settlement," a relatively rare phenomenon in British Columbia (Siemens, "Mennonite Settlement in the Lower Fraser Valley." MA Thesis, University of British Columbia, 1960, 114).

[11] See David Giesbrecht, "The Early Years of the Mennonite Brethren Church," in *Yarrow, British Columbia: Mennonite Promise*, vol. 2, *Village of Unsettled Yearnings*, ed. Leonard Neufeldt (Victoria, BC: TouchWood Editions, 2002), 34-43 and Veronica Barkowsky Thiessen, "History of the Yarrow United Mennonite Church," in ibid., 44.

[12] Derksen's son, Jacob, attended the school during the late 1920s prior to the family's move to BC. Penner, "Glimpses of Elim Bible School," in Ibid., 81.

[13] Mennonites had only just begun Bible schools in Russia when the Soviets brought such initiatives to an abrupt halt. The Tschongrav school, officially registered under the name "Mennonite Theological Seminary," was one of the more successful Mennonite Bible schools in Russia. It was started by Johann G. Wiens, a returned missionary from India and a graduate of the Baptist seminary in Hamburg, Germany. The school was permanently closed by the Red Army in 1924 after only six years of operation. For more information see Margaret

Reimer, *The Crimea Bible School, 1918-1924.* trans. Edwin Reimer (Kingsville, ON: Author, 1972).

[14] For more on Winkler Bible Institute see Guenther, "Training for Service," 133-142, and the detailed institutional biography by Pries.

[15] "The Bible School Movement in British Columbia," *MBBI Bulletin* (October-December 1963): 2-3.

[16] Peter Daniel Loewen, *Memoirs of Peter Daniel Loewen: A Story of God's Grace and Faithfulness* (Abbotsford, BC: Fraser Valley Custom Printers, 1999), 70-75. He developed a reputation as a vigorous advocate for Christian education and the training of Sunday school teachers.

[17] Many young people sought employment in order to help their families repay their *Reiseschuld* (the cost incurred by the Canadian Pacific Railway in transporting them from Russia to Canada). This made it difficult for them to attend Bible school on a full-time basis (Penner, "Glimpses of Elim . . . ," 81; and Loewen, 78).

[18] I was unable to find precise statistics for the Mennonite Brethren Bible schools, but a comparative study of Conference of Mennonites in Canada schools (whose development often lagged a few years behind that of the Mennonite Brethren schools) indicated that in 1958 between 2% and 27% of Bible school students had completed high school. By 1965, the percentage ranged between 53%-78% ("Academic Standing of Students at the Bible Schools" Bethel Bible Institute Papers, Box 990.5.1, MHSBCA).

[19] In 1951, shortly before its closure, a fifth-year post-graduate program restricted to men who were considering pastoral ministry or missionary service was added.

[20] Their involvement with the Western Children's Mission in the 1930s, during their time as Bible school students at Bethany Bible School inspired a group of people from the Abbotsford area in British Columbia to form a similar organization called the Western Children's Mission in British Columbia (later changed to West Coast Children's Mission). Their first worker was John Wiebe, a graduate of Winnipeg Bible Institute, who had worked with the Canadian Sunday School Mission in Manitoba. By the mid 1950s, it was active in more than thirty localities across British Columbia (Peter Penner, *Reaching the Otherwise Unreached: An Historical Account of the West Coast Children's Mission of BC* [Clearbrook, BC: West Coast Children's Mission, 1959]).

[21] The collapse of the raspberry industry during the late 1940s, the flood of the Vedder River in 1948, and the unresolved tensions among the different Mennonite communities precipitated financial difficulties not only for the Bible school, but also for the new high school in Yarrow. See Edward H. Dahl, "Sharon Mennonite Collegiate Institute, 1945-1949." Unpublished Paper, University of British Columbia, 1968, 9-19, for a detailed discussion of the financial needs that eventually precipitated a request on the part of the new school for assistance from the Chilliwack School District Board of Trustees. Subsequent citations will appear in the text.

[22] The enrolment statistics of Elim stand in contrast to the general pattern of sharp increases during the post-war years within the overall Bible school movement that included most other Mennonite schools. This anomaly adds additional emphasis to the significance of the factors pressuring the school at this time.

[23] Klassen, in *Yarrow*, 89-92; and the more detailed survey by Harvey Neufeldt, "'You've Changed Too':The Education of the Yarrow Mennonite Community, 1928-1960," *Studies in Education* 7.1 (1995): 71-95.

[24] The population of the Fraser Valley doubled between 1941 and 1961. Although the farming population remained relatively stable during this period, the urban centres absorbed most of this increase. Moreover, as the automobile became the dominant means of transportation and an infrastructure of roads developed, increased mobility helped disperse the Mennonite population throughout the valley. See Meyer,"The Evolution of Roads in the Lower Fraser Valley," in *Lower Fraser Valley: Evolution of a Cultural Landscape*, ed. Alfred Siemens (Vancouver: Tantalus Research Ltd., 1968), 69-88. As a result, during the 1950s, Clearbrook gradually began to eclipse Yarrow as the centre of Mennonite influence in the central Fraser Valley (Siemens, "Mennonite Settlement," 115-125).

[25] *MBBI Annual Catalogue*, 1956-57, 17; cited in Irwin Warkentin, "The Mennonite Brethren Bible Institute," Unpublished Paper, Clearbrook, BC: 1968. Mennonite Archives of Ontario.8.

[26] Henry C. Born, "Growth of the MBBI, Clearbrook," *Mennonite Brethren Herald* 6.22 (9 June 1967): 29-30; and Warkentin, 3.

[27] Report of Self-Study of the Mennonite Brethren Bible Institute, December 1964. See also Krahn, "A History of Mennonites in British Columbia." Graduation Thesis, University of British Columbia, 1955, 63.

[28] See "The Bible School Movement in British Columbia," 2-3; "Report of the Self-Study of the Mennonite Brethren Bible Institute"; Warkentin; 7-8; Born, 7-8 and David Giesbrecht, "Mennonite Schools in BC," *Mennonite Historical Society of BC Newsletter* 5. 5 (1999): 5-7. Subsequent citations will appear in the text.

[29] Katherine Harder, ed. *The Greendale Mennonite Brethren Church, 1931-1981* (Sardis, BC: The Greendale Mennonite Brethren Church, 1980), 161-63.

[30] Leaders in the school tried hard to make the case for young people to attend Bible school even after they completed high school (see Jacob Thielmann, *"Kann Eine Christliche Hochchule den Platz einer Bibleschule Ausfuellen?"* in *East Chilliwack Bible School* Botschafter (1953-54): 29.

[31] Bahnmann was a graduate of the Pedagogical School in Halbstadt, Russia, and had studied at both the Basel Bible School in Switzerland and Bethel College in Newton, Kansas (see Gerhardt I. Peters, *Remember Our Leaders: Conference of Mennonites in Canada, 1902-1977* [Clearbrook, BC: Mennonite Historical Society of British Columbia, 1982], 54).

[32] Cornelia Lehn, *Frontier Challenge: A Story of the Conference of Mennonites in BC* (Abbotsford, BC: Conference of Mennonites in British Columbia, 1990), 168.

[33] David Giesbrecht, "Bethel Bible Institute," *Canadian Mennonite Encyclopedia Online* www.mhsc.ca/encyclopedia/search.html. Underlying the conflict were longstanding differences concerning the nature of conversion and the relationship of conversion to discipleship (See Lehn, 75-78).

[34] In 1969, a proposal had been made that Bethel be amalgamated with Swift Current Bible Institute and that Christian education centres be established in three regional locations. The General Conference of Mennonites in British Columbia, however, wanted the school to remain in the province. Other possi-

bilities under consideration included moving to the facilities of Camp Squeah, relocating near Trinity Western College, or relocating to Burnaby near Simon Fraser University (Rose Retzlaff, "The History of Bethel Bible Institute." Unpublished paper, April, 1984. Vertical Files, Mennonite Heritage Centre Archives, 10-13).

[35] Without minimizing the role denominational schools played within their own constituencies, it is fair to say that, on their own, few of these schools could be considered particularly significant in the overall development of the Bible school movement. But when placed together, they reveal that evangelical Protestantism in western Canada was significantly more denominational than transdenominational in its orientation during the first half of the twentieth century.

[36] Isaac I. Friesen, "The Mennonites of Western Canada with Special Reference to Education." M.Ed. Thesis, University of Saskatchewan, 1934.

[37] Ted Regehr, *Mennonites in Canada, 1939-1970: A People Transformed* (Toronto: University of Toronto Press, 1996), 224. Subsequent citations will appear in the text.

[38] By 1937 there were eleven secondary schools in the eastern part of the Fraser Valley, with Chilliwack being the first in 1903; many of the others were started during the 1920s. Considering Mennonites did not arrive in the Fraser Valley until the late 1920s, and considering the way linguistic and cultural characteristics set them apart, it is worth noting the speed with which the Mennonites were able to establish a multi-level educational infrastructure for their young people during the 1940s. In the space of only three years (1944-1947), Mennonites across Canada started nine private high schools, bringing the total number of private Mennonite high schools in Canada to thirteen.

[39] For more on the story of Mennonite Brethren involvement in the accreditation of Bible colleges see Guenther, "Slithering Down the Plank of Intellectualism?"

[40] This is somewhat lower than the national figures, at least among the Mennonite Brethren during the 1940s, when annual enrolments equalled approximately 7-8% of the entire membership (during the 1940s the total annual enrolment in Mennonite Brethren schools in western Canada ranged between 540 and 610).

[41] A. J. Klassen, ed. *The Bible School Story, 1913-1963: Fifty Years of Mennonite Brethren Bible Schools in Canada* (Clearbrook, BC: Canadian Board of Education, 1963), 15-16. Subsequent citations will appear in the text.

[42] John A. Toews reluctantly acknowledges, "at certain times and in certain institutions the desire for the preservation of cultural values may have overshadowed the primary objective of Christian education" (254).

[43] The issue of language transition within the Bible schools was intricately linked to the matter of missions and outreach. All Mennonite Brethren shared in common a general spiritual concern for the Mennonite people, but Mennonite Brethren had come to understand missions—at least since the early-twentieth century—in more universal terms. The preoccupation on the part of *Russlaender* Mennonite Brethren who were interested in maintaining the German language as a boundary between their own Mennonite communities and Canadian culture resulted in a narrowing of their understanding of mission. Many but not all denominational leaders conveniently created distinctions between *die innerste*

Mission (the innermost mission, meaning a concern for the spiritual life of those already within the Mennonite Brethren stronghold, particularly the youth), and *die innere Mission* or *Randmission* (the inner or home mission, meaning a spiritual concern for other, scattered Mennonites or German-speaking people around them). Outreach activity beyond their linguistic boundaries was not readily endorsed or encouraged except for the work of missionaries in foreign countries (*die auessere Mission*). See Penner, *No Longer at Arms Length*, 4-5, 17-19, for a fuller discussion. Bible school leaders who had been influenced by fundamentalism frequently led the way in adopting English as the primary language of instruction. The desire on the part of enthusiastic, mission-minded students to obtain training in order to minister in non-German, non-Mennonite settings mitigated against a rigid insistence on the preservation of the German language and a distinct "Mennonite" ethnicity.

[44]Columbia Bible College's two-semester Quest discipleship program and the recently established Mark Centre in Abbotsford come closer to the spirit and intention of the early Bible schools than does the vision for an accredited college.

[45] "40s and 50s Alumni Celebration of Worship and Praise Bulletin." John and Doris Redekop were instrumental in organizing a remarkable reunion in February 2003 of British Columbia Bible School alumni from the 1930s, 1940s and 1950s.

Bibliography

Minutes, reports

Bargen, John. File 990.1.4.1, Yarrow Bible School, 1930-1955, Box 990.1, Mennonite Historical Society of British Columbia Archives, Abbotsford, BC (MHSBCA).

"Academic Standing of Students at the Bible Schools," Bethel Bible Institute Papers, Box 990.5.1, MHSBCA.

Report of Self-Study of the Mennonite Brethren Bible Institute, December, 1964, MHSBCA.

Books, Periodicals and Dissertations.

Barkowsky Thiessen, Veronica. "History of the Yarrow United Mennonite Church." *Yarrow, British Columbia: Mennonite Promise.* Vol. 2. *Village of Unsettled Yearnings.* Ed. Leonard Neufeldt. Victoria, BC: TouchWood Editions, 2002.

BC Baptist 4 no.7 (1929): 5.

"The Bible School Movement in British Columbia," *MBBI Bulletin* (October-December 1963).

Born, Henry C. "Growth of the MBBI, Clearbrook," *Mennonite Brethren Herald*, 6.22 (9 June 1967).

——. "Reflections on the Mennonite Brethren Bible School Movement in British Columbia," *Mennonite Historian*, 19.3 (September 1993).

Brereton, Virginia. *Training God's Army: The American Bible School, 1880-1940.* Indianapolis: Indiana University Press, 1990.

Burkinshaw, Robert, K. *Pilgrims in Lotus Land.* Montreal: McGill-Queens University Press, 1995.

Dahl, Edward H. "Sharon Mennonite Collegiate Institute, 1945-1949." Unpublished Paper, University of British Columbia, 1968.

"40s and 50s Alumni Celebration of Worship and Praise Bulletin," 16 February 2003.

Friesen, Isaac, I. "The Mennonites of Western Canada with Special Reference to Education." M. Ed. Thesis, University of Saskatchewan, 1934.

Giesbrecht, David. "Bethel Bible Institute," *Canadian Mennonite Encyclopedia Online.* www.mhsc.ca/encyclopedia/search.html

——. "The Early Years of the Mennonite Brethren Church." *Yarrow, British Columbia: Mennonite Promise.* Vol. 2. *Village of Unsettled Yearnings.* Ed. Leonard Neufeldt. Victoria, BC: TouchWood Editions, 2002.

——. "Mennonite Schools in BC," *Mennonite Historical Society of BC Newsletter.* 5.5 (1999).

Guenther, Bruce. "Slithering Down the Plank of Intellectualism? The Canadian Conference of Christian Educators and the Impulse Towards Accreditation Among Canadian Bible Schools During the 1960s." *Historical Studies in Education.* 16.2 (Fall 2004). Forthcoming.

Guenther, Bruce L. "Training for Service: The Bible School Movement in Western Canada, 1900-1960." PhD. Diss. McGill University, 2001.

Harder, Katherine, ed. *The Greendale Mennonite Brethren Church, 1931-1981.* Sardis, BC: The Greendale Mennonite Brethren Church, 1980.

Harris, Robin S. *A History of Higher Education in Canada, 1663-1960.* Toronto: University of Toronto Press, 1976.

Klassen, Agatha E. *Yarrow: A Portrait in Mosaic.* Yarrow, BC: Author, 1980.

Klassen, A. J., ed. *The Bible School Story, 1913-1963: Fifty Years of Mennonite Brethren Bible Schools in Canada.* Clearbrook, BC: Canadian Board of Education, 1963.

Krahn, John Jacob. "A History of Mennonites in British Columbia." Graduation Thesis, University of British Columbia, 1955.

Lehn, Cornelia. *Frontier Challenge: A Story of the Conference of Mennonites in BC.* Abbotsford, BC: Conference of Mennonites in British Columbia, 1990.

Loewen, Peter Daniel. *Memoirs of Peter Daniel Loewen: A Story of God's Grace and Faithfulness.* Abbotsford, BC: Fraser Valley Custom Printers, 1999.

Meyer, Ronald H. "The Evolution of Roads in the Lower Fraser Valley." In *Lower Fraser Valley: Evolution of a Cultural Landscape.* Ed. Alfred Siemens. Vancouver: Tantalus Research Ltd., 1968, 69-88

Neufeldt, Harvey. "'You've Changed Too': The Education of the Yarrow Mennonite Community, 1928-1960." *Studies in Education* 7.1 (1995): 71-95.

Neufeldt, Leonard, Lora Sawatsky and Robert Martens, eds. *Yarrow, British Columbia: Mennonite Promise.* Vol. 2. *Village of Unsettled Yearnings.* Victoria, BC: Touch Wood Editions, 2002.

Penner, Peter. "Glimpses of Elim Bible School, 1930-1955." *Yarrow, British Columbia: Mennonite Promise.* Vol. 2. *Village of Unsettled Yearnings.* Ed. Leonard Neufeldt, Victoria, BC: TouchWood Editions, 2002.

——. *No Longer at Arms Length: Mennonite Brethren Church Planting in Canada.* Winnipeg, MB: Kindred Press, 1987.

——. *Reaching the Otherwise Unreached: An Historical Account of the West Coast Children's Mission of BC*. Clearbrook, BC: West Coast Children's Mission, 1959.

Peters, Gerhardt, I. *Remember Our Leaders: Conference of Mennonites in Canada, 1902-1977*. Clearbrook, BC: Mennonite Historical Society of British Columbia, 1982.

Pickford, John H. *What God Hath Wrought: Sixty Years of God's Goodness in the Fellowship of Regular Baptist Churches of British Columbia*. Vancouver: Baptist Foundation of British Columbia, 1987.

Pries, George. *A Place Called Peniel: Winkler Bible Institute. 1925-1975*. Altona, MB: D. W. Friesen and Sons, Ltd., 1975.

Regehr, Ted. *Mennonites in Canada, 1939-1970: A People Transformed*. Toronto: University of Toronto Press, 1996.

Retzlaff, Rose. "The History of Bethel Bible Institute." Unpublished paper, April, 1984. Vertical Files, Mennonite Heritage Centre Archives.

Reimer, Margaret. *The Crimea Bible School, 1918-1924*. Trans. Edwin Reimer. Kingsville, ON: Author, 1972.

Richards, John B. *Baptists in British Columbia: A Struggle to Maintain "Sectarianism."* Vancouver: Northwest Baptist Theological College and Seminary, 1977.

Siemens, Alfred, ed. *Lower Fraser Valley: Evolution of a Cultural Landscape*. Vancouver: Tantalus Research Ltd., 1968.

——. "Mennonite Settlement in the Lower Fraser Valley." MA Thesis, University of British Columbia, 1960.

Statistics Canada. *Historical Compendium of Education Statistics from Confederation to 1975*. Ottawa: Statistics Canada, Education, Culture and Tourism Division, Projections and Analysis Section, Online edition.

Thielmann, Jacob. "Kann Eine Christliche Hochchule den Platz einer Bibleschule Ausfuellen?" *East Chilliwack Bible School* Botschafter. (1953-54): 29

Thiessen, Elmer J. *Teaching for Commitment: Liberal Education, Indoctrination and Christian Nurture*. Montreal: McGill-Queen's Press, 1993.

Toews, John A. *A History of the Mennonite Brethren Church: Pilgrims and Pioneers*. Hillsboro, KS: Mennonite Brethren Publishing House, 1963.

Warkentin, Irwin. "The Mennonite Brethren Bible Institute," Unpublished Paper, Clearbrook, BC: 1968. Mennonite Archives of Ontario.

"Yarrow Bible School" *The MBBI Recal*. 1.1(Winter, n.d.): 1

The Tradition Continues in Canada: Mennonite High Schools in Abbotsford and Yarrow, 1944-1969

Harvey Neufeldt

On March 5, 1944, a group of Fraser Valley Mennonites gathered at the South Abbotsford Mennonite Brethren Church to consider the need for and prospects of establishing a Mennonite high school in the valley. The end of the Depression in the 1930s in Canada brought with it increased educational and occupational aspirations for the Mennonite youth. The war also heightened the tension between the immigrant communities and their Anglo-Canadian neighbors, which often spilled over into the public high schools. Having concluded at the March 5 meeting that there was an urgent need to establish a Mennonite High School (*Mennonitische Fortbildungschule*), Fraser Valley Mennonites moved quickly to establish two Mennonite high schools; the Mennonite Educational Institute (MEI) in Abbotsford in 1944 and the Mennonite Educational Institute, renamed the Sharon Mennonite Collegiate Institute (SMCI), in Yarrow in 1945.[1] By 1947, the success of the two schools seemed certain. A combined enrolment of over 500 students and the construction of two new schools must have surpassed even the most optimistic projections of the schools' founders.

The purpose of this paper is to analyze the missions of the Mennonite high schools from the mid 1940s to the late 1960s. That the schools' missions changed over time is evident. That various individuals and constituencies had different reasons for either supporting or opposing the schools is also clear. In this paper, I have given special attention to the public discourse that framed the discussion relative to the schools' mission. In addition, I have analyzed modifications in school practices, including curricular and extracurricular offerings as well as rules and regulations. It is evident that the debate over the missions of the schools reflected changes within the supporting church constituencies. Above all, the debates reveal differences over time in the community's understandings of the meaning of the word "Mennonite," especially its essential markers.

At the risk of oversimplification, this paper divides the discourse on the schools' missions into three time periods. The first period, 1944 to the early 1950s, can be described as the era of the Russian Mennonite immigrants' schools. The second, the 1950s, witnessed a drive to move the schools into the North American evangelical mainstream and an attempt by some to delete what were formerly viewed as ethnic Mennonite markers. The term "evangelical mainstream," as used in this paper, refers to a movement within Protestantism, which, according to George Marsden, stresses "eternal salvation as possible only by regeneration" (being born again), the "Bible as authoritative and reliable," and the need for a "spiritually transformed life. "[2] The third period, the 1960s, is characterized by ambivalence within the Mennonite constituencies. On the one hand, there is some evidence of an attempt to reclaim an Anabaptist heritage, influenced by Harold Bender's concept of an Anabaptist vision combining aspects of evangelicalism and discipleship. But there is also the continuing movement begun in the 1950s to de-emphasize the schools' identification with Mennonitism and to move the Mennonite Brethren churches even further into the North American evangelical mainstream. It should be pointed out there that there is considerable overlap among the three periods.

The Early Period: The Russian Immigrant Experience

The establishment of the Mennonite Educational Institute in 1944 and of the Sharon Mennonite Collegiate Institute in 1945 can be linked to economic and political changes within the immigrant Mennonite communities in the Fraser Valley. The challenges of getting started in a new country and of the Great Depression had provided little opportunity for advanced education, limiting the educational and occupational aspirations of Mennonite youth. World War II changed the economic landscape significantly. For Mennonite youth, it was now possible to envision making a living aside from farming, clearing stumps off the land, working in the hop yards, or, for women, working as domestic servants in Vancouver. While the schools came too late for Jacob Loewen, a long-time translation consultant with the American and United Bible Societies, some of the students enrolling in Yarrow or Abbotsford might well have understood his need for education. As he explained, "I took one look at my dad and said, 'I did not want to stay there.'"[3] Bill Friesen, a teacher and principal at the Sharon Mennonite Collegiate (SMC) during the 1950s, also rebelled at the notion that all young people needed in life was to attend elementary school as far as the law required, enroll in Bible school, farm and get married (Interview, Bill Friesen). Analysis of the SMCI student population in the school's first year of existence suggests that Loewen and Friesen were not atypical. The 1945-1946 class of 151 students listed their educational and occupational aspirations as follows: planning to enter university, 29; to become a nurse, 23; to become a teacher, 15; to enter business, 11; and to attend a Bible School, 4. While the small number planning to attend Bible School can be explained, at least in part, by the fact that 56 of the 151 students had attended Bible School prior to enrolling, it also suggests that high school was beginning to replace Bible School as the school of choice for Mennonite youth. Included among the 151 students were 23 over-age students enrolled in a special class, grade 9X, for whom the Mennonite high school offered an opportunity to realize educational aspirations that seemingly had not been available for them prior to World War II.[4]

The schools were also established in part to provide a safe haven for Mennonite youth that would shield them from the hostility encountered in public schools. During the 1930s and 1940s, Mennonites were often made to feel like unwanted neighbors. In 1943, Gordon Tower, the newly elected president of the Fraser Valley Boards of Trade, warned that Mennonites were "a menace" and that unless steps were taken to control the expansion of their settlements, they would "eventually swamp the valley as the Japanese did."[5] Such attitudes, not surprisingly, spilled over into several public schools. It was not uncommon for Mennonite youth attending public schools to experience both physical and verbal harassment. Bill Friesen, who attended the Chilliwack High School prior to the MEI opening its doors in 1944, described the hostile environment that he encountered there during the war years. "It wasn't hostility," he remarked, "it was open warfare." From the perspective of the non-Mennonite students, "we were the enemy and collaborated with the enemy" (Interview, Bill Friesen). After facing physical harassment at the Mount Lehman School, Henry Klassen, an alumnus of and long-time teacher at MEI, and his classmates "yearned" for the day the MEI would open its doors" (Interview, Klassen).

In addition to providing a safe haven, the schools were set up to guard against cultural and religious assimilation. Central to the 1940s mission statements of both the MEI and the SMCI was an emphasis on cultural, ethnic and religious separatism. The first set of MEI minutes from March 5, 1944 provides the founders' rationale for establishing a school. Since Mennonite youth who were determined to attend high school would be receiving their education from sources that were contrary to the Mennonite principles of faith (*"welche unsere Glaubensprinzip abgeneigt sind"*), it was deemed essential to establish a high school. Like the Mennonite settlers who had immigrated into Canada in the late-nineteenth century, they also "assumed that their own schools were absolutely essential for the preservation of Mennonitism."[6]

Both Yarrow and Abbotsford leaders drew heavily upon their Russian experience in formulating the purpose and philosophy of the schools. A case in point is Franz Thiessen, a key leader in the movement to establish a Mennonite high school in Abbotsford. At a meeting in 1944, attended by representatives from 7 of the 14 British Columbia Mennonite Brethren churches, Thiessen laid out his case for a school. Undoubtedly drawing upon the Mennonites' Russian experience, he argued that the development of Mennonites as a people was based on religion taught in their institutions. It was essential that the community establish its own schools to provide a foundation for an understanding of the Bible and knowledge of the German language. As John Redekop, an MEI graduate observed, Thiessen represented what the churches wanted: Music, German, and Mennonite culture.[7]

In 1946, the MEI School Board sent an open letter to its supporting churches, soliciting money for the purchase of a school site. (MEI used buildings on the South Abbotsford Church grounds before moving into a new structure on the corner of Old Yale Road and Clearbrook Road in December 1946.) God, they argued, had not rescued the Mennonites from the "Red Terror" for them to lose their identity by succumbing to the forces of assimilation (minutes MEI, 1 Feb. 1946).

Promoting and preserving a culturally separatist environment was also a key factor in the establishment of the first Sharon High School in Yarrow, the SMCI, in 1945. Like the MEI, it also opened on church grounds, in this case those of the Yarrow MB Church. Enrolment surpassed all projections, with 151 in the initial year and over 300 in the second. The desire to maintain a culturally separatist position is not surprising, given the fact that the vast majority of students were either first or second-generation immigrants. Of the 333 students attending the SMCI from 1945-1949 for whom information is available, twenty-two were born in Russia, and over 96 percent listed Russia as their parents' birthplace, making it a truly a *Russlaender* institution (SMCI Information forms, 1945-1949).

When planning for a new high school building, the Yarrow MB Church and the School Board faced the question of whether to include plans for adding grades 7 and 8. This question was quickly answered in the affirmative. It was as if a cry had risen from the hearts of the parents. The community feared the loss of their children should they attend the junior and senior high schools in Chilliwack.[8]

Maintaining a safe haven required the sanction of true religion. Chapel, organized prayer groups and inclusion of religious instruction in the curriculum were all deemed essential for maintaining cultural and religious separatism. In a letter drafted in 1945 by the Yarrow Committee to George Cruickshank, Liberal Member of Parliament for the Chilliwack District, requesting a building permit to house the Bible and high school, the Committee argued that a "Mennonite without religion ...[is] like a house without foundation"(Letter, C.C. Peters). As the 1945 *Laurel* Editorial (the SMCI Yearbook) stated,

> Regardless ... of how the world may view our interpretations of the Bible we are resolved to imbue and indoctrinate our children with the beliefs of our forefathers in so far as they will serve to halt in some small measure the mad rush of the world towards material idolatry, social chaos and atheism.[9]

Along with the teaching and practice of religion, the use of German was viewed as central to maintaining a culturally separatist community. At a June 11, 1946 SMCI Parent and Teacher meeting, Anna Bartsch, a former missionary to Africa, argued that maintaining the German language was necessary if the immigrant community was "to be able to preserve ...[its] confession and...[its] faith." Furthermore, preserving the German language was essential if the young were to share in the inheritance of their forefathers, including their thoughts, spirit, mind and customs (*Ihr Denken, der Geist, ihr Sinn, ihre Art*). The School Board agreed. In 1948 it declared German and religion to be essential aspects of the school's mission, necessary for citizenship as well as for effective membership in one's own society (*zu nuetzlichen Glieder der Geselschaft einziehen.*)[10] For F. C. Thiessen, the preservation of the German language was absolutely essential. He taught all his subjects in German. In 1949, Thiessen, representing the Mennonite high schools in British Columbia, presented a report to a conference of MB Bible schools and high schools in Canada. Thiessen reminded the audience that "Mennonite Brethren had been born into German-speaking families not by chance," but rather by "the express will of God." Preservation of the German language thus included more than cultural preservation; it meant nothing less than doing God's will.[11]

The education and preservation of an immigrant community also required adherence to specific behavioral traits. Not surprisingly, both the MEI and the SMCI sought to incorporate rules and regulations that defined the Mennonite life style. Some of these cultural markers had special relevance for female students. In this respect, Mennonites were not atypical compared with other immigrant groups in North America. As Michael

Olneck has pointed out, it is especially girls who have been called upon by immigrant communities to maintain distinctive ethnic markers.[12] One such marker included dress codes, especially uniforms. Both MEI and SMCI enacted dress codes that included uniforms for girls. Prior to 1953, the MEI boys' basketball team always wore long pants. However, girls' teams did not dress in shorts until the early 1960s. The MEI Board stipulated that when performing on stage, male and female members of the cast must enter separately (*nicht zumischt auftreten*). In 1954 it expressed its concern that students were seen frequenting "worldly sports sites" (*Weltlichen Sportsplaetzen*), including roller rinks.[13] On the one hand, these rules can be seen as markers of a separatist Mennonite community, and as part of a Russian Mennonite heritage. But these Russian practices also coincided with those advocated in the broader North American fundamentalist community as enunciated by men like John R. Rice. As such they reflected not only aspects of ethnic preservation, but also of contemporary evangelical fundamentalism.[14]

Given the Mennonites' Russian experience, a desire to maintain cultural boundaries, including religious and linguistic separatism, are understandable. As Jacob Loewen observed, for Johannes Harder, the SMCI Board Chair throughout the school's four-year history, assimilation was never a question; only the ungodly assimilated (Interview, Jacob Loewen). In 1947 Harder opposed inter-church cooperation with the Youth for Christ rallies because the Pentecostal Churches participated in them. Cooperation by the Mennonite church community meant the danger "of being assimilated and thus losing what it had received from God, those values for which its parents had died." While comparing the mission of the SMCI Board with that of the Chilliwack School Board, Harder virtually defined "Christian" and "assimilation" as opposing categories. The Chilliwack Board assumed that through assimilation one created good citizens. The goal of the SMCI, however, was to provide a school with a Christian atmosphere and instruction.[15]

Support for the MEI and the SMCI, while overwhelming, was never without opposition. In the fall of 1946, the MEI Board reported with sadness that some individuals failed to understand the mission of the school and, sadder still, even spoke out against it. In 1947, the SMCI supporting churches, faced with a sizeable debt brought on by an ambitious building program, agreed, with faith in God, to continue in their efforts to raise the required sums, despite the unwillingness of several brethren to join in. As the school faced severe economic pressures in 1949, the Yarrow Church sadly reported that there were still individuals who were not convinced of the absolute necessity of a Christian school.[16]

Moving beyond Mennonite separatism

The 1950s witnessed a movement both in Yarrow and Abbotsford to move beyond a Mennonite separatist position. The 1948 flooding of Sardis and Greendale by the Fraser River and the economically devastating collapse of the berry market in the same year (which had a devastating impact on the Yarrow economy) forced the closure of the SMCI in 1949 and the eventual sale of its building in 1952 to the Chilliwack School Board. After the demise of the SMCI, supporters of a private high school organized themselves into a society and established another high school in 1951, which ultimately became the Sharon Mennonite Collegiate (SMC). The SMC soon gave ample evidence that its function would be somewhat different than that of its predecessor. Its principal, Henry Voth, had served in the military, albeit in a non-combative role, and appeared to have worn the uniform proudly. Preservation of the German language and Mennonitism never appeared to be his primary concern. Mennonite history was replaced with other religious subjects. With the shift in religion came an increased emphasis on evangelism in the schools. This focus, however, was not typical of the earlier Mennonite schools in Russia.[17]

William Friesen, Henry Voth's successor as principal in 1955, accelerated the shift away from a culturally separatist orientation. Friesen chafed under what he saw as the conservative orientation of the Yarrow MB Church, complaining that, "How was this decided in Russia?" was the guiding principle in most decisions. Harder, he felt, had been too much of a cultural isolationist. While a student at the University of British Columbia, Friesen had been introduced to the Inter Varsity Christian Fellowship. The IVCF approached Bible studies from an inter-church, evangelical perspective, a perspective he sought to include in religion courses at SMC. He advocated teaching Christian History not from a Mennonite perspective, but rather from the "viewpoint of Christian civilization" (Interview, Bill Friesen).

The German language at SMC lost the exalted position it had enjoyed in the first high school. The study of German as a foreign language replaced German/English bilingualism. The fact that the language issue remained a most contentious one in the school reflected an ongoing struggle in the Yarrow MB Church. In 1958, following a two-year debate on the language issue, the Yarrow MB Church agreed to include both a German and English sermon in the Sunday morning service. SMC hired two Bible School teachers, C. C. Peters and Herman Voth, to teach Bible and German in the spring sessions. Despite this, the school faced criticisms that it was neglecting the German language. However, by 1960, German was no longer included in the twelfth grade curriculum. Promoting academic excellence in an evangelical environment increasingly defined the mission of the school.[18]

Undoubtedly, William Friesen had support from some of the Board members for his attempt to move the school from being a separatist Mennonite institution to becoming an evangelical Christian school that happened to be located in a Mennonite community. A case in point was Peter Neufeldt, one of the school's founders, who served as a Board member (1951-1959) and Board Chair (1957-59). Neufeldt had been exposed to a North American evangelical-fundamentalist orientation both as a student in the Yarrow Bible School and in his work with the West Coast Children's Mission. Maintaining distinctive Mennonite markers, including the German language, were never his priority, both while on the Board and also while pastor of the Yarrow MB Church in the late 1950s.

The MEI also moved away from its early culturally separatist orientation. Franz Thiessen had never taught a course in English, and his musical productions, such as *Das Lied von der Glocke*, were always performed in the German language. In 1954, MEI principal Isaac Dyck defended the school's decision to teach a Christian doctrines course (*Glaubenslehre*) in English. He stated that in the future students would be required to explain their faith to members of society in the English language. Cultural, including religious, separatism was gradually being reappraised in the 1950s. Musical and drama presentations shifted in the 1950s from all German productions to include both an English play, *Esther*, in 1950, and a German production, *Glaube und Heimat*, the following year. MEI's hiring of C.C. Peters in the late 1950s, a *Russlaender* fluent in the German language, might be interpreted as a belated attempt by the MEI Board to shore up the school's German and Mennonite identity.[19]

While the MEI, like the SMC, moved away from affirming a separatist religious community to position itself within the broader North American evangelical community; this shift may have been lessened somewhat with the presence of the General Conference Mennonite Churches within the MEI family of supporting churches. The General Conference churches, more so than their Mennonite Brethren counterparts, maintained strong ties with inter-Mennonite organizations. In addition, post-World War II Mennonite refugees from the Soviet Union disproportionately joined General Conference rather than Mennonite Brethren churches. Their presence led to a renewed emphasis on the use of the German language within the church community. In 1954, the West Abbotsford Mennonite Church, a General Conference congregation combining both an evangelical orientation and a Mennonite identity, formally joined the MEI Society of Churches. On the other hand, the Yarrow SMC Board never seriously considered inviting the General Conference Church to join in their venture.[20]

The 1960s—period of ambivalence

The 1960s were difficult years for both schools. The SMC, after facing decreasing enrolment for several years, finally closed its doors in 1969. The MEI also struggled in the 1960s. After dropping grades 7 and 13 in 1967, the MEI struggled to limit the decrease in enrolment occurring during the late 1960s. Whereas enrolment stood at 397 in September 1964, it had declined to 288 in the fall of 1967. After that, enrolment picked up once again, reaching 321 and 379 in 1969 and 1970 respectively. SMC's drop in enrolment can be explained in large part by the changing demographics. The exodus from Yarrow, which began with the collapse of the berry market in 1948, only accelerated in the 1950s and 1960s. Finally, in 1969, Sharon High, as it was popularly known, was closed, and one year later it was sold to the Canadian Reformed School Society in Abbotsford for $54,000.[21] MEI's decline in enrolment can be explained in part by a governmentally mandated revision of the high school programs, especially its decision to move the seventh grade from the secondary to the elementary school (minutes, MEI Bd, 1 August 1967). In addition, both the MEI and the SMC faced increasing pressure as Mennonite communities continued to redefine their place within the larger Canadian society. This was especially evident in the Central Heights MB Church, which voted in 1967 to withdraw as a member of the MEI Society (Interview, Klassen).

SMC still struggled with the issue of maintaining traditional markers in student conduct and curriculum. In 1960, the Board authorized the students' use of wigs and of costumes for school dramas, but not makeup (*roetliche Farben*). Several years later, the Board registered its concern that some students had been observed walking as couples on the street and loitering for lengthy periods of time on street corners. By 1960, the girls' basketball teams, which previously had worn long pants or peddle pushers, dressed in shirts with short sleeves and knee-length Bermuda shorts.[22]

Providing a curriculum that met the needs of senior high students became increasingly problematic. In order to concentrate more on the subjects required for governmental exams, SMC, in 1960, deleted German from the twelfth grade curriculum. Three years later, Principal Vern Ratzlaff reported that to accommodate students who were considering transferring to Chilliwack for their senior year unless more curricular options were made available, instruction in German or Bible was being reduced by one hour per week. In

1966, the school decided to drop its senior grades, enrolling students only in grades six to nine.[23]

At the same time that some of the former Mennonite markers of a separatist, immigrant community were disappearing, attempts were made by some to reclaim an Anabaptist heritage. A case in point is Hugo and Jean Friesen who joined the faculty in the mid 1950s. Attendance at Goshen College and service in the MCC had deepened their commitment to and love for their Anabaptist heritage. Vern Ratzlaff, Hugo Friesen's successor as principal in 1963, was heavily influenced by Guy Hershberger's and Harold Bender's discussion on the recovery of the Anabaptist vision, and he attempted to inculcate an Anabaptist perspective in the school. He saw SMC as a "Mennonite school, where peace, service and discipleship were central." Whether Friesen's and Ratzlaff's positions were more individualistic and isolated rather than part of a formal institutional response is not clear. Mennonite history or Anabaptist studies were not a formal part of SMC's curriculum.[24]

In the mid 1960s, MEI's School Board established a Self Study Commission, whose findings were released in 1965. The commission began the report by claiming continuity in the school's mission over the past two decades. "After having studied the reports," it stated, "the Commission has arrived at the same conclusion as our leaders 22 years ago—'We need a Christian High School.'" It then went on to state, "The reasons for it are very much the same as they were at the founding of the school. Basically the objectives have not changed." The main objective in the 1940s as well as in the 1960s was to provide for their children "a Christian education."[25]

But even as the commission explained the need for a Christian school, its explanations suggested not continuity but change. It stated, "Contrary to common talk and rumours, our school, therefore, does not exist merely to separate our children from secular schools and influences, and to continue them in traditional Mennonitism to become superficial conformists to the church." One cannot imagine either the founders of the first Sharon High School or of the MEI making such a statement. The total emphasis in the introduction was on the word "Christian"; the only time the word "Mennonite" appeared was in the negative connotation mentioned above. In fact, what seems of greatest importance is the language used in the opening statement: "We need a Christian High School." In 1944, MEI's founders were convinced that they needed a Mennonite High School. The Self Study Commission raised the question, "Concerning objectives, the question of priority might be raised. Is the school to serve first a people and culture, or does it have first of all a spiritual objective that rises above culture? If faith and culture pose as mere partners, faith will likely lose out in the end." The commission was ambivalent as to whether the name of the school should be changed, suggesting merely that should the school be renamed: it "should be a place name and not a denominational name." As for the German language, the commission concluded, it no longer was a necessary marker of the Mennonite community. Its status, the commission concluded, was "simply that of another foreign language." It is evident that the discourse of 1965 was quite different from that of 1944.[26] The question is, to what extent did the shift in language signal a change in the school's mission as well?

One distinct change was evident in the Mennonite community itself. Many still viewed the school as a safe haven, a place to shore up the young people's faith (Interview, Dave Loewen). The Mennonite community, however, no longer required a safe haven to shield its young people from hostility in the public sector. By the 1960s Mennonites in the Valley no longer felt themselves to be second-class citizens. The success of MEI students in academics, athletics and music instilled a great deal of pride, a feeling that the students could hold their own with the best in the province. In the end, nothing provided more community spirit and pride than the basketball program. In 1963, the senior boys won their first provincial championship, after having placed 3rd and 4th in 1961 and 1962 respectively. Meanwhile, the junior boys team won the provincial championship in 1965. The success of the program led to the building of a new gym in 1970. The gym, which an observer called one of the best in the province, cost slightly less than 200,000 dollars.[27]

The athletic program, the construction of the gym, and concert choirs restricted to students of musical talent, were not without their critics. The Self Study itself raised concern that "a possible over-emphasis on basketball" might be detracting from a physical education program that involved the entire student body. It also suggested that although selective participation in music "might provide a better quality program, it is advantageous to have total participation and thus discourage rivalry, cliquishness, and inferiority complexes." Concerning drama, the commission recommended that "no consideration of light operas be given; rather that work with activities be encouraged. If truly spiritual, they will help resolve such problems as cliquishness and an unhealthy emphasis on boy-girl relationships" (MEI Self Study, 23, 31, 33).

By the mid 1960s, providing a safe haven was restricted to shielding the young from an undue exposure to a secular educational philosophy. At the annual 1968 Society meeting, the Board Chair, Jake Friesen, rejected the notion that the school had served its purpose and that the youth should now attend public schools in order to help evangelize the world (minutes, MEI Bd. 22 October, 1968). His remarks may have been, at least in part, a response to the decision of the Central Heights Church to withdraw from the MEI Society. In 1967, the Central Heights MB Church, following a majority vote to drop its membership in the MEI Society of Churches, notified the MEI Board of its intention to discontinue its support of the school on a "member-levy basis." In the fall of 1967, only 12 students from Central Heights as compared to 45 from the Bakerview MB Church enrolled in the MEI. Nick Dyck, the senior pastor of Central Heights, questioned the concept of a safe haven. He asserted that in the public schools, unlike at MEI, Christian students could not be complacent; rather they were compelled to take a stand. Looking back, Nick Dyck observed that the MEI's promotion of Mennonitism, even if done more covertly, did not seem to be as compelling at that time. Reflecting on his previous stance, Nick Dyck remarked, "I was reacting against that Mennonite thing."[28]

The 1960s witnessed the gradual erosion of Mennonite markers, especially in women's dress codes. The senior boys' basketball team had already appeared in shorts in 1953, some nine years before their girls' counterparts. In 1962 and then again in 1969, the MEI Board opposed the formal organization of cheerleader squads. The school finally organized its first female cheerleaders' squad in 1974. While girls' uniforms remained mandatory throughout the 1960s, they were finally discontinued in 1971.[29]

Conclusion

From the mid-forties to the sixties, change as well as continuity characterized the missions of the Mennonite high schools in Yarrow and Abbotsford. Both continuity and change were reflected in the perceived need to maintain schools as safe havens for Mennonite adolescents. The schools were initially regarded as necessary institutions to help safeguard Mennonite youth from the dangers of secularism and assimilation. By the 1960s it was evident, however, that Mennonites no longer perceived themselves as an embattled minority. It was also evident that the need for schools to serve as safeguards against cultural assimilation was being questioned and rejected by an increasing number of members in the Mennonite community at large. While there was continuity in the idea that the schools should be Christian schools, what was not clear by the 1960s was the extent to which they should be Mennonite schools.

It is clear that the markers of ethnicity underwent considerable change over the two-and-one-half decades. This shift was especially evident in the school's language policies and in the debate over dress codes. The decreasing emphasis on retention of these markers reflected a shift in the Mennonite communities in the Fraser Valley, as they increasingly identified themselves as a religious denomination rather than as an ethnic group. In so doing, the schools and the Mennonite communities distanced themselves from their Russian heritage.

Endnotes

[1] Minutes, MEI Bd. 5 March 1944. Subsequent citation of minutes will appear in the text. See the bibliography for full details.

[2] George Marsden, "Evangelical and Fundamental Christianity," in *The Encyclopedia of Christianity,* vol. 5, ed. Mircea Eliade (New York: McMillan, 1987), 190. Subsequent citations will apear in the text.

[3] Personal interview with Jacob Loewen, August 1985 and August 1986. Subsequent citation of interviews will appear in the text. See the bibliography for full details.

[4] Minutes, SMCI, 4 March 1946, Office Copy Marks, First Term Students Class Lists, MEI Yarrow, BC, 1945-1946, Grade 9X Class Lists, 1945-1946, 1946-1947, 1947-1948, SMCI Records.

[5] "Mennonites Protested as Valley Evil," *Vancouver Sun,* 20 March, 1943, 16; "Are Mennonites Taboo?" *Vancouver Sun,* 23 May 1940, 6. For protests against Mennonite settlements in areas outside the Fraser Valley see "Fort George Member Opposes Mennonite Settlements in BC," *Vancouver Province,* 7 June 1941, 12.

[6] Minutes, MEI, 5 March 1944,1-3; Frank Epp, *Education with a Difference: The Story of Rosthern Junior College* (Waterloo, ON: Conrad Press, 1975), 14.

[7] Minutes, MEI, 14 May 1944, p.5; Interview, Redekop; interview Ratzlaff. For a brief laudatory biography on F.C. Thiessen, see Klassen, *My Father.* Aspects of rural and popular education in Russian society in the eighteenth and nineteenth centuries are discussed in Ecklof, "The Adequacy of Basic Education in Rural Russia," and Walker, "Popular Responses to Public Education in the Reign of Tsar Alexander." On education in the Mennonite Commonwealth in Russia see Rempel, "The Mennonite Commonwealth in Russia;" Urry, "None but Saints"; Friesen, *The Mennonite Brotherhood in Russia*; and Toews, "Cultural and Intellectual Aspects of the Mennonite Experience in Russia." Educational developments in selected Mennonite settlements are discussed in Cherkazianova, "The Mennonite Schools in Siberia"; Goertz, *The Molotschna Settlement,"* and Brucks and Hooge, *Neu Samara.* A case study of one Zentralschule in Russia is Regehr, *For Everything a Season.*

[8] Minutes, YMBC, 9 February 1946, p. 138; Minutes, SMCI, PTA, 28 January 1947, np.

[9] *Laurel, 1945-1946*, p. 3. On the inclusion of religion in a Russian high school see Regehr, *For Everything a Season*, 59-60.

[10] Edward Dahl, "Sharon Mennonite Collegiate Institute: 1945-1949," 24; Minutes, SMCI, PTA, Meeting, 11 June, 1946; Minutes, SMCI, 15 June 1946. On the importance of German in Russian Mennonite schools see Regehr, *For Everything a Season.*

[11] Gerald Ediger, *Crossing the Divide,* 43, 54-59. For a discussion on the language issue in the Canadian MB Churches, see Ediger, *Crossing the Divide*, 1-88; on the German identity among the Mennonite Brethren see Redekop, "The German Identity of Mennonite Brethren Immigrants in Canada." In "Transferred Crisis," Wagner presents a negative assessment of Mennonite identification with German "Volkish" thought.

[12] Michael Olneck, "Immigrants and Education," in *Handbook on Research in Multicultural Education,* ed. James Banks and Cherry Banks (New York: MacMillan, 1995), 317-18.

[13] Minutes, YMBC, 21 August 1945, 95; Minutes, SMCI, 31 August 1946, 37-39, 6 May 1947, 2763-64; Minutes, SMCI PTA Meeting, 6 June 1947, np; *Evergreen*, 21,74-75; Minutes, MEI, 13 May 1947, 71, 2 Nov.1954,259-60. On uniforms for girls at Rosthern Academy, see Epp, *Education with a Difference*, 161.

[14] Regehr, *For Everything a Season*, 62-63; interview, Redekop. On the maintenance of Mennonite markers in the Yarrow Mennonite community see Neufeldt, "Creating the Brotherhood," 224-27.

[15] Neufeldt, "Creating the Brotherhood," 233; minutes, SMCI, 24 September 1947, 614-15; Dahl, "Sharon Mennonite Collegiate Institute," 21.

[16] Minutes, MEI, 10 October 1946, 2-4; Minutes, SMCI, 4 November 4 1947, 94; Minutes, YMBC, 25 January 1949, 54.

[17] Interview, Neufeldt; oral communication, Giesbrecht; Regehr, *For Everything a Season*, 59-60.

[18] Minutes, YMBC, 19 December 1956, p. 314; 9 January 1957, pp. 317-18; 3 December 1957, 337-38; 16 December 1957, p. 349; 3 November 1958, 370; Minutes, SMC, 10 April 1955, np., 10 May 1952, np., 22 January 1953, np., 5 February 1954, np., 29 January 1958, np.; 27 September 1960, np.; interview, William Friesen; interview, John Friesen.

[19] Minutes, MEI, 2 November 1954, pp. 259-60; interview, Wiebe; interview, Redekop; *Evergreen*, 49; interview, Klassen; interview, Ratzlaff.

[20] Minutes, MEI, 3 November, and 1 December 1953, pp. 218-21; 2 November 1954, 225-26. For a history of the West Abbotsford Church see Loewen, *Living Stones.* In Russia, schools were usually joint ventures, enrolling students from all Mennonite churches. A case in point was the Alexanderkrone School. See Regehr, *For Everything a Season,* 60.

[21] Minutes, MEI, 8 September 1964, np.; MEI Annual Meeting, 17 October 1967, np.; MEI Annual Meeting, 22 October 1970, np.; Minutes, YMBC, 31 March 1970, 145.

[22] Minutes, SMC, 19 February 1960, np.; 21 September 1961, np., 26 April 1963, np.

[23] Minutes, SMC, 27 September 1960, np., 25 September 1962, np., 26 September, 1963 np., 29 June 1966, np.

[24] Memo, Ratzlaff ; Regehr, *Mennonites in Canada*, 13-14; Bender, "The Anabaptist Vision," 29-54; oral communication, Martens; *Sharon Chatterer*, November, 1962.

[25] MEI Self Study Commission, 6 May 1966 (Unpublished report), 9. Subsequent references will appear in the text.

[26] Ibid., 1-2, 5, 9-10, 16, 35.

[27] Interview, Ratzlaff; interview, Klassen, interview, Baerg; *Evergreen*, 65-66, 70; Minutes, MEI, 15 December 1970. The actual cost of the gymnasium was $199,212.82.

[28] Minutes, MEI, 1 August 1967; minutes, Annual Meeting, MEI, 17 October 1967; interview, Dyck. Nick Dyck had begun his pastoral career with the West Coast Children's Mission, where Mennonite identity was often viewed as being problematic.

[29] Minutes, MEI, 6 November 1962 and 7 October 1969; *Evergreen*, 21, 72; Minutes, Annual Meeting, MEI, 19 October 1971.

Bibliography

Bender, Harold. "The Anabaptist Vision," in *The Recovery of the Anabaptist Vision*. Ed. Guy Hershberger. Scotdale PA: Herald Press, 1957.

Brucks Jacob and Hooge, Henry, compilers. *Neu Samara: A Mennonite Settlement East of the Volga*. Trans. John Isaac. Edmonton: Jackpine House Ltd., 2002.

Cherkazianova, Irina. "The Mennonite schools in Siberia from the Late Nineteenth Century to the 1920s," *Journal of Mennonite Studies*. 20(2002): 9-26.

Dahl, Edward. "Sharon Mennonite Collegiate Institute: 1945-1949." Unpublished paper, University of British Columbia, 1968.

Ecklof, Ben. "The Adequacy of Basic Schooling in Rural Russia: Teachers and their Craft, 1880-1914." *History of Education Quarterly*. 26 (Summer 1986): 199-223.

Ediger, Gerald. *Crossing the Divide: Language Transition Among Canadian Mennonite Brethren, 1940-1970*. Winnipeg: Center for Mennonite Studies, 2001.

Ens, Adolph. "Mennonites Education in Russia," in *Mennonites in Russia, 1788-1998: Essays in Honour of Gerhard Lohrenz*. Ed. John Friesen. Winnipeg, Manitoba: CMBC Publications, 1989. 75-79.

Ens, Gerhard. *"Die Schule muss sein": A History of the Mennonite Collegiate Institute*. Altona, Manitoba: Friesen Printers, 1990.

Epp, Frank. *Education with a Difference: The Story of Rosthern Junior College*. Waterloo, Ont.: Conrad Press, 1975.

Friesen, P.M. *The Mennonite Brotherhood in Russia, 1789-1910*. Translated from German. Fresno, CA.: Board of Christian Literature- Gen Conference of Mennonite Brethren Churches, 1978.

Goertz, Heinrich. *The Molotschna Settlement*. Transl. Al Reimer and John B. Toews. Winnipeg: CMBC Publications, 1989.

Klassen, Katie. *My Father, Franz C. Thiessen*. Trans. Mary Enns. Self- published, 1979.

Klassen, Peter. "A History of Mennonite Education in Canada." Dissertation, University of University of Toronto, 1970.

Loewen, David. *Living Stones: A History of the West Abbotsford Mennonite Church, 1936-1986*. Abbotsford, B.C.: West Abbotsford Church, 1987.

Marsden George. "Evangelical and Fundamental Christianity." *The Encyclopedia of Christianity*, Vol. 5. Ed. Mircea Eliade. New York: McMillan, 1987. 190-97.

MEI Evergreen Jubilee edition, 1944-1994: *His Faithfulness Continues*. Altona, Manitoba: Friesen Yearbooks, 1994.

Neufeldt, Harvey. "Creating the Brotherhood: Status and Control in the Yarrow Mennonite Community, 1928-1960." *Canadian Papers in Rural History*. Vol 9. Ed. Don Akenson. Gananoque, Ontario: Langdale Press, 1994. 211-38.

Olneck, Michael. "Immigrants and Education." *Handbook on Research in Multicultural Education*. Ed. James Banks and Cherry Banks. New York: MacMillan, 1995. 310-27.

Redekop, Benjamin. "The German Identity of Mennonite Brethren Immigrants in Canada, 1930-1960." Masters thesis, U. of British Columbia, 1990.

Regehr, T.D. *For Everything a Season: A History of the Alexanderkrone Zentralschule*. Winnipeg: CMBC Publications, 1988.

———. *Mennonites in Canada, 1939-1970: A People Transformed*. Toronto:University of Toronto Press, 1996.

Rempel, David. "The Mennonite Commonwealth in Russia: A Sketch of its Founding and Endurance, 1789-1919." *Mennonite Quarterly Review* 48 (April 1973): 5-54.

Toews, John B. "Cultural and Intellectual Aspects of the Mennonite Experience in Russia." *Mennonite Quarterly Review* 47 (April 1973): 83-110.

Wagner, Johnathan. "Transferred Crisis: German Volkish Thought Among Russian Mennonite Immigrants to Western Canada." *Canadian Review of Studies in Nationalism* 1 (Spring 1974): 202-220.

Urry, James. *None but Saints: the Transformation of Mennonite Life in Russia, 1789-1889*. Winnipeg: Hyperion Press, 1989.

Walker, Franklin. "Popular Responses to Public Education in the Reign of Tsar Alexander (1810-1825)." *History of Education Quarterly*, 24 (Winter, 1984): 527-43.

Newspapers

"Are Mennonites Taboo?" *Vancouver Sun*, 23 May 1940, p. 6.

"Fort George Member Opposes Mennonite Settlements in BC." *Vancouver Province*, 7 June 1941, p. 12.

"Trade Board Opens Meeting, *The Daily Province*, 4 September, 1940, np.

Minutes, reports and records

MEI Self Study Commission, 6 May 1966 (Unpublished report).

Minutes, Mennonite Educational Institute, Book 1944-1972 (cited as minutes, MEI.).

Minutes, Sharon Mennonite Collegiate Institute Board, 1945-1949 (cited as minutes, SMCI).

Minutes, Sharon Mennonite Collegiate Board, 1952-1969 (cited as minutes, SMC).

Minutes, Yarrow Mennonite Brethren Church (cited as minutes YMBC).

Sharon Mennonite Collegiate Institute Records (cited as SMCI records).

Sharon Mennonite Collegiate Institute Information Forms, 1945-1959. Box 990.111/990.112 (cited as SMCI information forms).

Interviews

Baerg, Rudy. Personal interview. 21 October 2002.
Dyck, Nick. Personal interview. 10 December 2002.
Friesen, Bill. Personal interview. 10 November 2000 and 23 May 2001.
Friesen, John. Personal interview. 9 March 2003.
Giesbrecht, David. Personal interview. 3 August 1993.
Klassen, Henry. Personal interview. 23 and 24 September 2002.
Loewen, Dave. Personal interview. 21 October 2002.
Loewen, Jacob. Personal interview. August 1985 and August 1986.
Neufeldt, Leonard. Personal interview. Summer 1990.
Neuman, Peter. Personal Interview. 22 October 2002.
Ratzlaff John. Personal interview. 10 March 2003.
Redekop John. Personal Interview. 10 December 2002.
Wiebe, Bill. Personal Interview. 21 September 2002.

E-mail

Vern Ratzlaff. "Re: Interview questions." E-mail to the author. 23 April 2003.

Oral Communication

Bob Martens. Oral communication. "Re: Interview question." 8 March 2003.
MEI Yearbook
The Laurel, 1945-1946.
SMC School Paper, "The Chatterer."

Letter

C. C. Peters. Letter to the Honorable George Cruikshank. 9 March 1945.

PART V
Economic Development and Urbanization of Ethnic Mennonites

A Gift from Providence: the Hop Industry in the Fraser Valley and its Impact on Yarrow

Ron Denman

From the early 1890s until 1997, the hop growing industry in Canada was centred around Chilliwack, with thousands of people participating in the annual hop picking harvest. Workers from throughout British Columbia, Idaho and Washington converged on the fields to separate the hop cone from the hop vine.[1] The workforce included Aboriginals, Chinese, Japanese, South Asians and Euro-Canadians. Though all these groups were dependant on the cash income provided by the work, each was motivated by different reasons.

For aboriginal people, the annual sports days complete with cash prizes, dances, boxing matches, bone games (*Slahal*), trading of various types of salmon, soapberries and basketry, and visiting were as much a part of the gatherings as the picking. Keith Carlson, Professor of History at the University of Saskatchewan, states that hop picking informally substituted, although not adequately, for potlatching, which was banned in 1884.[2] For the aboriginals, potlatches had been the main social institution for acknowledging and meeting social obligations and for affirming and reinforcing ownership of various resources.

Some single Chinese male workers worked in the hop industry throughout the year, and these workers were able to send money to their families in China. Japanese farm workers from Abbotsford, Matsqui and Mission also worked in the industry until World War Two, when Japanese-Canadians were removed to internment camps because they were perceived as a threat to Canadian security. Mennonites joined the hop workforce when a series of global and local events led to their acceptance into Canada and eventual immigration to the Fraser Valley. For Mennonite families, impoverished by war and displacement, work in the hopfields meant economic survival.

When Mennonite families migrated to Yarrow in 1927 and the following years, most arrived with little or no cash and very few assets. These families eventually formed the community of Yarrow and added substantially to the population of the neighbouring community of Greendale. Hav-

From the early 1890s to the mid-1950s, aboriginal people ended their seasonal rounds of work at the hop yards in Sardis and Sumas Prairie. Stó:lō pickers, at their own request, were segregated from non aboriginals. Segregation allowed for the types of social interaction that helped preserve important aspects of aboriginal cultures. When Mennonites joined the industry, workers continued to be culturally segregated. This meant that different aspects of Mennonite culture could be preserved. (Chilliwack Archives P1622)

ing fled the Soviet Union because of religious and economic persecution following the Russian Revolution of 1917, these Mennonite families were lured to the area hoping that plentiful and cheap land would provide them with an opportunity to create a new Mennonite settlement modeled after the settlements they had left behind.

The refugees' first few years in Canada were spent mostly in the older Mennonite communities on the Prairies, whose inhabitants had fled Russia in the 1870s when new governmental changes threatened their independence and compromised their historic rights relative to exemption from military service. Life on the Prairies was not easy. Harsh living conditions, crop failures and an overall lack of economic opportunities were reasons that most families remained open to further change in their already disrupted lives. Fortuitously, by 1927, Chauncey Eckert, a successful Chilliwack developer, chose to subdivide his vast landholdings located south of Chilliwack in the lush Fraser Valley. Advertisements for Eckert's land in the *Mennonitische Rundschau*, a Mennonite newspaper published in the Prairies, caught the attention of John Bargen and others. With nothing to lose, Bargen traveled to British Columbia in November 1927 and soon secured a job and land from Eckert. Isaak Sawatsky joined him in December. An enthusiastic letter sent by John Bargen back to the

Rundschau about conditions in the Fraser Valley "caused an explosion of interest among our Mennonite immigrant friends in the Prairies."[3] The opportunity for jobs and land in a hospitable climate enticed many other families to follow. Fortunately, these families arrived in the Fraser Valley at a time when the production of hops was undergoing massive expansion. The need for workers was acute. As a result of this influx, Yarrow soon became the centre of Mennonite settlement in British Columbia.

Until 1926, there were only two hop producing companies operating in the Chilliwack area. Henry Hulbert, a transplanted Englishman, harvested the first commercial crop in 1893. Hulbert's English background provided him with some knowledge of the hop industry. From 1884 to about 1892, he had owned a tea and rubber plantation in Ceylon (present day Sri Lanka). Malaria likely caused him to leave Ceylon, and his return journey to England led to a stop in Vancouver where he visited his two sisters. A side trip to Chilliwack sealed his fate.[4] Hop growing was evolving beyond the experimental stage, and he saw an opportunity to join the industry. His timing was fortunate, since infestations of the hop louse, a type of aphid, were devastating hop growing regions on Vancouver Island and in Western Washington. However, in the Fraser Valley, some farmers, such as John Broe in Aldergrove, were having success in growing hops on an experimental basis. In Chilliwack, Adam Vedder and Theopholis Dumville were also experimenting with the new crop. The decline in production in the other growing areas together with the favorable growing conditions in the Fraser Valley meant that Hulbert's operation was a commercial success from the beginning.[5]

E. Clemons Horst, a German born American, entered the business in 1902. Horst worked as a hop merchant throughout the 1890s in New York, but by 1902 moved to San Francisco to develop his interests in fruit growing and canning. He purchased part of Adam Vedder's property in 1902 and within a few years owned over 300 acres of land in Sardis. Horst then expanded to Agassiz, so that by 1912 his operation, the B.C. Hop Company, was the largest producing farm in the area.[6] Little expansion took place in the industry in Chilliwack over the next twenty-five years. However, beginning in the mid 1920s, events in both Canada and the United States resulted in rapid, large-scale expansion.

The Volstead Act (National Prohibition Enforcement Act) passed by the United States Congress in 1919 and in effect by 1920 effectively ended the legal production of alcoholic beverages in America. For the most part, however, the Act was unenforceable and alcohol continued to be produced. Also, illegal imports from Europe and Canada found their way into American homes and speakeasy clubs. Canadian products, including beer, were funneled into the United States by newly emerging entrepreneurs and organized crime groups. Despite prohibition, consumption of alcohol continued. The failure of the Volstead Act to curb consumption led to its repeal in 1933.[7] During this period, the Canadian brewing industry experienced phenomenal growth. Capital invested in the industry grew from $29,580,433 in 1917 to $45, $375 and $529 in 1925. Demand for hops far outstripped supply. Canada was only able to supply about 50 percent of the hops required for the domestic market (*Progress*, 8 September 1926, 6). The expanding market demanded a rapid increase in hop production. The Fraser Valley, already Canada's major hop producing region, was ideally suited to absorb this growth. Well drained alluvial soils, a plentiful supply of land and the potential for a large labour force made the area suitable for expanded hop production.

The draining of Sumas Lake in 1924 opened a vast tract of new farmland. The Canadian Hop Company purchased 600 acres in 1926, and by 1927 the first crops were being harvested. This company was formed when Henry Norton Ord, who had gained experience in Horst's American hop yard operations, joined forces with Thomas Livesley and Hugo Loewi to create the company. Ord became the managing partner of the company.[8] At the same time John I. Haas, an American hop broker, purchased the Evans farm in Sardis and was soon harvesting hops (*Progress*, 10 March 1926, 1). Within five years, 1925 to 1930, the amount of acreage devoted to hops in the Fraser Valley more than doubled. This increased production brought about the need for a greatly expanded labour force of an additional 1500 to 2000 workers.

Although, according to the *Chilliwack Progress* (12 September 1912, 6), East Indian, Chinese and Japanese workers were also employed in the industry, up to the mid 1920s most of the labour needed to pick the crop came from aboriginal communities scattered throughout British Columbia and Washington State. Aboriginal people would travel from Port Simpson on the BC coast, the Nass and Skeena Rivers, Vancouver Island (*Progress*, 11 September 1907, 1), Lytton, Lillooet (*Progress*, 4 September 1912, 6), the Fraser valley, and Washington and Oregon States to pick hops in the local fields. By 1927, however, the Dominion Department of Immigration was refusing Washington State aboriginals entry to Canada, exacerbating labour shortages (*Progress*, 1 September 1927, 1). Additionally, by the mid 1920s, a perception was developing that an "all-white picking force would be more efficient and economical than an all-native or mixed force." According to E. D. Barrow, the Provincial Minister of Agriculture, a complete change in the ethnicity of the work force was coming.[9]

While the BC Hop Company and the Hulbert Hop Company continued to employ aboriginals, the new companies looked to local and Vancouver

When Sumas Lake was drained in 1924, over 10,000 acres of land became available for sale. The Canadian Hop Company was the first to buy land for hop growing purposes. When Mennonites arrived in Yarrow after 1928, the company became an important employer for the community. (Chilliwack Archives P.Coll 106, File 11)

communities for help (*Progress*, 8 September 1926,1). The growers felt that by using local, non-aboriginal picking crews "this much additional purchasing power, as understood in terms of white standards of living, will have a beneficial effect upon the economic life in the part of the Lower Mainland in which development will be taking place" (*Progress*, 2 June 1926, 1). Thus the entry of Mennonites into the local labour force could not have been better timed. The growers were looking for new labour, preferably white, while Mennonites were looking for sources of cash income. Initially, the Canadian Hop Company, while still employing some aboriginals, turned to the Mennonite community for help. Other companies followed and were also soon employing Mennonites. For Mennonites, paid work in the hop fields meant economic survival. Cash was needed to repay the Canadian Pacific Railway for travel costs from Russia to Canada, as well as for land, housing and everyday expenses.

Chauncey Eckert along with Ernest Crain owned 749 acres in Yarrow. In 1928, the first full year that the land was available, nearly 50 Mennonite families purchased land. Terms for the mostly ten to twenty acre lots were generous, typically $200.00 as a down payment and $20.00/acre annually at six percent interest However, these yearly payments required that cash be accumulated.[10] Hopyard work provided the financial bridge necessary for families to survive the initial years in Yarrow. As Peter P. Giesbrecht observed, "Without the hops, Yarrow would not have survived" (Neufeldt, 159).

However, while working in the hop fields provided a dependable source of income for Mennonites, a contradiction arose between the nature of the work and the Mennonite belief system. Since alcohol was not permitted in Mennonite homes, some Mennonites, while knowing that hops were used in the production of beer, rationalized this contradiction with the assertion that "...they were picking for yeast not for beer." This perception lasted even into the 1940s, as Chuck Regehr, writing about his parents, Cornelius and Katharina (Katie) Regehr, points out:

> In addition to looking after their son, Katie worked in the hop yards. One morning on her way to work, one of the men pointed out to her that her husband, a pacifist Mennonite, was aiding Canada's war effort by working in the shipyard. Not one to take such criticism lightly, Katie pointed out to this man that he was picking hops used to make beer. He quickly replied that the hops he picked were used for yeast (Neufeldt, 282).

Although at times unease about hop picking was expressed, survival of the family unit and the ethnic community was a value that superseded any qualms about the nature of the hop picking industry. In an interview, Esther Harder emphasized that "...life and survival were more important than what the hops were going for."[11]

Several other economic factors combined to ensure that the entry of Mennonites into the hopfield workforce was relatively seamless. Canadian producers were always looking for different ways to reduce production costs and protect the industry from cheaper, American hops. Lobbying efforts to increase duties charged on imported American hops had occurred as early as 1929, if not earlier. At that time, the duty levied on Canadian hops imported into the United States was over three times that charged for American hops imported into Canada (*Chilliwack Progress*, 15 August 1929, 1). The growers believed that a higher duty on imported American and European hops was required to protect the industry. By 1935, their efforts brought some success, and a high tariff on imported American hops was established (*Chilliwack Progress*, 22 August 1935, 1).

Companies internally absorbed the costs of hiring and retaining a steady, stable work force. For years, this meant offering a variety of incentives to workers. Travel costs, whether by BC Electric Railway from Vancouver or by CNR or CPR rail travel from the interior, were covered by the growers. Cabins in the hop yards were provided and sometimes free wood, potatoes (*Chilliwack Progress*, 8 September 1926, 6), medical services, and security were offered as additional incentives. For the hop companies, reducing these costs meant increased profits. A steady supply of local workers who could be

Men, women and children found work in the hop fields. These two women, believed to be Mennonites, are picking hops, a job generally given to women and children. (Chilliwack Archives, P2203 30 11)

transported to the hop fields was needed, and the newly arrived Mennonites were available and willing.

Initially, most Mennonite pickers resided in hop yard cabins. Susie Alice Giesbrecht Derksen recalls, "At the end of August, hop picking began. We moved there with our entire family on a wagon with the cow tied to the back, our collie named Sport, and all eleven of us, except Margaret, moved" (Neufeldt, 160). It didn't take long, however, for some enterprising individuals to purchase trucks for transporting people to the hop fields in the early morning hours. Susie recalls that "in later years, when transportation was provided by trucks from Yarrow, mother and the small children lived at home. They cooked, baked, milked the cows and then caught the truck at 5:00 am, thus bringing us some fresh produce and baking daily" (Neufeldt, 161).

By the 1940s, the scene was familiar to everyone. Anna Bartsch described those early morning pickups: "After the berry season we picked hops. We had breakfast at 5 am and hurried out with our lunch kits to stand at the street corner in the dark. Here we waited with others to be picked up by a large open truck, which took us to the hopfields" (Neufeldt, 231-32). This arrangement undoubtedly helped the producers reduce their costs, and it was more practical for the families of the hop yard workers, since early mornings and late evenings could be devoted to farm and domestic work at home.

Additionally, the hopyards' policies addressed the issue of ethnic and racial segregation within the workforce. Since the inception of the hop industry in the 1890s, the pickers had been racially and ethnically segregated. Hop yards were organized into camps, such as, for example, the white camp, the Indian camp and the Japanese camp. Lorna Shaw and Cecil Shaw talk about hopyard stores in the Indian camps located in the B.C. Hop Company yards.[12] A sketch of the Sardis hop fields by Fred Haas clearly shows an area designated as the Japanese camp. This method of organizing labour, to some extent, facilitated the preservation of language and culture. For Mennonites, this arrangement undoubtedly brought some degree of comfort, since the desire to create a closed Mennonite settlement was still uppermost in the minds of community leaders. Hopyard work offered the opportunity to maintain cultural homogeneity. Heinrich Harms recalls that:

The most mysterious, chaotic, and exciting time of hop picking came when we finished picking a field. In those hours, two communities would meet in the middle of the field, each having worked from opposite ends. As young pickers, we were not only excited at the prospect of that day; we were also frightened. ...Perhaps there would be other Mennonites from such communities as Chilliwack, Abbotsford, or Greendale. Sometimes cousins from another community revealed the group's identity. Seldom would the explorer find people he knew from his own community (Neufeldt, 181).

Although motivations for working in the hopyards differed, the experiences of Mennonites mirrored those of Aboriginal, Chinese, Japanese and other Euro-Canadian workers. Because of segregation, languages and certain aspects of the differing cultures could be preserved or at least temporarily protected from change. Thus family and community ties could be maintained.

For the producers, this segregation had two major ramifications. First, family units working together tended to pick more hops than individual pickers.[13] The CHMS Newletter records Cecil and Lorna Shaw, who operated a hopyard store, talking about the Depression years and the problems of relying on transient workers.

Cecil Shaw remembers: " We had a bunch come up here once I remember. They were on welfare. Well welfare in Vancouver in those days was pretty slim. You had to go and beg to get it. ...They came up here and those fellows were individuals. They picked alone."

Lorna Shaw comments: "They could never get their boxes full."

Cecil Shaw agrees and asserts strongly that "Never! Never! They'd get a bag full and pour it into the box and be half full or a third full. I think it took about three bags. Come out the next morning, it was down a quarter. This went on. It was just after I started, '34 or '35" (CMHS Newsletter 3).

In contrast, Mennonites picked in family units and thus increased production, adding to the family's income. Money earned in the hop fields by individual family members was pooled and used to support the family. Thelma Reimer Kauffman reports that "all earnings went into the family account to pay for school expenses, new clothes for the fall, and a few incidentals badly needed in the home."[14]

Walter Harder echoes this attitude, stating:

We went straight from harvesting the hops to the Eaton's catalogue didn't we? Mother would make a list of all the things that we needed together with the price and then when she had finished then she added up the cost and it was nearly always much more than we were able to pay. Well then she said 'now I will have to scratch out the ones that are a lower priority.' And what she did, she took the things off that she needed.[15]

Economic necessity required that family members work together, an approach willingly accepted by the producers.

In addition to gaining increased production from family-centred picking crews, a second benefit for the producers was the pejorative view of strikes taken by Mennonites. The concept of going on strike for more money was simply not part of Mennonite thinking. Peter Harder recalls that when he was five or six years old he saw a group huddled together a little distance from where they should be picking. He learned from his father that this was a sit-down strike. He remembers:

Yeh, they wanted more money per pound. But the company, they knew the ethnic Mennonite people would not go on strike because that is against our principles for one thing, and there wasn't enough unity among us to speak the language. The ethnic Mennonite people were quite safe when it came to labour action and the Japanese likewise. They were not indoctrinated into labour action to gain high prices....[16]

Many Mennonite families continued to move to Yarrow from the 1930s to 1950s, providing the local hop yards with a dependable source of labour. This was an arrangement that suited both Mennonites and the producers. However, by the mid 1950s picking machines were introduced, and large crews were no longer needed. Newspaper reports from 1953 mention that 70 per cent of the production from the Kent Hop Gardens (the original Hulbert farm) was harvested by machine (*Chilliwack Progress*, 16 September 1953, 1). It is estimated that one picking machine could handle up to 50,000 pounds of hops per day, or the equivalent production of 400 to 500 pickers.[17] It was just a matter of time before picking machines were introduced to all hop farms. Fortunately, by this time, Mennonites were firmly established both economically and socially within the Canadian cultural mosaic and no longer depended on the hop harvest for survival.

When Chauncey Eckert subdivided his landholdings in Yarrow, beginning in 1927, an opportunity arose for Mennonite families to settle together in a new community. At the same time, the nearby hop companies were experiencing phenomenal growth that required a greatly expanded labour force. Mennonites arrived just in time to fill the need. In an interview, Peter Harder articulated how an amazing coincidence of various events—the Mennonite emigration from Russia, availability of land in Yarrow, a sympathetic developer, an expanding industry, and jobs that allowed a community of people to survive, grow and flourish—led him to conclude that divine intervention must have been at work. He emphasized that work at the hopyards "... seemed like a providential gift to the Mennonites just when they needed it, and once they didn't need it anymore it was taken away" (Peter Harder, interview).

Endnotes

[1] The hop contains brachts or brachioles, which, in turn, are made up of microscopic, ice-creamed cone shaped glands, called lupulin glands. More than 200 active essential oils, found in lupulin gland, are used to provide beer with its taste, smell, foam, flavour and physical stability.

[2] Personal Communication, Carlson, 2004. See also Robert L. A. Hancock, "The Hop Yards", 70. Amendments to the Indian Act in 1844 made it illegal for aboriginal people to gather together in ceremonial dance, funeral, marriage, naming ceremony or any other kind of event where gifts were given out. This type of gathering, or potlatch, was the main economic and social institution whereby social and economic obligations were recognized publicly. Typically, a family would accumulate wealth over a lengthy period of time, and at a ceremony acknowledging the event, it would give gifts to those who came to witness the ceremony. Potlatches were also times for speeches and dances that allowed for the re-affirmation of a chief's and his family's place within the *Stó:lō* society. For a more thorough analysis of the effect of various governmental interventions on the lives of the *Stó:lō* see Carlson, "Early Nineteenth Century *Stó:lō* Structures and Government Assimilation Policy," 87-105.

[3] Leonard Neufeldt, Lora Sawatsky and Robert Martens, eds., *Yarrow, British Columbia: Mennonite Promise*, vol. 1, *Before We Were the Land's* (Victoria, BC: Touch Wood Editions, 2002), 113. Subsequent citations will appear in the text.

[4] *Chilliwack Progress*, 16 July 1931, 1. Subsequent citations will appear in the text.

[5] Greg Evans, "Hop Industry Origins of Washington and British Columbia." *Celebrator Beer News* (April/May 1997). Subsequent citations will appear in parentheses in the text.

[6] There are no books written on the history of the hop industry in British Columbia. However, there are excellent archival repositories that have records on the history of the industry. The Chilliwack Archives has some company records for the British Columbia Hop Company (Add. Mss. 189), the Canadian Hop Company (Add. Mss. 853) and the John I. Haas Company. Henry Hulbert, who started the Hulbert Hop Company, details the early history of his business in the Hulbert Letterbooks, available at the British Columbia Archives and Record Service. The Yakima Valley Museum is an excellent source of information about hop growing in the Yakima Valley in Washington. Hop production began there in the 1890s. Today Yakima is the North American centre for hop growing. The Ezra Meeker Historical Society in Puyallup, Washington, is a wonderful source for information about Ezra Meeker, once known as the "hop king of the world." Meeker pioneered hop growing in Western Washington, beginning in 1865. For Canadian growers on the Saanich Peninsula and on the mainland, his book *Hop Culture in the United States* was necessary reading. While Chilliwack/Sardis and Agassiz remained the centres for hop growing in Canada, the plant was also grown in Vernon, Lillooet, the Squamish Valley, Kamloops, Creston and Kelowna, with varying degrees of success.

[7] Numerous books have been written about prohibition. Edward Behr's *Prohibition: Thirteen Years that Changed America* chronicles the rise of organized crime groups as they successfully created new businesses from the illegal importation, distribution, and sale of alcoholic beverages.

[8] In 1991, the Chilliwack Archives was able to photocopy Henry Norton Ord's business records. These records, mostly correspondence, detail the history of the company from 1926 to 1957. Add. Mss. 853, Chilliwack Archives.

[9] *The Progress*, 2 June, 1926, 1. E.D. Barrow, Minister of Agriculture, predicted an all-white labour force was imminent.

[10] Peter Penner, "Chauncey Eckert, the CCA and Early Settlement," in *Yarrow, British Columbia*, 132.

[11] Esther Harder, interview. In a 19 February 2004 email, Ralph Olsen, General Manager of the Hop Union, CBS, LLC in Yakima, Washington suggested that "hop growers used to call them 'medicinal hops' in order to allow Mennonites to become pickers. ...It may be that the pickers did not know they were actually going to make beer."

[12] Lorna Shaw and Cecil Shaw, Transcript Interview, 15 November 1989. Acc.# 990.12.

[13] *Chilliwack Museum and Historical Society Newsletter* (CMHS) (Fall 1990): 3. Subsequent citations will appear in the text.

[14] Thelma Reimer Kauffman, "Our Raspberry World," *Yarrow, British Columbia*, vol. 2, *Village of Unsettled Yearnings*, ed. Leonard Neufeldt (Victoria, BC: Touch Wood Editions, 2002), 174.

[15] Walter Harder, interviewed by Greg Evans and Linda Eversole, 29 October 2001. Transcript, Chilliwack.

[16] Peter Harder, transcript interview, 29 October 2001. Chilliwack Museum and Archives.

[17] Greg Evans, *The History of the Hop Picking Industry in British Columbia*. Text Panel, 2003. Chilliwack Museum and Archives.

Bibliography

Behr, Edward. *Prohibition: Thirteen Years that Changed America*. New York: Arcade Publisher, 1996.

Carlson, Keith Thor, Albert McHalsie and Jan Perrier, ed. *A Sto:lo-Coast Salish Historical Atlas*. Vancouver and Toronto: Douglas and McIntyre, 2001.

Carlson, Keith Thor. "Early Nineteenth Century Sto:lo Structures and Government Assimilation Policy." *You are Asked to Witness: The Sto:lo on Canada's Pacific History*. Ed. Keith Thor Carlson. Chilliwack, BC: Sto:lo Heritage Fund, 1997.

——, ed. *You are Asked to Witness: The Sto:lo on Canada's Pacific History*. Chilliwack, BC: Sto:lo Heritage Trust, 1997.

Chilliwack Museum and Historical Society Newsletter (CMHS). (Fall 1990): 3.

Epp, George. "Widow Epp." *Yarrow, British Columbia: Mennonite Promise* Vol 2. *Village of Unsettled Yearnings,* Ed. Leonard Neufeldt.. Victoria, BC: Touchwood Editions, 2002.

Evans, Greg. "Hop Industry Origins of Washington and British Columbia." *Celebrator Beer News* (April/May 1997).

——. *The History of the Hop Picking Industry in British Columbia*. Text Panel, 2003. Chilliwack Museum and Archives.

Hancock, Robert L. A. "The Hop Yards." *A Sto:lo-Coast Historical Atlas*. Ed. Keith Thor Carlson, et al. Vancouver and Toronto: Douglas and McIntyre, 2001.

Kauffman, Thelma Reimer. "Our Raspberry World." *Yarrow, British Columbia: Mennonite Promise*. Vol. 2. *Village of Unsettled Yearnings*. Ed. Leonard Neufeldt. Victoria, BC: Touch Wood Editions, 2002.

Meeker, Ezra. *Hop Culture in the United States*. Pyallup, Washington Territory: E. Meeker, 1883.

Neufeldt, Leonard, Lora Sawatsky and Robert Martens, ed. *Yarrow, British Columbia: Mennonite Promise.* Vol. 1. *Before We were the Land's.* Ed. Leonard Neufeldt. Victoria, BC: Touch Wood Editions, 2002.
——. *Yarrow, British Columbia: Mennonite Promise.* Vol. 2. *Village of Unsettled Yearnings.* Victoria, BC: Touch Wood Editions, 2002.
Penner, Peter. "Chauncey Eckert, the CCA and Early Settlement." *Yarrow, British Columbia: Mennonite Promise.* Vol. 1. *Before We were the Land's.* Ed. Leonard Neufledt. Victoria, BC: Touch Wood Editions, 2002.
Regehr, Cornelius (Chuck). "Building a Life Through Necessity: Cornelius Regehr." *Yarrow, British Columbia: Mennonite Promise.* Vol. 2. *Village of Unsettled Yearnings.* Ed. Leonard Neufeldt. Victoria, BC: Touch Wood Editions, 2002.

E Mail Correspondence

Olsen, Ralph. 19 February 2004.

Interviews

Harder, Esther. Interviewed by Greg Evans and Linda Eversole. 29 October, 2001. Transcript, Chilliwack Museum and Archives
Museum and Archives.
Harder, Peter. Transcript Interview, 29 October 2001. Chilliwack Museum and Archives.
Harder, Walter. Interviewed by Greg Evans and Linda Eversole, 29 October 2001. Transcript, Chilliwack Museum and Archives.
Shaw, Lorna and Cecil Shaw. Transcript Interview, 15 November 1989. Acc.# 990.12
Personal communication
Carlson, Keith. Persoanl communication with Ron Denmann, Chilliwack, B.C., summer 2004.

Newspapers

The Chilliwack Progress, 15 August 1929:1.
The *Chilliwack Progress,* 16 July 1931: 1.
The Chilliwack Progress, 22 August 1935:1.
The Chilliwack Progress, 16 September 1953:1.
The Progress, 11 September 1907:1.
The Progress, 4 September 1912:6.
The Progress, 12 September 1912:6.
The Progress, 10 March, 1926:1.
The Progress, 2 June 1926:1.
The Progress, 8 September 1926: 1,6.
The Progress, 1 September 1927:1.

Sketch

Fonds, John I Hass, Sketch. Acc# 1999.31.

Urbanization, Religious Dispersion and Secularization: Personal Reflections on Mennonites in the Fraser Valley, 1940s and 1950s

John Redekop

A. Introduction

Given the scope of this essay, the challenge of defining the term Mennonite must be addressed. The word Mennonite has at least three meanings: the religious, the ethnic, and the ethno-religious; the latter term refers to those people who are part of the recognized Mennonite ethnic group and also hold to the distinctive Mennonite religious beliefs. I have elsewhere provided an analysis of the various definitions.[1] In this essay I employ the inclusive ethno-religious definition.

Further, in the Mennonite experience, during the 1940s and 1950s, urbanization, religious dispersion and secularization were closely interwoven. But they were not coterminous or equally consequential. Since urbanization was, in large part, a precursor for the other two developments, and also the more basic and dominant trend, this aspect will receive the most attention. This investigation will examine the major economic, religious, sociological and educational factors shaping the three key trends of urbanization, religious dispersion and secularization. It concludes with four hypotheses concerning the way these factors have impacted Fraser Valley Mennonites.

B. Approach and Research Methods

For the most part, this introductory survey is personal and subjective. Given that almost no scientifically valid data on Fraser Valley Mennonite urbanization, dispersion or secularization is available, we must rely on other sources. This analysis therefore relies on media reports, biographical accounts, interviews, and, especially, on personal experience and observation, beginning with the year 1944 when our family relocated from Saskatchewan to Abbotsford, British Columbia. In recent years, on numerous occasions, I have discussed the relationship of urbanization to secularization with both Mennonites and non-Mennonites, who have provided useful comments and insights. At various times, I have addressed various aspects of this topic in both popular[2] and scholarly publications[3]. Clearly, in a survey such as this, we encounter many generalizations. They obviously need refinement and clarification. Even so, they can function as useful hypotheses or starting points.

C. Economic Factors which Influenced Urbanization as well as Religious Diversification and Secularization

The initial influx of Mennonites to the Fraser Valley, people who came almost entirely from the Depression-plagued prairie provinces, was motivated mainly by economic considerations. Cheap land beckoned. The mild climate was an added attraction as was the virtually assured absence of devastating crop failures. Economic progress seemed certain. The hardy settlers of the late 1920s, the 1930s and the 1940s were therefore prepared, despite the difficulties in their initial pioneering ventures on the Canadian prairies, to undertake a second phase of difficult pioneering.

Some specifics should be noted. First, in contrast to the prairie norms, the Mennonite newcomers in the valley were initially able to undertake viable agricultural pursuits with low capital costs on small acreages. Poultry operations, mixed farming, and later, raspberry production could be done profitably on a small scale. Child labour, moreover, could be put to good use. Many farm-related skills such as welding, construction, motor repair, finish carpentry, plumbing, machine maintenance, and electrical work, learned well in the larger prairie operations, facilitated vocational diversification, mostly on a part-time basis, to augment income, but could also be pursued on a full-time basis for those thus inclined.

With a little on-the-job training, many of these early settlers and their first generation children quickly achieved success in a broad spectrum of careers ranging from plumbing and carpentry to auto repair and general construction. Phone book listings of the day contain the names of many Mennonites who had undertaken such vocations. The various service categories, ranging from housework by domestic maids to sales, as well as retail business itself, also provided ample job opportunities. With a substantial population of other ethnic groups in close proximity— in Sardis, Chilliwack, Abbotsford, Mission, and Langley—the growing Mennonite enclave soon developed a mutually beneficial economic relationship with non-Mennonites often eager to hire such reliable and hard-working people. We should, however, note that in the 1930s, '40s, and '50s, various vocations, including teaching, were, in most school districts, not yet open to Mennonites.

After 1939, all of the above factors must be viewed against the backdrop of World War II. The large-scale induction of young men, including scores of Mennonites from the Fraser Valley, into the military and the sudden surge in demand for agricultural products, both for the Canadian military machine and for allies such as the United Kingdom, produced extensive employment opportunities as well as a strong demand at good prices for whatever could be produced. The 1942 removal by Ottawa of Japanese farmers, who produced most of the strawberries and raspberries in British Columbia, from the Fraser Valley suddenly gave the Mennonites great opportunities.[4] While the removal of the Japanese made additional berry-growing land available to Mennonites in Abbotsford, Coghlan, Aldergrove, and Langley, this increased production was processed almost entirely in Abbotsford and Mission. Meanwhile, the small Yarrow Growers Cooperative, which in 1941 handled less than 1 percent of the local berry crop, handled more than half of it in 1943 (Regehr 112). Because of the high wartime prices and the wartime demand, Mennonite farmers in the eastern Fraser Valley very rapidly increased their acreage of berries.

Concurrently, beginning about 1940, significant trends set in, which within a few years saw the substantial relocation of Mennonites from the farms to urban areas, occasionally to towns such as Chilliwack, Langley, and New Westminster, but mainly to Vancouver. By the mid 1950s, the new area of Clearbrook, about two miles west of Abbotsford, began to emerge as an urban center attracting Mennonite relocation. In fact, to a large extent, the Mennonites who relocated to the Clearbrook area created their own urban region. Some other urban areas, especially in Surrey, Delta and Richmond, also absorbed large numbers of Mennonites from the eastern and central Fraser Valley.

What economic factors produced this rather early departure from farming for more than half of the Mennonite population? We can identify at least six factors. First, as both the standard of living and economic expectations rose, it quickly became evident that the mostly small farm operations could not provide adequate opportunity for all of the children as they became adults. This is a major reason why fewer than 10 percent of the children of these pioneers took up farming.[5] But in contrast to the earlier Mennonite experience in the Ukraine, where landless families were considered to be in a lower social class and generally had no vote on community economic policies, the landless Mennonites of the Fraser Valley were not particularly disadvantaged. They could either acquire their own farms at relatively low cost elsewhere, as some did, or they could relocate to urban areas and take up new vocations and professions, as most did. About half of the members in the new Vancouver Mennonite churches established themselves in these new trades, mostly in construction. In the labour-short economy which characterized both the 1940s and the 1950s, job opportunities in the urban areas were both appealing and rewarding. There were also, of course, the hundreds of Mennonite domestic maids who worked, mostly in Greater Vancouver, to augment the income of their financially struggling pioneer families. This situation continued until the mid 1950s.

Second, as the first settlers prospered and acquired capital, an increasing number looked for entrepreneurial opportunities. While some, such as the proprietors of Funk's grocery stores, managed to develop substantial businesses locally, others, such as the Block Brothers in real estate and Abe Warkentin in auto sales, along with numerous owners of construction companies, found that the larger urban areas offered by far the most promising opportunities. Third, with the end of the war in 1945, the demand for various agricultural products weakened. Some prices also fell. Simultaneously, some large-scale and more efficient agricultural operations were being established, mostly at the outset by non-Mennonites, which increasingly marginalized the early, small mixed-farming endeavours. The farmer with a few hundred chickens, three or four cows, and an acre or two of berries could not successfully compete. It was also soon realized that the small mixed farms would not be able to meet the rising economic expectations of the next generation. For this reason also, large numbers left for urban areas.

Fourth, because of the loss of overseas wartime markets, the thriving Newberg raspberry industry virtually collapsed in 1948. Yarrow and some other communities were economically devastated. Some of these communities also had to cope with the huge 1948 flood as the Fraser River spilled onto all of the low farmland in Matsqui Prairie and much of the low farmland in the eastern half of Sumas Prairie. The Matsqui and the Greendale Mennonite churches were also devastated by these events. The economic effect was immediate. This important sector of the agricultural economy thus contracted and virtually collapsed, although the less extensive strawberry production continued. A significant number of families and scores of young adults, formerly in the raspberry business, moved to urban areas because of this reality.

Fifth, after the war, and especially during the 1950s, the Fraser Valley and the entire Lower Mainland experienced strong real estate markets. My own parents' ten-acre farm had been purchased in 1945 for $2 500. By 1955, it was worth $10 000. The sale of small farms and acreages produced significant capital gains, a form of income not taxed at that time. This situation provided extensive land development and construction opportunities, sales jobs, and work for sub-trades, as well as jobs for casual labour. While a minor part of this expansion occurred in rural areas, the bulk occurred in urban areas such as Chilliwack, Sardis, Abbotsford, Mission, Langley, and greater Vancouver.

Sixth, as a result of the general improvement in the economy and the much improved income opportunities, in which working in urban areas as even an unskilled labourer or employee paid much more than did picking hops or hoeing berries, the Mennonite population in the Fraser Valley gradually shifted from low income to middle class. In fact, once World War II began, Fraser Valley Mennonites rapidly improved their socio-economic status. This shift was evident, at least by the mid 1950s, in the sudden interest in recreational vehicles, in the new emphasis on music lessons (for example, hundreds of students were taught by Menno and Walter Neufeld), in the patronizing of travel agencies and hair salons, in the purchase of second family cars, in professional home renovation, in the surge of interest in pleasure boats, and in the establishment of Mennonite credit unions in which to deposit the growing surplus funds. By the end of the 1950s, many Mennonites in the Fraser Valley had become prosperous. Church parking lots contained many new cars, many Mennonites took expensive holidays, and neighbourly visits often included discussions about investments. More than a few, such as, for example, the Block Brothers in real estate, established large companies and soon became wealthy.

This extensive Mennonite urbanization influenced religious dispersion and produced some secularization, including the rejection of traditional Christian beliefs. These trends cannot, unfortunately, be quantified, but their reality cannot be denied. A significant number of young people, especially those who moved to the greater Vancouver area, terminated their church membership or were excommunicated because of their overt rejection of the Christian faith. While in the early years, virtually all Valley Mennonites attended church, and almost all attended German-speaking Mennonite churches, urbanization, together with the transition to English as the dominant church language (mostly in the 1950s) produced changes. While the transition to English was delayed and painful in some congregations, and resulted in the loss of large numbers of younger people to the Christian and Missionary Alliance and Nazarene churches, in itself it did not precipitate rejection of Christianity.

For some Mennonites who moved to the cities, and to a lesser extent also for some who remained in the rural areas or the small towns, the shift to

English and the weakening of the Mennonite enclaves, both economically and socially, produced new church options. As Mennonite churches processed a series of ethical and ecclesiological challenges ranging from language transition to television debates and from wedding forms to worship styles, newly urbanized Mennonites began investigating other versions of church. Unfortunately, statistical documentation is not available. Mennonite churches do not generally keep records of members who transfer to non-Mennonite congregations. In addition, many of the young people who left their parental congregations had not yet become official members.

While the above factors explain part of the gradually increasing religious diversification, they do not tell the whole story. For some Mennonites, this religious dispersion was triggered by frustration with the old ecclesiastical order, the rather legalistic and austere ethical code set down by the congregational leaders. For some, it was the result of living too distantly from an existing Mennonite church. Some younger Mennonites wanted to pursue vocational options such as nursing and social work, with which they had become familiar during student days. For others it involved a search for something less spiritually regimented or was the result of intermarriage. Especially during World War II, some Mennonites no longer wanted to identify with a group that was ethnically Mennonite or German-speaking. And for others, it was probably nothing more than curiosity. In any event, by 1960, Mennonites, by the hundreds, were attending other churches. Mostly these were Christian and Missionary Alliance and Baptist, but also Pentecostal, Evangelical Free, Nazarene, Plymouth Brethren and even some mainline congregations gained new Mennonite attendees and adherents. That trend has continued to this day.

For more than a few Mennonites the increased affluence available in the cities shifted their focus, to a significant extent, to more on this world and less to the world to come. Reliance on God seemed "less essential" for financially successful people who prepared their new boats or RVs for weekend activity than for prairie farmers who saw their crops burning in the sun or being devoured by grasshoppers. It is probably correct to say that outright and total secularization, that is, a definite and conscious rejection of all religion, was rare among Mennonites: more common was a rearranging of priorities. Thus, for an increasing minority of Mennonites, not only in urban areas, the local church and a Christian commitment was no longer the encompassing framework within which all else was placed and rationalized. The history of humanity suggests that substantial prosperity has frequently been a significant challenge to the retention of orthodox beliefs. The Mennonite experience in the decades under consideration, as well as in later years, seems to support this observation.

D. Religious Factors which Influenced Urbanization as well as Religious Diversification and Secularization

We can identify at least four religious factors, broadly defined, which played a part in Mennonite urbanization as well as in religious diversification and secularization during the 1940s and 1950s.

1. The Protestant work ethic.

Sociologists may still be debating the causes and the dimensions of what is termed the "Protestant work ethic." Be that as it may, Mennonites, especially in those early years in the Fraser Valley, seem to have possessed the Protestant work ethic in remarkable abundance. Many took second jobs or worked extra hours to get ahead faster. Working hard, as R. H. Tawney has documented, was seen as being a mark of a true Christian. Whether their industriousness was generated by the memory of hard times in the Prairies or rooted in the desire to prosper or even get wealthy or in viewing work as a service to God, Mennonite families exhibited an astonishing eagerness to work, especially in the 1940s and 1950s. If cleanliness was deemed to be next to godliness, working was probably a close third. Not only the main adult work force, but also children and seniors worked hard in the berry fields and other agricultural labours, contributing what they could to advance a family's economic well being. They seem to have extended the old axiom about an idle mind being the devil's workshop by adding the notion that idle hands are a sinful waste of opportunity.

This strong work ethic, also present in other immigrant groups such as the Scandinavians, Ukrainians, Poles, and Germans, doubtless played a major role in the fairly widespread decisions of Mennonites to move to the cities where both opportunities and rewards were greater. Many a young Mennonite adult left the shelter of home and community to get ahead in the city. The readiness to relocate to places, whether near or far away, where economic prospects were greater, also brought with it exposure to other religious options and subsequent religious diversification. Taken to the extreme, namely, when the pursuit of money overshadows virtually all else and money becomes god, the Protestant work ethic can, in an ironic manner, undermine the faith in which it seems to be rooted and produce varying degrees of materialistic secularization. It would appear that such an outcome may also have been widespread among the Mennonites in these decades.

2.The general Christian ethic.

No people group has a monopoly on any element of the Christian ethic. Nonetheless, those groups, such as the Mennonites in the 1940s and 1950s in the Fraser Valley, who make great efforts to cultivate habits of thrift, frugality, integrity and honesty, key elements of the Christian ethic, find their economic prospects and their reputation enhanced. I well recall my father challenging all six of us children as we headed out to jobs, particularly in our early youth. To the boys he would say, "*Sohn, erwerb dir Kredit!*" (Son, earn a good reputation for yourself!). The axiom was appropriately modified for the girls.

The cultivation of the virtues mentioned above, while important for their own sake, also produced relatively greater job and income opportunities. Employers looked for workers who were diligent, reliable, and honest. It can perhaps be argued that the fairly widespread transition to urban areas was made easier by the fact that, generally speaking, Mennonite folk had a good reputation as workers. The very positive reputation of the hundreds of Mennonite girls who worked as domestics constitutes a key example.[6]

3. The "confining" theology.

The early Mennonite settlers lived by a clearly delineated conservative evangelical, in part fundamentalist, theology. It was conservative and evangelical in insisting that Christianity was the only true faith and that proselytizing was essential; it was partly fundamentalist in its strict ethical code and its rejection of Christian groups which took a more liberal view of Christianity. Whatever the merits of this theological stance may be, more than a few young folk repudiated some of its ethical strictures, such as the rejection of movies and the use of cards, prohibitions which they deemed to be overly restrictive or legalistic. At times they also rejected also some of its doctrinal assertions, such as the belief that all non-Christians will go to a literal hell. In reaction, some opted for a non-Mennonite religious affiliation and drifted off to other branches of the Christian church.

For more than a few, the conscious withdrawing from what they deemed to be a confining church community was achieved by a move to urban areas, either as a student or as a member of the workforce. For them urbanization was a form of religious release. No one would be keeping track of church attendance or of movie attendance, for that matter. In passing, we should also note that for some Mennonites who migrated to urban areas, students as well as others, life in the secular city produced increased appreciation and gratitude for their particular religious roots. They came home on weekends and took their Christian heritage more seriously, sometimes to the point of making it part of their university studies. These people also tended to marry within their own ethno-religious group.

4. Weakening of the ethno-religious enclave.

We learn from history that it is difficult to retain an ethno-religious enclave when many of the mutually reinforcing boundaries weaken or disappear.

Gradually, the Mennonite communities in the Fraser Valley experienced the weakening of ethnic and religious boundaries. During the 1940s and '50s, the major Mennonite communities, in fact most Mennonite congregations, while involved extensively in the surrounding community economically, were still largely a people apart.[7] Their distinctive pacifist theology, underscored and publicized by many wartime Mennonite conscientious objectors, distinguished them from the other Christian groups. The use of German in virtually all Mennonite churches, the widespread but not universal prohibition against marrying non-Mennonites, and the generally strong ethnic ties; these all served to reinforce ethno-religious separation. Geographically clustered settlement patterns and various Mennonite-oriented economic structures such as berry co-ops and credit unions provided additional boundary demarcation.

This situation began changing in the 1940s, and by the mid-fifties, certain centrifugal trends were well underway. Economic opportunities or career necessity drew many away from the initial settlement communities. Given the proximity of numerous other denominational options, hundreds of Mennonites shifted their church allegiances. Numerous instances of intermarriage with people from other faith communities, initially without church approval, was another key factor which drew people to non-Mennonite congregations.

E. Sociological Factors which Influenced Urbanization as well as Religious Diversification and Secularization

We have already alluded to several sociological factors which impacted the Mennonite communities in the Fraser Valley during the 1940s and 1950s. We have noted how the largely faith-based work ethic, the increasing incidence of intermarriage with outsiders, and the weakening of the ethnic glue all played a role in transforming the initially largely homogeneous ethnoreligious communities and facilitated urbanization as well as religious diversification and, in some instances, shades of secularization.

In the 1940s and 1950s, most Mennonite families in the Fraser Valley were still comparatively large; families with six, eight or even ten children were common. During the earlier hard times in the Prairies, as well as during the pioneer years in the Fraser Valley, people with large families often lived in very small houses. Children doubled or tripled up in bedrooms. Houses were crowded. Toilet facilities were outside. Since furniture was sparse, small homes seemed adequate. And children provided cheap labour!

Wartime prosperity, the generally rising economic conditions, and finally the increasing awareness and raised expectations triggered by interaction with friends and strangers in the non-Mennonite surroundings changed matters. The erstwhile realities were no longer deemed adequate. Some families tore down their small houses and built much larger ones. But many members of large families left modest homesteads in East Chilliwack, Sardis, Greendale, Yarrow, Arnold, Abbotsford, Coghlan, Aldergrove, Langley, Mission, etc., and headed for the city lights. As the younger people became more comfortable with big city life, some parents followed. Others moved to urban areas because of their own vocational opportunities. Some moved there to retire near their children and grandchildren. By 1960, about half of the Mennonite church membership in the Fraser Valley and Lower Mainland was urban.

Second, the rising economic conditions in Mennonite communities generated more leisure time as well as more discretionary income. By the mid to late 1950s, both of these trends enabled many Mennonites in the Fraser Valley to have the time, the resources, and the inclination to come to better terms with the big lights and the challenges of urban areas. In the 1930s and early 1940s, many Valley Mennonites had traveled to various well-known spots such as the Salvation Army used clothing store, the "Old Church" (*"Alte Kirche"*), and other second hand stores in Vancouver to buy used clothing. Those with a bit more money bought goods at the Army and Navy. By the late 1950s, some of these same families, particularly the younger adults, were patronizing exclusive stores, touring art galleries, attending concerts, and enjoying fine restaurants.

Third, with increased economic and social assimilation, many Fraser Valley Mennonites opted for, or drifted to, increased individualism as contrasted with the communalism of their ethno-religious communities. In most instances, this new emphasis on individual ethical choices was not so much a rejection of family as of certain aspects of particularly conservative Valley Mennonite communities and congregations which had been, in the eyes of some, overly restrictive or even legalistic. In part it was also triggered by economics. Greater opportunities drew many to the urban areas, to non-traditional jobs, and to various activities not associated with traditional Mennonite communities. Most such workplaces were not part of an ethnic, let alone religious, community.

Finally, even though some segments of the Mennonite constituency in the Fraser Valley looked to the past for guidance, especially in moral matters, increasing numbers, even among the leaders, were open to change. They looked to the future, and they realized that for various reasons, ranging from education to economic opportunity, urban centres would play a large role in the future of the Mennonite people. This gradual shift in attitude was also a factor in facilitating Mennonite urbanization and social assimilation. Some of the earlier taboos and restrictions concerning movie attendance, playing cards, social drinking and marrying non-Mennonites were seriously under-mined in the non-enclave urban settings.

A few words need to be said about the influx of Mennonite refugees after World War II. While most of these came with no financial resources, did not speak or write English, and initially found adjustment very difficult, the fact that they generally had relatives as sponsors and hosts, and that times were prosperous, enabled virtually all of them to improve their lot rather rapidly and to catch up economically with the earlier waves of settlers. Most learned English quickly and quite easily moved into various trades and professions. The fact that these newcomers generally associated with or lived with Mennonite hosts who had already been acculturated to a considerable degree into Canadian society facilitated their own acculturation.

F. Educational Factors which Influenced Urbanization, Religious Diversification and Secularization

Educational developments played a major role in facilitating Mennonite urbanization in the decades under consideration. Significantly, the roots of the new reality go back to typical immigrant values. Pioneering immigrant families generally want their children to have an easier life than the parents are having, and many see education as the main means of achieving that goal. The early Mennonite communities in the Fraser Valley expressed this desire in two ways. In the first place, Mennonite children, with very few exceptions, were strongly encouraged by their parents to get as much education as possible. In difficult economic times, particularly in the 1930s, some children and young people had to drop out of school to help provide sustenance for the family. However, committed parents did their best to keep their children in school. With the increasing prosperity after 1939, most Mennonite young people attended high school, and by 1950, about three-quarters of the Mennonite young people in the Fraser Valley were completing high school.

In the second place, by the early 1940s, partly because of societal back-lash against German-speaking Mennonites and the Mennonite conscientious objection to war—some Mennonite boys were physically beaten by other boys because they spoke German and were known to be pacifist—and partly because of the greater availability of funds, Mennonite leaders began plan-ning for their own secondary schools. Of the various initiatives, two were particularly noteworthy: the founding of the Mennonite Educational Insti-tute in Clearbrook in 1944 and the establishment of Sharon Mennonite Col-legiate Institute in Yarrow in 1945. Both high schools were established to teach Mennonite young people the standard provincial curriculum along with additional intra-mural Mennonite subjects and extra-mural Mennonite cultural and religious programs intended to nurture Mennonite values and beliefs.

In a sense, the establishment of these schools, especially of the MEI which has survived to this day, succeeded too well. Although they were created to nurture the young people in the Mennonite way of life, they served largely to educate many young people away from their home communities, especially in terms of professional careers but, for more than a few students, also ideologically and theologically. Even at the high school level, the exposure to great literature in both English and German, several full-year courses in Canadian and world history, and research in the sciences produced a broadening of thought which made it difficult for many Mennonite students to hold to the traditional ways of viewing the non-Mennonite world. Probing discussions with some outstanding teachers also facilitated considerable change in perspective.

Many hundreds if not thousands of Mennonite young people attended these schools and then proceeded on to post-secondary education and professional training in secular universities and other institutes in urban areas. Many of them, as well as many hundreds who had attended public high schools, investigated other religious options. Some rejected their religious roots and a few moved in varying degrees to secularism. Many, however, perhaps the majority, did continue in their traditional faith or in similar alternative faiths. Significantly, many took up careers which removed them from Mennonite congregations and communities. After all, there were relatively few teaching, nursing, social work or engineering jobs in Chilliwack, Abbotsford, or Langley.

In summary, the educational developments for Valley Mennonites in the 1940s and '50s produced major changes. There was widespread exposure to other branches of evangelical Christianity as well as to mainline beliefs, especially in the public high schools but also in the private Mennonite schools. This exposure challenged much of the stereotypical thinking common in these previously tight ethno-religious communities about non-Mennonites. It also resulted in many transfers to non-Mennonite congregations. The result, in many instances, was also a new social and economic status, often a transition to the professional class, as well as a broadened and better-informed worldview. Urbanization and even relocation to non-Mennonite rural areas thus seriously weakened ties to congregations and communities still functioning at least partly within traditional ethno-religious boundaries.

G. Some Hypotheses

How does one explain the major developments in the urbanization and the sometimes attendant religious dispersion and secularization of Valley Mennonites in the 1940s and 1950s? The causes are clearly complex and not entirely understood. Even so, I shall spell out four key hypotheses or theories. The four focus mainly on why most Mennonites ultimately opted for urbanization. These hypotheses may be useful as starting points for further research.

1.The matter of individualism.

The hypothesis*: Because the Mennonite people in the Fraser Valley had developed a great emphasis on individualism, they were, by and large, open to the idea of relocating to urban areas, especially for reasons of financial gain. Such economic dispersion brought with it exposure to more religious options and, for some, a shift towards such options.*

For many generations, Mennonites have emphasized the importance of community. The nature of this emphasis is important. Despite its inclusive theological underpinning, it actually focuses mainly on religious and spiritual matters and, for Canadian Mennonite Brethren after 1930, decreasingly on enclave relationships. While it incorporates notions of mutual aid and benevolence for the needy, Mennonite communitarianism, except in some minority branches of Mennonites not represented in the Fraser Valley, does not emphasize economic activity. In that realm individualism reigns supreme. Economically, Mennonites have generally embraced free enterprise and classic individualism. It is a case of "Every man for himself!"

Whatever its merits or shortcomings, the Mennonite emphasis on economic individualism, on the individual acquisition of assets, results in a readiness to relocate to places where individual financial gain can be advanced most successfully, in the actual accumulation of investment capital and in individual rather than community accountability concerning personal assets. The result, not surprisingly, is that Mennonites have generally been open to relocating to urban areas to achieve financial advancement. Such relocation and achievement are more likely to bring with them religious dispersion and, at times, slippage into secularization.

2. Attitude toward land.

The hypothesis*: Mennonites tend to see land primarily as a means to an economic end and generally do not hesitate to sever connection to any given piece of real estate.*

Generally speaking, Mennonites have no spiritual connection to land. Granted, land is viewed as part of God's great creation, but it is not in any way seen as holy or as an extension of the deity, nor is it tied in with religious beliefs and observances. Any interest in identifying ancestral land focuses mainly on where ancestors lived, not on the land itself. While emphasizing good stewardship of God's creation, Mennonites generally view land basically as a means to an end, an economic end. Therefore, they do not hesitate to move from one piece of property to the other, whether from grudgingly productive prairie farms to the acreages in the Fraser Valley, or from an inadequate raspberry farm to a house in Vancouver. Since leaving land is not a problem, relocation has no religious component.

3. The question of economic values.

The hypothesis. *Despite their theological emphasis on community, Mennonites in the Fraser Valley have generally allowed economic values to trump community unity.*

The propensity towards enclave settlement, both geographical and social, is part of the Mennonite tradition. In initiating pioneer settlement in the prairies, such patterns were followed as closely as possible, often based on formal contracts with governments for large blocks of land. In the Fraser Valley, early Mennonite settlers attempted to establish similar enclaves, especially in Yarrow, but community homogeneity, never complete, soon broke down. A main reason was the readiness of Mennonite individuals and families to leave the community for better economic opportunities. Jobs, educational opportunities, professional careers, and general economic advancement were deemed to be adequate reasons to move elsewhere, even to locations without a Mennonite place of worship or any other Mennonite residents. The guiding axiom seems to have been, "I earn, therefore I am; I acquire, therefore I am a success."

4. Attitudes towards tradition.

The hypothesis: *Generally speaking, most Mennonites have not emphasized community traditions: they have tended to focus on the future.*

Other than harking back on occasion to some near idyllic situations in self-contained Mennonite communities in Ukraine during the nineteenth and early-twentieth centuries, Fraser Valley Mennonites have not let their appreciation of the past prevent them from being future-oriented.

The past is something to learn from and to build on, not something to revere as the best of all times. While some archivists, historians, ethnologists, and some devoted retirees focus on the past, most Fraser Valley Mennonites, perhaps because of hard times in the past or stories of such hard times, focus more on the future. They have tended to see their Golden Age, typically defined in economic terms, as awaiting them in the future. They want to move on, get ahead, and improve their lot. They tend to be optimistic.

Not surprisingly, the consequences of such a mindset are substantial. Mennonites, especially the later generations, have been surprisingly ready to change and adapt to new situations. As a result, they tend to welcome new opportunities and challenges. Thus, transition to urban settings and even to new faith experiences, despite lingering ethno-religious connections, are not to be feared or avoided; they constitute new opportunities and tend to give rise to increased optimism.

Endnotes

[1] John H. Redekop, *A People Apart: Ethnicity and the Mennonite Brethren* (Winnipeg: Kindred Press, 1987), 170-173. See also Redekop, "Three Kinds of Mennonites," *Mennonite Brethren Herald* 12 February 1982: 12.

[2] Examples include "Three Kinds of Mennonites," 12; "Class and Brotherhood," *Mennonite Brethren Herald*. 21 April 1972: 17; "Learning from the 'Leavers,'" *Mennonite Brethren Herald*. 21 May 1982: 13; "The Winds of Change," *Mennonite Brethren Herald*. 26 June 1964: 2; and "The Work Ethic." *Mennonite Brethren Herald*. 19 January 1979: 24.

[3] Examples include "Mennonites in Politics in Canada and the United States." *Journal of Mennonite Studies* 1 (1983): 79-105; "Decades of Transition: North American Mennonite Brethren in Politics," in *Bridging Troubled Waters: Mennonite Brethren in Mid-Century*, ed. Paul Toews (Winnipeg: Kindred Press, 1995), 19- 84; "Mennonite Brethren in a Changing Society," in *For Everything a Season: Mennonite Brethren in North America, 1874-2002*, ed. Paul Toews and Kevin Enns-Rempel (Winnipeg: Kindred Productions, 2002), 151-165.

[4] T. D. Regehr, *Mennonites in Canada, 1939-1970* (Toronto: University of Toronto Press, 1996), 110-16. Subsequent citations will appear in the text.

[5] Based on numbers taken from a non-published survey of vocational choices of Mennonite graduating seniors from area high schools in the 1950s.

[6] Ruth Derksen Siemens,"Quilt as Text and Text as Quilt: The Influence of Genre in the Mennonite Girls' Home of Vancouver (1930-1960)," *Journal of Mennonite Studies* 17 (1999), 118-29.

[7] Redekop, *A People Apart*, ch. 4.

Bibliography

Derksen Siemens, Ruth. "Quilt as Text and Text as Quilt: The Influence of Genre in the Mennonite Girls' Home of Vancouver (1930-1960)." *Journal of Mennonite Studies* 17 (1999).

Redekop, John H. *A People Apart: Ethnicity and the Mennonite Brethren*. Winnipeg: Kindred Press, 1987.

——. "Class and Brotherhood." *Mennonite Brethren Herald*. 21 April 1972: 17.

——. "Decades of Transition: North American Mennonite Brethren in Politics." In *Bridging Troubled Waters; Mennonite Brethren in Mid-Century*. Ed. Paul Toews. Winnipeg: Kindred Press, 1995: 19 - 84.

——. "Learning from the 'Leavers.'" *Mennonite Brethren Herald.* 21 May 1982: 13.

——. "Mennonite Brethren in a Changing Society." *For Everything a Season; Mennonite Brethren in North America, 1874-2002.* Eds. Paul Toews and Kevin Enns-Rempel. Winnipeg: Kindred Productions, 2002.

——. "Mennonites in Politics in Canada and the United States." *Journal of Mennonite Studies* 1 (1983).

——. "Three Kinds of Mennonites." *Mennonite Brethren Herald* 12 February 1982: 12.

——. "Why is Christian Non Resistance Weakening Among MBs?" *Mennonite Brethren Herald.* 14 November 1986:10.

——. "The Winds of Change." *Mennonite Brethren Herald.* 26 June 1964: 2.

——. "The Work Ethic." *Mennonite Brethren Herald.* 19 January 1979: 24.

Regehr, T. D. *Mennonites in Canada, 1939-1970.* Toronto: University of Toronto Press, 1996.

Tawney, R.H. *Religion and the Rise of Capitalism.* Gloucester, MA: P. Smith, 1962.

Name Index

Topic Index

List of Contributors

Ron Dart has taught in the Department of Political Science/Philosophy/ Religious Studies at the University College of the Fraser Valley since 1990. He has published twelve books, the most recent being *The Canadian High Tory Tradition: Raids on the Unspeakable*.

Baljeet Dhaliwal has an MA from Simon Fraser University and is a Development Consultant for the Centre for Indo-Canadian Studies at the University College of the Fraser Valley. She is also a member of the Resources Committee for Xaytem.

Ron Denman is the Director of the Chilliwack Museum and Archives. One of his passions is the role that the hop industry played in the lives of Fraser Valley residents.

Ruth Derksen Siemens is a professor of Rhetoric in the Department of English at the University of British Columbia. Her PhD dissertation at the Bakhtin Centre, University of Sheffield, UK examines a corpus of letters written from Stalin's Gulags.

Anne Doré recently completed her MA in History at Simon Fraser University and is currently a PhD student at Dalhousie University in Halifax, Nova Scotia.

Reverend Mark Dumont, O.S.B., born in Vancouver BC, has been a member of Westminster Abbey in Mission, B.C. since 1964. He was ordained a priest in 1971 and studied History and Education at Oxford University, University of British Columbia and Western Washington University. For the past thirty years, he has been teaching History and Science in the Seminary of Christ the King, Mission. He is also Guestmaster of Westminster Abbey.

Marlene Epp is an Associate Professor of History and Peace & Conflict Studies at Conrad Grebel University College, Waterloo, Ontario. She is the author of *Women without Men: Mennonite Refugees of the Second World War* (University of Toronto Press, 2000).

Bruce Guenther is Associate Professor of Church History and Mennonite Studies at the Mennonite Brethren Biblical Seminary campus, which is part of the ACTS Seminaries Consortium in Langley, B.C.

John Harder retired to Kelowna, British Columbia from the Canadian Combined Military Forces. Here he served as educator and later as Director of Social Development Services with a specialization in the treatment and prevention of addictions.

Maryann Tjart Jantzen teaches English and co-directs the Writing Centre at Trinity Western University in Langley, B.C. Her research interests include Canadian Mennonite writers and post-colonial African literatures.

Royden Loewen is the Chair in Mennonite Studies and Professor of History at the University of Winnipeg. He has researched and published on the social and cultural history of North American Mennonites. He lives in Steinbach, Manitoba with his family.

Albert (Sonny) McHalsie has, for the last eighteen years, been the cultural advisor and acting executive director of the Aboriginal Rights and Title Department of the Stó:lō Nation located in Sardis, B.C. His home is in Laidlaw, B.C.

Catherine Marcellus graduated with a Master's Degree from Simon Fraser University, and has lived in Mission since 1947. As a local historian and community activist, she has co-authored *Mission's Living Memorial*, a history of the Mission Hospital (1992).

Harvey Neufeldt completed a Ph.D at Michigan State University and is Professor Emeritus at Tennessee Technological University. He serves as coordinator of the Yarrow Research Committee. His research interests are immigrant, community and educational history.

John Redekop holds a Ph.D. and D.Hum.(hon) and is Professor Emeritus of Wilfred Laurier University. He is presently an Adjunct Professor of Political Science at Trinity Western University. His major research areas include Religion and Politics, Church and State, Comparative Politics, and Canadian Politics.

Lora Sawatsky has been a high-school teacher in Kansas and Winnipeg, and an instructor in Adult Education. She presently lives in Chilliwack, B.C. Born and raised in Yarrow, B.C., she was most recently the assistant editor and contributor to the two-volume set, *Yarrow, British Columbia: Mennonite Promise*.

Bob Smith has been a member of the History Department at the University College of the Fraser Valley since 1976.

About Pandora Press

Pandora Press is a small, independently owned press dedicated to making available modestly priced books that deal with Anabaptist, Mennonite, and Believers Church topics, both historical and theological. We welcome comments from our readers.

Visit our full-service online Bookstore:
www.pandorapress.com

Rodney James Sawatsky, *History and Ideology: American Mennonite Identity Definition through History* (Kitchener: Pandora Press, 2005). Softcover, 216 pp. Includes bibliography and index. ISBN 1-894710-53-3 ISSN 1494-4081

Harvey Neufeldt, Ruth Derksen Siemens and Roberyt Martens, eds., *First Nations and First Settlers in the Fraser Valley (1890-1960)* (Kitchener: Pandora Press, 2005). Softcover, 287 pp. Incudes bibliography and index. ISBN 1-894710-54-1

David Waltner-Towes, *The Complete Tante Tina: Mennonite Blues and Recipes* (Kitchener: Pandora Press, 2004) Softcover, 129 pp. ISBN 1-894710-52-5

John Howard Yoder, *Anabaptism and Reformation in Switzerland: An Historical and Theological Analysis of the Dialogues Between Anabaptists and Reformers* Anabaptist and Mennonite Studies Series (Kitchener: Pandora Press, 2004) Softcover, 509 pp., includes bibliography and indices. ISBN 1-894710-44-4 ISSN 1494-4081

Antje Jackelén, *The Dialogue Between Religion and Science: Challenges and Future Directions* (Kitchener: Pandora Press, 2004) Softcover, 143 pp., includes index. ISBN 1-894710-45-2

Ivan J. Kauffman, ed., *Just Policing: Mennonite-Catholic Theological Colloquium 2001-2002* The Bridgefolk Series (Kitchener: Pandora Press, 2004). Softcover, 127 pp., ISBN 1-894710-48-7.

Gerald W. Schlabach, ed., *On Baptism: Mennonite-Catholic Theological Colloquium 2001-2002* The Bridgefolk Series (Kitchener: Pandora Press, 2004). Softcover, 147 pp., ISBN 1-894710-47-9 ISSN 1711-9480.

Harvey L. Dyck, John R. Staples and John B. Toews, comp., trans. and ed. *Nestor Makhno and the Eichenfeld Massacre: A Civil War Tragedy in a Ukrainian Mennonite Village* (Kitchener: Pandora Press, 2004). Softcover, 115pp. ISBN 1-894710-46-0.

Jeffrey Wayne Taylor, *The Formation of the Primitive Baptist Movement* Studies in the Believers Church Tradition (Kitchener: Pandora Press, 2004). Softcover, 225 pp., includes bibliography and index. ISBN 1-894710-42-8 ISSN 1480-7432.

James C. Juhnke and Carol M. Hunter, *The Missing Peace: The Search for Nonviolent Alternatives in United States History* Second Expanded Edition (Kitchener: Pandora Press, 2004; co-published with Herald Press.) Softcover, 339 pp., includes index. ISBN 1-894710-46-3

Louise Hawkley and James C. Juhnke, eds., *Nonviolent America: History through the Eyes of Peace* Wedel Series 5 (North Newton: Bethel College, 2004, co-published with Pandora Press) Softcover, 269 pp., includes index. ISBN 1-889239-02-X

Karl Koop, *Anabaptist-Mennonite Confessions of Faith: the Development of a Tradition* (Kitchener: Pandora Press, 2004; co-published with Herald Press) Softcover, 178 pp., includes index. ISBN 1-894710-32-0

Lucille Marr, *The Transforming Power of a Century: Mennonite Central Committee and its Evolution in Ontario* (Kitchener: Pandora Press, 2003). Softcover, 390 pp., includes bibliography and index, ISBN 1-894710-41-x.

Erica Janzen, *Six Sugar Beets, Five Bitter Years* (Kitchener: Pandora Press, 2003). Softcover, 186 pp., ISBN 1-894710-37-1.

T. D. Regehr, *Faith Life and Witness in the Northwest, 1903–2003: Centenninal History of the Northwest Mennonite Conference* (Kitchener: Pandora Press, 2003). Softcover, 524 pp., includes index, ISBN 1-894710-39-8.

John A. Lapp and C. Arnold Snyder, gen.eds., *A Global Mennonite History. Volume One: Africa* (Kitchener: Pandora Press, 2003). Softcover, 320 pp., includes indexes, ISBN 1-894710-38-x.

George F. R. Ellis, *A Universe of Ethics Morality and Hope: Proceedings from the Second Annual Goshen Conference on Religion and Science* (Kitchener: Pandora Press, 2003; co-published with Herald Press.) Softcover, 148 pp. ISBN 1-894710-36-3

Donald Martin, *Old Order Mennonites of Ontario: Gelassenheit, Discipleship, Brotherhood* (Kitchener: Pandora Press, 2003; co-published with Herald Press.) Softcover, 381 pp., includes index. ISBN 1-894710-33-9

Mary A. Schiedel, *Pioneers in Ministry: Women Pastors in Ontario Mennonite Churches, 1973-2003* (Kitchener: Pandora Press, 2003) Softcover, 204 pp., ISBN 1-894710-35-5

Harry Loewen, ed., *Shepherds, Servants and Prophets* (Kitchener: Pandora Press, 2003; co-published with Herald Press) Softcover, 446 pp., ISBN 1-894710-35-5

Robert A. Riall, trans., Galen A. Peters, ed., *The Earliest Hymns of the Ausbund: Some Beautiful Christian Songs Composed and Sung in the Prison at Passau, Published 1564* (Kitchener: Pandora Press, 2003; co-published with Herald Press) Softcover, 468 pp., includes bibliography and index. ISBN 1-894710-34-7.

John A. Harder, *From Kleefeld With Love* (Kitchener: Pandora Press, 2003; co-published with Herald Press) Softcover, 198 pp. ISBN 1-894710-28-2

John F. Peters, *The Plain People: A Glimpse at Life Among the Old Order Mennonites of Ontario* (Kitchener: Pandora Press, 2003; co-published with Herald Press) Softcover, 54 pp. ISBN 1-894710-26-6

Robert S. Kreider, *My Early Years: An Autobiography* (Kitchener: Pandora Press, 2002; co-published with Herald Press) Softcover, 600 pp., index ISBN 1-894710-23-1

Helen Martens, *Hutterite Songs* (Kitchener: Pandora Press, 2002; co-published with Herald Press) Softcover, xxii, 328 pp. ISBN 1-894710-24-X

C. Arnold Snyder and Galen A. Peters, eds., *Reading the Anabaptist Bible: Reflections for Every Day of the Year* introduction by Arthur Paul Boers (Kitchener: Pandora Press, 2002; co-published with Herald Press.) Softcover, 415 pp. ISBN 1-894710-25-8

C. Arnold Snyder, ed., *Commoners and Community: Essays in Honour of Werner O. Packull* (Kitchener: Pandora Press, 2002; co-published with Herald Press.) Softcover, 324 pp. ISBN 1-894710-27-4

James O. Lehman, *Mennonite Tent Revivals: Howard Hammer and Myron Augsburger, 1952-1962* (Kitchener: Pandora Press, 2002; co-published with Herald Press) Softcover, xxiv, 318 pp. ISBN 1-894710-22-3
Lawrence Klippenstein and Jacob Dick, *Mennonite Alternative Service in Russia* (Kitchener: Pandora Press, 2002; co-published with Herald Press) Softcover, viii, 163 pp. ISBN 1-894710-21-5

Nancey Murphy, *Religion and Science* (Kitchener: Pandora Press, 2002; co-published with Herald Press) Softcover, 126 pp. ISBN 1-894710-20-7

Biblical Concordance of the Swiss Brethren, 1540. Trans. Gilbert Fast and Galen Peters; bib. intro. Joe Springer; ed. C. Arnold Snyder (Kitchener: Pandora Press, 2001; co-published with Herald Press) Softcover, lv, 227pp. ISBN 1-894710-16-9

Orland Gingerich, *The Amish of Canada* (Kitchener: Pandora Press, 2001; co-published with Herald Press.) Softcover, 244 pp., includes index. ISBN 1-894710-19-3

M. Darrol Bryant, *Religion in a New Key* (Kitchener: Pandora Press, 2001) Softcover, 136 pp., includes bib. refs. ISBN 1-894710- 18-5

Trans. Walter Klaassen, Frank Friesen, Werner O. Packull, ed. C. Arnold Snyder, *Sources of South German/Austrian Anabaptism* (Kitchener: Pandora Press, 2001; co-published with Herald Press.) Softcover, 430 pp. includes indexes. ISBN 1-894710-15-0

Pedro A. Sandín Fremaint y Pablo A. Jimémez, *Palabras Duras: Homilías* (Kitchener: Pandora Press, 2001). Softcover, 121 pp., ISBN 1-894710-17-7

Ruth Elizabeth Mooney, *Manual Para Crear Materiales de Educación Cristiana* (Kitchener: Pandora Press, 2001). Softcover, 206 pp., ISBN 1-894710-12-6

Esther and Malcolm Wenger, poetry by Ann Wenger, *Healing the Wounds* (Kitchener: Pandora Press, 2001; co-pub. with Herald Press). Softcover, 210 pp. ISBN 1-894710-09-6.

Otto H. Selles and Geraldine Selles-Ysselstein, *New Songs* (Kitchener: Pandora Press, 2001). Poetry and relief prints, 90pp. ISBN 1-894719-14-2

Pedro A. Sandín Fremaint, *Cuentos y Encuentros: Hacia una Educación Transformadora* (Kitchener: Pandora Press, 2001). Softcover 163 pp ISBN 1-894710-08-8.

A. James Reimer, *Mennonites and Classical Theology: Dogmatic Foundations for Christian Ethics* (Kitchener: Pandora Press, 2001; co-published with Herald Press) Softcover, 650pp. ISBN 0-9685543-7-7

Walter Klaassen, *Anabaptism: Neither Catholic nor Protestant*, 3rd ed (Kitchener: Pandora Press, 2001; co-pub. Herald Press) Softcover, 122pp. ISBN 1-894710-01-0

Dale Schrag & James Juhnke, eds., *Anabaptist Visions for the new Millennium: A search for identity* (Kitchener: Pandora Press, 2000; co-published with Herald Press) Softcover, 242 pp. ISBN 1-894710-00-2

Harry Loewen, ed., *Road to Freedom: Mennonites Escape the Land of Suffering* (Kitchener: Pandora Press, 2000; co-published with Herald Press) Hardcover, large format, 302pp. ISBN 0-9685543-5-0

Alan Kreider and Stuart Murray, eds., *Coming Home: Stories of Anabaptists in Britain and Ireland* (Kitchener: Pandora Press, 2000; co-published with Herald Press) Softcover, 220pp. ISBN 0-9685543-6-9

Edna Schroeder Thiessen and Angela Showalter, *A Life Displaced: A Mennonite Woman's Flight from War-Torn Poland* (Kitchener: Pandora Press, 2000; co-published with Herald Press) Softcover, xii, 218pp. ISBN 0-9685543-2-6

Stuart Murray, *Biblical Interpretation in the Anabaptist Tradition,* Studies in the Believers Tradition (Kitchener: Pandora Press, 2000; co-published with Herald Press) Softcover, 310pp. ISBN 0-9685543-3-4 ISSN 1480-7432.

Loren L. Johns, ed. *Apocalypticism and Millennialism,* Studies in the Believers Church Tradition (Kitchener: Pandora Press, 2000; co-published with Herald Press) Softcover, 419pp; Scripture and name indeces ISBN 0-9683462-9-4 ISSN 1480-7432

Later Writings by Pilgram Marpeck and his Circle. Volume 1: The Exposé, A Dialogue and Marpeck's Response to Caspar Schwenckfeld. Trans. Walter Klaassen, Werner Packull, and John Rempel (Kitchener: Pandora Press, 1999; co-published with Herald Press) Softcover, 157pp. ISBN 0-9683462-6-X

John Driver, *Radical Faith. An Alternative History of the Christian Church,* edited by Carrie Snyder. Kitchener: Pandora Press, 1999; co-published with Herald Press) Softcover, 334pp. ISBN 0-9683462-8-6

C. Arnold Snyder, *From Anabaptist Seed. The Historical Core of Anabaptist-Related Identity* (Kitchener: Pandora Press, 1999; co-published with Herald Press) Softcover, 53pp.; discussion questions. ISBN 0-9685543-0-X
Also available in Spanish translation: *De Semilla Anabautista,* from Pandora Press only.

John D. Thiesen, *Mennonite and Nazi? Attitudes Among Mennonite Colonists in Latin America, 1933-1945* (Kitchener: Pandora Press, 1999; co-published with Herald Press) Softcover, 330pp., 2 maps, 24 b/w illustrations, bibliography, index. ISBN 0-9683462-5-1

Lifting the Veil, a translation of *Aus meinem Leben: Erinnerungen von J.H. Janzen.* Ed. by Leonard Friesen; trans. by Walter Klaassen (Kitchener: Pandora Press, 1998; co-pub. with Herald Press). Softcover, 128pp.; 4pp. of illustrations. ISBN 0-9683462-1-9

Leonard Gross, *The Golden Years of the Hutterites,* rev. ed. (Kitchener: Pandora Press, 1998; co-pub. with Herald Press). Softcover, 280pp., index. ISBN 0-9683462-3-5

William H. Brackney, ed., *The Believers Church: A Voluntary Church*, Studies in the Believers Church Tradition (Kitchener: Pandora Press, 1998; co-published with Herald Press). Softcover, viii, 237pp., index. ISBN 0-9683462-0-0 ISSN 1480-7432.

An Annotated Hutterite Bibliography, compiled by Maria H. Krisztinkovich, ed. by Peter C. Erb (Kitchener: Pandora Press, 1998). (Ca. 2,700 entries) 312pp., cerlox bound, electronic, or both. ISBN (paper) 0-9698762-8-9/(disk) 0-9698762-9-7

Jacobus ten Doornkaat Koolman, *Dirk Philips. Friend and Colleague of Menno Simons*, trans. W. E. Keeney, ed. C. A. Snyder (Kitchener: Pandora Press, 1998; co-published with Herald Press). Softcover, xviii, 236pp., index. ISBN: 0-9698762-3-8

Sarah Dyck, ed./tr., *The Silence Echoes: Memoirs of Trauma & Tears* (Kitchener: Pandora Press, 1997; co-published with Herald Press). Softcover, xii, 236pp., 2 maps. ISBN: 0-9698762-7-0

Wes Harrison, *Andreas Ehrenpreis and Hutterite Faith and Practice* (Kitchener: Pandora Press, 1997; co-published with Herald Press). Softcover, xxiv, 274pp., 2 maps, index. ISBN 0-9698762-6-2

C. Arnold Snyder, *Anabaptist History and Theology: Revised Student Edition* (Kitchener: Pandora Press, 1997; co-pub. Herald Press). Softcover, xiv, 466pp., 7 maps, 28 illustrations, index, bibliography. ISBN 0-9698762-5-4

Nancey Murphy, *Reconciling Theology and Science: A Radical Reformation Perspective* (Kitchener, Ont.: Pandora Press, 1997; co-pub. Herald Press). Softcover, x, 103pp., index. ISBN 0-9698762-4-6

C. Arnold Snyder and Linda A. Huebert Hecht, eds, *Profiles of Anabaptist Women: Sixteenth Century Reforming Pioneers* (Waterloo, Ont.: Wilfrid Laurier University Press, 1996). Softcover, xxii, 442pp. ISBN: 0-88920-277-X

The Limits of Perfection: A Conversation with J. Lawrence Burkholder 2nd ed., with a new epilogue by J. Lawrence Burkholder, Rodney Sawatsky and Scott Holland, eds. (Kitchener: Pandora Press, 1996). Softcover, x, 154pp. ISBN 0-9698762-2-X

C. Arnold Snyder, *Anabaptist History and Theology: An Introduction*
(Kitchener: Pandora Press, 1995). ISBN 0-9698762-0-3 Softcover, x,
434pp., 6 maps, 29 illustrations, index,bibliography.

Pandora Press

33 Kent Avenue Kitchener, ON   N2G 3R2

Tel.: (519) 578-2381 / Fax: (519) 578-1826
E-mail: info@pandorapress.com
Web site: www.pandorapress.com